The Company They Kept

Writers on Unforgettable Friendships

The Company They Kept

Writers on Unforgettable Friendships

PREFACE BY
Robert B. Silvers

EDITED BY
Robert B. Silvers and Barbara Epstein

NEW YORK REVIEW BOOKS

New York

THIS IS A NEW YORK REVIEW BOOK

PUBLISHED BY THE NEW YORK REVIEW OF BOOKS

Contents

PREFACE by Robert B. Silvers   *1*

1   Stanley Kunitz on Theodore Roethke   *5*
2   Robert Lowell on Randall Jarrell   *13*
3   Edward Dahlberg on Hart Crane   *23*
4   Robert Oppenheimer on Albert Einstein   *35*
5   Dwight Macdonald on Delmore Schwartz   *43*
6   Alfred Kazin on Josephine Herbst   *53*
7   Jason Epstein on Edmund Wilson   *57*
8   Susan Sontag on Paul Goodman   *67*
9   Anna Akhmatova on Amedeo Modigliani   *75*
10 Robert Craft on Igor Stravinsky   *85*
11 Saul Bellow on John Cheever   *101*
12 Mary McCarthy on F. W. Dupee   *105*
13 Derek Walcott on Robert Lowell   *115*
14 Darryl Pinckney on Djuna Barnes   *133*
15 Maurice Grosser on Gertrude Stein and Alice Toklas   *153*
16 Prudence Crowther on S. J. Perelman   *165*
17 Michael Ignatieff on Bruce Chatwin   *189*
18 Joseph Brodsky on Isaiah Berlin   *193*
19 Caroline Blackwood on Francis Bacon   *201*
20 Elizabeth Hardwick on Mary McCarthy   *207*
21 Tatyana Tolstaya on Joseph Brodsky   *219*
22 Enrique Krauze on Octavio Paz   *227*
23 Richard Seaver on Jérôme Lindon   *237*
24 Seamus Heaney on Thomas Flanagan   *247*
25 Larry McMurtry on Ken Kesey   *253*
26 Brad Leithauser on Anthony Hecht   *267*
27 Oliver Sacks on Francis Crick   *275*

ABOUT THE AUTHORS AND SUBJECTS   *291*

Preface

A MEMOIR OF a talented friend risks sentimentality. It may sound cautious, protective, promotional, false. Yet by some miracle, none of this seems true of the reminiscences from *The New York Review* collected here. It is hard to say how any of them came about. For the most part, they are not the sort of essays an editor can ask for. They are not obituaries, not literary appreciations. In practically every case the writers felt they had to write something about someone they had known very well, and whose work had mattered in their lives, and they told us so. Petty anecdotes and the sly observations that people often make about their friends have little place here; instead, the writers concentrate on moments of comradeship and originality, on a presence and on work that gave pleasure.

Some of the best moments are about the start of something, as when Prudence Crowther called on S. J. Perelman:

> One night early on I was walking home late from a ballet class —"twirling," Sid called it—and swung by his hotel. I thought of phoning him from the lobby but hesitated, picturing him in the middle of a more or less permanent salon in his rooms, which I hadn't yet seen. After circling the block once I finally dialed and

asked him what he was doing. "I'm poised here looking like I'm going to make an epigram, and all I've got in my head is butter-scotch." I asked if he wanted to go have some dessert, and he sounded overjoyed to be sprung from his solitude. That was my first inkling that his life was not the Olympian bower I'd imagined. He looked very sharp as usual, like an old artist, and wore a plaid shirt with a dark tie.

Without the affection that runs through these memoirs, they would be lifeless. Without the literary judgments they imply, they would be hollow. In each one, high critical standards count for practically everything but are seldom stated. In such company it isn't necessary.

—Robert B. Silvers

I

STANLEY KUNITZ
ON THEODORE ROETHKE

THE POET OF my generation who meant most to me, in his person and in his art, was Theodore Roethke. To say, in fact, "poet of my generation" is to name him. Immediately after Eliot and Pound and Hart Crane and Stevens and William Carlos Williams, to mention only a handful, it was difficult to be taken seriously as a new American poet; for the title to "the new poetry" was in the possession of a dynasty of extraordinary gifts and powers, not the least of which was its capacity for literary survival. When Roethke was a schoolboy in Michigan in the Twenties, these poets born late in the nineteenth century had already "arrived." Today, in the general view, they are still the rebels and inventors beyond whom even a college course in contemporary literature scarcely dares to venture.

Roethke took his own work seriously indeed, as he had every reason to do. Lashed by his competitive and compulsive temper, he committed himself fully to the exhausting struggle for recognition—a desperately intimate struggle that left its mark on him. Only a few years ago he could refer to himself sardonically as "the oldest younger poet in the U.S.A." America wants to wither its artists with neglect or kill them with success. When recognition came, it came in full measure, except for the seductive blessing of a mass audience. Roethke won the Pulitzer Prize in 1954 for *The Waking*; in 1959, after the publication of *Words for the Wind*, his collected verse, he received eight awards in all, including some prizes, grants, and honors that nobody had even heard of before. The flattery that meant most of all came in the form of imitation by dozens of even "younger" poets, including some with gray hair. Ted would occasionally make a fuss about these pretenders who were "stealing (his) stuff," but one did not take the complaints at face value.

More than twenty-five years have passed since he blew into my life like the "big wind" of one of his poems. I was living in the Delaware Valley then. He came, unannounced, downriver from Lafayette College, where he was instructor in English and—more satisfying to his pride—tennis coach. My recollection is of a traditionally battered jalopy from which a perfectly tremendous raccoon coat emerged, with my first book of poems tucked under its left paw. The introductory mumble that followed could be construed as a compliment. Then he stood, embarrassed and inarticulate, in my doorway, waiting to gauge the extent of my hospitality. The image that never left me was of a blond, smooth, shambling giant, irrevocably Teutonic, with a cold pudding of a face, somehow contradicted by the sullen downturn of the mouth and the pale furious eyes. He had come to talk about poetry, and we did talk vehemently all through the night. There were times, in the years that followed, when I could swear that I hadn't been to bed since.

All those evenings seemed to move inexorably toward a moment of trial for both of us when he would fumble for the crinkled manuscript in his pocket and present it for approval. During the reading of his poem he waited in an attitude of excruciating tension and suspicion. If the praise failed to meet his expectation, he would grow violently defensive or lapse into a hostile silence. Nevertheless, despite these instant manifestations, he was by no means impervious to criticism or to suggestions. When I proposed "Open House" as the title for his first book of poems (1941), he not only adopted it gratefully but proceeded to write the title-poem that still stands at the head of his collected verse:

My secrets cry aloud.
I have no need for tongue.
My heart keeps open house,
My doors are widely swung.
An epic of the eyes
My love, with no disguise.

On another country visit perhaps a decade later, he asked me long after midnight to read something choice to him. I picked up Sir John Davies's neglected Elizabethan masterpiece *Orchestra, a Poem of Dancing*, which he had somehow never chanced on despite his omnivorous appetite for verse, and I can still recall the excitement and the joy with which he greeted the clear-voiced music.

From that encounter, combined with his deep attachment to the beat of Yeats—it was beat, above all, that enchanted him—he composed the memorable sequence *Four for Sir John Davies*, which was to set the cadence for a whole new cycle of later poems:

Is that dance slowing in the mind of man
That made him think the universe could hum?
The great wheel turns its axle when it can;
I need a place to sing, and dancing-room,
And I have made a promise to my ears
I'll sing and whistle romping with the bears.

Ted was not easy on his friends, but neither was he easy on himself. For a while, when our dialogue arrived at an impasse, we could always fight it out on the courts. For all his six-foot-three, two-hundred-plus-pound bulk and his lumbering walk, he was amazingly nimble on his feet and—less amazingly—ruthless at the kill, with a smashing service and a blistering forehand drive. The daemon in him played the game just as it wrote the poems. Whatever he did was an aspect of the same insatiable will to conquer self and art and others. He could not bear to lose. If you managed to beat him by cunning and by luck, you could not expect to be congratulated by him: he was more likely to smash his racket across his knees. It was typical of him that after the progressive wear and tear of his body had forced him to give up the game, he displayed no further interest in it.

As a young man he felt humiliated and disgraced by the periodic mental breakdowns that were to afflict him all his life. There were outbreaks and absences and silences that he had to cover up, partly because he realized what a threat they offered to his survival in the academic world. He was one of the supreme teachers of poetry, as his students will surely testify, but not until he came—after Bennington—to the University of Washington in 1947 did he have any assurance of tenure. There he found a staunch advocate in the person of Robert Heilman, chairman of the English department, who remained loyal to him through the worst of weathers.

By the time of his arrival in Seattle, Roethke had found the means of transforming his ordeal into language, notably in the wild and masterful sequence of longer poems initiated by *The Lost Son.* A more recent formal suite on the ordeal and the ecstasy seems, like Hopkins's terrible sonnets, to be "written in blood." Eventually he more than half-believed that the springs of his disorder were inseparable from the sources of his art, and he could brag of belonging to the brotherhood of mad poets that includes William Blake, John Clare, and Christopher Smart, with each of whom he was able to identify himself as "lost." His affection for Dylan Thomas had much the same base; but on the other hand some of his longest friendships, including those with Louise Bogan and W. H. Auden, signified his unswerving admiration for those who stood in his mind as representatives of a sacred discipline.

What I wrote in *Poetry* about *The Lost Son* on its publication in 1948—this is the book of his that I continue to think of as the great one—still sounds pertinent to me: "The ferocity of Roethke's imagination makes most contemporary poetry seem pale and tepid in contrast. Even the wit is murderous.... What Roethke brings us is news of the root, of the minimal, of the primordial. The sub-human is given tongue, and the tongue proclaims the agony of coming alive, the painful miracle of growth." Let me add now that one of Roethke's remarkable powers, particularly evident in the later productions, is that of the compassionate flow of self into the things of his experience. His poems become what they love; and mostly he loves a creature-world smaller and purer than his own.

> *I study the lives on a leaf: the little*
> *Sleepers, numb nudgers in cold dimensions,*
> *Beetles in caves, newts, stone-deaf fishes,*
> *Lice tethered to long limp subterranean weeds,*
> *Squirmers in bogs,*
> *And bacterial creepers....*

No other modern poet seems so directly tuned to the natural universe: his disturbance was in being human. The soul trapped in his ursine frame yearned less for the infinite than for the infinitesimal. This florist's son never really departed from the moist, fecund world of his father's greenhouse in Saginaw. In "Cuttings," one of a bouquet of greenhouse poems, he gives a clue to his root-image:

> *This urge, wrestle, resurrection of dry sticks,*
> *Cut stems struggling to put down feet,*
> *What saint strained so much,*
> *Rose on such lopped limbs to a new life?*

I can hear, underground, that sucking and sobbing,
In my veins, in my bones I feel it,—
The small waters seeping upward,
The tight grains parting at last.
When sprouts break out,
Slippery as fish,
I quail, lean to beginnings, sheath-wet.

In 1953 Roethke married one of his former Bennington students, Beatrice O'Connell, who justified in a number of ways, not the least of which were beauty, devotion, and courage, the love poems that he addressed to her, including the dazzling one that begins, "I knew a woman, lovely in her bones." During the weekend visit after their wedding I prodded him to write an autobiographical sketch for the First Supplement to *Twentieth Century Authors*, of which I was editor. The resulting document in longhand, still in my possession, provides an invaluable insight into his sense of himself. One passage reads: "I have tried to transmute and purify my 'life,' the sense of being defiled by it, in both small and formal and somewhat blunt short poems, and, latterly, in longer poems which try in their rhythm to catch the very movement of the mind itself, to trace the spiritual history of a protagonist (not 'I,' personally), of all haunted and harried men; to make in this series (now probably finished) a true and not arbitrary order which will permit many ranges of feelings, including humor."

Roethke's humor, of which he gave due warning, was no gentle, prattling thing. After all, one does not go to the axe to learn about politeness. He was convinced, nevertheless, that his humor, much of it ribald, was side-splitting when it was not devastating, and that nobody since Edward Lear had composed such hilarious verses for children. It was during the wedding visit that he proposed to demonstrate his comic genius by entertaining my three-year-old daughter with a recitation of his nonsense verse. His first selection was a quatrain entitled "The Cow." Dancing around her, thumping out the beat, illustrating the action with appropriate gestures, he roared the lines:

There Once was a Cow with a Double Udder.
When I think of it now, I just have to Shudder!
She was too much for One, you can bet your Life:
She had to be Milked by a Man and his Wife.

The result might have been anticipated. Gretchen burst into tears and tried to hide under the sofa.

I was to think of that incident seven years later, in the spring of 1960, when Roethke read at The Poetry Center in New York, where I introduced him. He had a high fever, and backstage he was jittery, sweating copiously from every pore as he guzzled champagne by the bottle. On stage, for the first portion of his program he clowned and hammed incorrigibly, weaving, gyrating, dancing, shrugging his shoulders, muttering to himself intermittently, and now and then making curiously flipper-like or foetal gestures with his hands. But gradually, as the evening wore on, he settled into a straight dramatic style that was enormously effective and moving. When he came to the new "mad" sequence, particularly the poem that begins, "In a dark time the eye begins to see," his voice rang out with such an over-whelming roll of noble anguish that many in the audience wept.

As we filed out of the hall, a painter-friend remarked on Roethke's strange affinity to that other lost and violent spirit, Jackson Pollock. "How true!" I thought, though the resemblance was not obvious. And I heard myself repeating a rather enigmatic phrase that I had picked up from Franz Kline when he was reminiscing once about his old companion: "He divined himself."

—1963

2

ROBERT LOWELL

ON RANDALL JARRELL

WHEN I FIRST met Randall, he was twenty-three or four, and upsettingly brilliant, precocious, knowing, naive, and vexing. He seemed to make no distinction between what he would say in our hearing and what he would say behind our backs. If anything, absence made him more discreet. Woe to the acquaintance who liked the wrong writer, the wrong poem by the right writer, or the wrong lines in the right poem! And how those who loved him enjoyed admiring, complaining, and gossiping about the last outrageous thing he had done or, more often, said. It brought us together—whispering about Randall. In 1937, we both roomed at the house of John Crowe Ransom in Gambier, Ohio. Ransom and Jarrell had each separately spent the preceding summer studying Shakespeare's *Sonnets*, and had emerged with unorthodox and widely differing theories. Roughly, Ransom thought that Shakespeare was continually going off the rails into illogical incoherence. Jarrell believed that no one, not even William Empson, had done justice to the rich, significant ambiguity of Shakespeare's intelligence and images. I can see and hear Ransom and Jarrell now, seated on one sofa, as though on one love-seat, the sacred texts open on their laps, one fifty, the other just out of college, and each expounding to the other's deaf ears his own inspired and irreconcilable interpretation.

Gordon Chalmers, the President of Kenyon College and a disciple of the somber anti-Romantic Humanists, once went skiing with Randall, and was shocked to hear him exclaiming, "I feel just like an angel." Randall *did* somehow give off an angelic impression, despite his love for tennis, singular mufflers knitted by a girlfriend, and disturbing improvements of his own on the latest dance steps. His mind, unearthly in its quickness, was a little boyish, disembodied, and brittle. His body was a little ghostly in its immunity to soil, entanglements, and rebellion. As one sat with him in oblivious absorption at the campus bar, sucking a fifteen-cent chocolate milkshake and talking eternal things, one felt, beside him, too corrupt and companionable. He had the harsh luminosity of Shelley—like Shelley, every inch a poet, and like Shelley, imperiled perhaps by an arid, abstracting precosity. Not really! Somewhere inside him, a breezy, untouchable spirit had even then made its youthful and sightless promise to accept—to accept and never to accept the bulk, confusion, and defeat of mortal flesh . . . all that blithe and blood-torn dolor!

Randall Jarrell had his own peculiar and important excellence as a poet, and out-distanced all others in the things he could do well. His gifts, both by nature and by a lifetime of hard dedication and growth, were wit, pathos, and brilliance of intelligence. These qualities, dazzling in themselves, were often so well employed that he became, I think, the most heartbreaking English poet of his generation.

Most good poets are also good critics on occasion, but Jarrell was much more than this. He was a critic of genius, a poet-critic of genius at a time when, as he wrote, most criticism was "astonishingly graceless, joyless, humorless, long-winded, niggling, blinkered, methodical, self-important, cliché-ridden, prestige-obsessed, and almost autonomous."

He had a deadly hand for killing what he despised. He described a murky verbal poet as "writing poems that might have been written *by* a typewriter *on* a typewriter." The flashing reviews he wrote in his twenties are full of such witticisms and barbs, and hundreds more were tossed off in casual conversation, and never preserved, or even repeated. Speaking of a famous scholar, he said, "What can be more tedious than a man whose every sentence is a balanced epigram without wit, profundity, or taste?" He himself, though often fierce, was incapable of vulgarity, self-seeking, or meanness. He could be very tender and gracious, but often he seemed tone-deaf to the amenities and dishonesties that make human relations tolerable. Both his likes and dislikes were a terror to everyone, that is to everyone who either saw himself as important or wished to see himself as important. Although he was almost without vices, heads of colleges and English departments found his frankness more unsettling and unpredictable than the drunken explosions of some divine *enfant terrible*, such as Dylan Thomas. Usually his wit was austerely pure, but sometimes he could jolt the more cynical. Once we were looking at a furnished apartment that one of our friends had just rented. It was overbearingly eccentric. Lifesize clay lamps like flowerpots remodeled into Matisse nudes by a spastic child. Paintings made from a palette of mud by a blind painter. About the paintings Randall said, "Ectoplasm sprinkled with zinc." About the apartment, "All that's missing are Mrs. X's illegitimate children in bottles of formaldehyde." His first reviews were described as "symbolic murders," but even then his most destructive judgments had a patient, intuitive, unworldly certainty.

Yet eulogy was the glory of Randall's criticism. Eulogies that not only impressed readers with his own enthusiasms, but which also, time and again, changed and improved opinions and values. He left many reputations permanently altered and exalted. I think particularly of his famous Frost and Whitman essays, and one on the last poems of Wallace Stevens, which was a dramatic reversal of his own earlier evaluation. His mind kept moving and groping more deeply. His prejudices were never the established and fashionable prejudices of the world around him. One could never say of one of his new admirations, "Oh, I knew *you* would like that." His progress was not the usual youthful critic's progress from callow severity to lax benevolence. With wrinkled brow and cool fresh eye, he was forever musing, discovering, and chipping away at his own misconceptions. Getting out on a limb was a daily occurrence for him, and when he found words for what he had intuited, his judgments were bold and unlikely. Randall was so often right, that sometimes we said he was always right. He could enjoy discarded writers whom it was a scandal to like, praise young, unknown writers as if he were praising and describing Shakespeare's *Tragedies*, and read Shakespeare's *Tragedies* with the uncertainty and wonder of their first discoverers.

He once said, "If I were a rich man, I would pay money for the privilege of being able to teach." Probably there was no better teacher of literature in the country, and yet he was curiously unworldly about it, and welcomed teaching for almost twenty years in the shade or heat of his little-known Southern college for girls in Greensboro, North Carolina. There his own community gave him a compact, tangible, personal reverence that was incomparably more substantial and poignant than the empty, numerical long-distance blaze of national publicity. He grieved over the coarseness, unkindness, and corruption of our society, and said that "the poet has a peculiar relation to this public. It is unaware of his existence." He said bitterly and lightheartedly that "the gods who had taken away the poet's audience had given him students." Yet he gloried in being a teacher, never apologized for it, and related it to his most serious criticism. Writing of three long poems by Robert Frost, poems too long to include in his essay, he breaks off and says, "I have used rather an odd tone about these poems because I felt so much frustration at not being able to quote and go over them, as I have so often done with friends and classes." Few critics could so gracefully descend from the grand manner or be so offhand about their dignity. His essays are never encrusted with the hardness of a professor. They have the raciness and artistic gaiety of his own hypnotic voice.

Randall was the only man I have ever met who could make other writers feel that their work was more important to him than his own. I don't mean that he was in the habit of saying to people he admired, "This is much better than anything I could do." Such confessions, though charming, cost little effort. What he did was to make others feel that their realizing themselves was as close to him as his own self-realization, and that he cared as much about making the nature and goodness of someone else's work understood, as he cared about making his own understood. I have never known anyone who so connected what his friends wrote with their lives, or their lives with what they wrote. This could be trying: whenever we turned out something Randall felt was unworthy or a falling off, there was a coolness in all one's relations with him. You felt that even your choice in neckties wounded him. Yet he always veered and returned, for he knew as well as anyone that the spark from heaven is beyond man's call and control. Good will he demanded, but in the end was lenient to honest sterility and failure.

Jarrell was the most readable and generous of critics of contemporary poetry. His novel, *Pictures from an Institution*, whatever its fictional oddities, is a unique and serious joke-book. How often I've met people who keep it by their beds or somewhere handy, and read random pages aloud to lighten their hearts. His book, *A Sad Heart at the Supermarket*, had a condescending press. When one listened to these social essays, they were like *dies irae* sermons, strange ones that cauterized the soul, and yet made us weep with laughter. A banal world found them banal. But what Jarrell's inner life really was in all its wonder, variety, and subtlety is best told in his poetry. To the end, he was writing with deepening force, clarity, and frankness. For some twenty-five years he wrote excellent poems. Here I only want to emphasize two of his peaks: what he wrote about the War, and what he completed in the last years of his life.

In the first months of the War, Jarrell became a pilot. He was rather old for a beginner, and soon "washed out," and spent the remaining war years as an aviation instructor. Even earlier, he had an expert's knowledge. I remember sitting with him in 1938 on the hill of Kenyon College and listening to him analyze in cool technical detail the various rather minute ways in which the latest British planes were superior to their German equivalents. He then jokingly sketched out how a bombing raid might be made against the college. Nine tenths of his war poems are air force poems, and are about planes and their personnel, the flyers, crews, and mechanics who attended them. No other imaginative writer had his precise knowledge of aviation, or knew so well how to draw inspiration from this knowledge.

> *In the turret's great glass dome, the apparition death,*
> *Framed in the glass of the gun-sight, a fighter's*
> *blinking wing,*
> *Flares softly, a vacant fire. If the flak's inked blurs—*
> *Distributed, statistical—the bomb's lost patterning*
> *Are death, they are death under glass, a chance*
> *For someone yesterday, someone tomorrow; and the fire*
> *That streams from the fighter which is there, not there,*
> *Does not warm you, has not burned them, though*
> *they die.*

More important still, the soldiers he wrote about were men much like his own pilot-students. He knew them well, and not only that, peculiarly sympathized with them. For Jarrell, the war careers of these young men had the freshness, wonder, and magical brevity of childhood. In his poetry, they are murderers, and yet innocents. They destroyed cities and men that had only the nominal reality of names studied in elementary geography classes.

In bombers named for girls, we burned
The cities we had learned about in school—
Till our lives wore out...

Or

In this year of our warfare, indispensible
In general, and in particular dispensible...

Finally, the pilot goes home for good, forever mutilated and wounded, "the slow flesh failing, the terrible flesh sloughed off at last...stumbling to the toilet on one clever leg of leather, wire, and willow..." There, knowledge has at last come to him:

And it is different, different—you have understood
Your world at last: you have tasted your own blood.

Jarrell's portraits of his pilots have been downgraded sometimes as unheroic, naive, and even sentimental. Well, he was writing beyond the War, and turning the full visionary powers of his mind on the War to probe into and expose the horror, pathos, and charm he found in life. Always behind the sharpened edge of his lines, there is the merciful vision, *his* vision, partial like all others, but an illumination of life, too sad and radiant for us to stay with long—or forget.

In his last and best book, *The Lost World*, he used subjects and methods he had been developing and improving for almost twenty years. Most of the poems are dramatic monologues. Their speakers, though mostly women, are intentionally, and unlike Browning's, very close to the author. Their themes, repeated with endless variations, are solitude, the solitude of the unmarried, the solitude of the married, the love, strife, dependency, and indifference of man and woman —how mortals age, and brood over their lost and raw childhood, only recapturable in memory and imagination. Above all, childhood! This subject for many a careless and tarnished cliché was for him what it was for his two favorite poets, Rilke and Wordsworth, a governing and transcendent vision. For shallower creatures, recollections of childhood and youth are drenched in a mist of plaintive pathos, or even bathos, but for Jarrell this was the divine glimpse, lifelong to be lived with, painfully and tenderly relived, transformed, matured— man with and against woman, child with and against adult.

One of his aging women says,

> *When I was young and miserable and pretty*
> *And poor, I'd wish*
> *What all girls wish: to have a husband . . .*

But later, thinking of the withering present, she says,

> *How young I seem; I am exceptional;*
> *I think of all I have.*
> *But really no one is exceptional,*
> *No one has anything, I'm anybody,*
> *I stand beside my grave*
> *Confused with my life that is commonplace*
>   *and solitary.*

In so reflecting, she is a particular woman—one sad, particular woman reaching into Jarrell's universal Everyman, poor or triumphant. Speaking in his own person and of his own childhood, he says,

> *. . . As I run by the chicken coops*
> *With lettuce for my rabbit, real remorse*
> *Hurts me, here, now: the little girl is crying*

Because I didn't write. Because—
                    of course,
I was a child, I missed them so. But justifying
Hurts too...

Then in a poem called "Woman," the speaker, a man, addresses the woman next to him in bed:

Let me sleep beside you, each night, like a spoon;
When starting from my dreams, I groan to you,
May your I love you send me back to sleep.
At morning bring me, grayer for its mirroring,
The heaven's sun perfected in your eyes.

It all comes back to me now—the just under thirty years of our friendship, mostly meetings in transit, mostly in Greensboro, North Carolina, the South he loved and stayed with, though no Agrarian, but a radical liberal. Poor modern-minded exile from the forests of Grimm, I see him unbearded, slightly South American–looking, then later bearded, with a beard we at first wished to reach out our hands to and pluck off but which later became him, like Walter Bagehot's, or some Symbolist's in France's *fin-de-siècle* Third Republic. Then unbearded again. I see the bright, petty, pretty sacred objects he accumulated for his joy and solace: Vermeer's red-hatted girl, the Piero and Donatello reproductions, the photographs of his bruised, merciful heroes: Chekhov, Rilke, Marcel Proust. I see the white sporting Mercedes Benz, the ever better cut and more deliberately jaunty clothes, the television with its long afternoons of professional football, those matches he thought miraculously more graceful than college football...Randall had an uncanny clairvoyance for helping friends in subtle precarious moments—almost always as only he could help, with something written: critical sentences in a letter, or an unanticipated published book review. Twice or thrice, I think, he must have thrown me a lifeline. In his own life, he had much public acclaim and more private. The public, at least, fell cruelly short of what he deserved. Now that he is gone, I see clearly that the spark from heaven really struck and irradiated the lines and being of my dear old friend—his noble, difficult, and beautiful soul.

—1965

3

EDWARD DAHLBERG
ON HART CRANE

THE LIFE OF Hart Crane was a bacchic orgy; he knew no other way to live or compose his poems. As Quevedo wrote: "He rode post to perdition." Though I realize that humdrum everyday existence cannot be a gloss upon the poem, it might be of niggish interest to the reader to have some intelligence of Crane as a person. I knew him, and there were some similarities in our lives which, though no more than gossip, tease the blood and the veins.

Hart Crane was born July 21, 1899, and I on July 22, 1900. When he was a soda fountain clerk in his father's fancy ice cream parlor and tearoom in Cleveland, Ohio, I was then an inmate of an orphanage in the same city. For a short space of time Hart Crane was a navvy in a munitions plant in Cleveland, and so was I. In 1928 he went to Paris where we met. Crane had already published *White Buildings*, of which I had never heard, and he asked me, though God knows why, to read the ms. of *The Bridge*. Though I had studied pre-Socratic philosophy and middle English in the graduate school at Columbia, I knew little about the Boulevard Montparnasse seers of the USA vulgate. I was exceedingly anxious to be a part of the covey of roaring, spastic exiles who contributed to *Transition* and *This Quarter*, little expatriate magazines. Hart Crane and I already had encountered Robert Mc-Almon, Kay Boyle, Eugene Jolas, one of the editors of *Transition*, and

Harry Crosby, a disciple of Lautréamont, author of *Maldoror*, and the high priest of surrealist satanism.

I was prepared to offer Crane all the genuflections necessary to quell his doubts. We became friendly and he introduced me to McCown, the artist, with whom he lived in a left bank atelier. Both had read my first novel, *Bottom Dogs* (for which D. H. Lawrence, one of Crane's deities, had written the Introduction), and Constant Huntington, director of G. P. Putnam's in London, had given me a contract for the book. Huntington asked me to look up somebody in Paris who would design the wrapper for the volume and Hart Crane had suggested that McCown should do it.

When McCown gave me the drawing for the dust-jacket, I conveyed it to Mr. Huntington who, after receiving it, sent me an acerb reply, saying that he knew that I had written a dirty, picaresque Americanese, but he had never imagined I had believed it was lewd. Eugene McCown had drawn a map of the United States emphasizing a phallical Florida which I had noticed with a nebulous and naive uneasiness. Of course, I had heard about pathics, but had not the scantiest suspicion that Hart Crane was homosexual. Crane was a stocky, virile male with a jovean square face, mizzling, foggy eyes, gun-metal, gray hair, and a smouldering, amorous mouth.

Though Crane and I knew many Americans in Paris both of us were overwhelmingly alone, castaways of American letters. On the outside of this riotous, visionary coterie, we were solitary mendicants looking for the rotten grapes of Pisgah, and living like cut-rate Montezumas in some dump near the Select or Coupole, parnassian meeting-places for deracinated chatterboxes of literature and gamy, venereal whores.

Crane and I were part of a senseless babel of economics. Impecunious most of his life, he was then receiving a handsome subsidy from the banker and patron of the arts, Otto H. Kahn. *The Bridge* was to be published by the millionaire sybarite of letters, Harry Crosby. No less poor than Crane, I was then involved with the niece of a very puissant industrialist who later became the fervid crony of Khrushchev. I mention these pocketbook ironies as an aside.

Harry Crosby also invited Crane to write in a castle whose eighteenth-century proprietor had been the Duc de La Rochefoucauld, hoping he would finish *The Bridge* there. Meanwhile, Crosby, a tenderhearted sufferer who also longed for dionysiac trances, and detesting a world suitable for pithless salesmen and fusty, monied dowds, committed suicide. It was Crosby's widow, Caresse, who published *The Bridge* in a beautiful, recherché edition of the Black Sun Press in Paris.

Although Crane had fallen into adust ecstasies over Paris, absinthe, Gertrude Stein, and the French language, he went back to America. Penniless by then myself, Hart Crane suggested that I go to Otto H. Kahn and say I was his friend, which I did, and with felicitous results. In New York I saw Hart Crane just when Boni and Liveright had brought out the American edition of *The Bridge*. He lived in a one-room apartment, somewhat beneath the sidewalk, with a gallon of whiskey on the floor next to his cot, and a pile of Sophie Tucker records for his Victrola. Though not thirty years old, his hair was the color of a seagull. In the daytime he was deeply pooled in mouldy sleep, and at night he ran about Red Hook, the libidinous docks of Tarshish in Brooklyn, soliciting the favors of sailors.

Many times Crane had been beaten by seamen; on one occasion, living on Columbia Heights hard by his iron seraph, the Brooklyn Bridge, he complained to me that a young man whom he thought had the milk-white shoulders of Pelops (I am paraphrasing Christopher Marlowe, Hart Crane's demigod) had stolen his clothes and forsaken him. He was sorely wounded by this ill hap, but, as I have said, when he was not humiliated, or had not drunk hyssop in some waterfront pot-house, he was unable to achieve that Apollonian composure which he needed to enable him to sit at a table—a poet's guillotine—and write. "Unless you are broken up, you are not alive," said Wyndham

Lewis in one of his remarkable letters, but as Hart Crane has worded it, he wrote verses, roared, and quarreled with all "the zest for doom."

What drove Crane crazy was the humid torpor between poems. An odalisque can be idle and recumbent, and her languor is the joy of Eve and the serpent in Eden, but when a poet is supine, just a rotting unthinking corpse, he is beside himself.

Still, he was glutted with remorse and shame; he wrote: "Our tongues recant like beaten weather vanes." Later I saw him at a party given in honor of Mae West, who had completed her autobiography, the usual elite *merde* of the cinema star. Crane arrived late; though extremely drunk his clothes were seemly and his manner cavalier. In one of his missives he said: "I've been cooking my own meals, and doing my best without the help of a flatiron to keep myself looking spruce." Crane, copying the dandyism of Heine, explains elsewhere: "Despite my objections to cane-carrying, I find it very pleasant. Puce-colored gloves complete the proper touch."

He doted on a soirée, and on this occasion he had found the side of a carton which he was offering to authors upon which to sign their names to petition Mae West to sing *Frankie and Johnnie*. Why Mae West, a mildewed and synthetic dame of the theater, was considered such an aphrodisiacal morsel I will never know. Edmund Wilson, who was there, thought she was as desirable as a Sabine virgin. I don't think any poet has ever had luck with these dumpy Hollywood dolls whose agents inform us they adore Proust and Dostoevsky. He had sent *White Buildings* to Chaplin, supposed to be the sorrowful and educated Quixote clown: Chaplin's secretary sent him a sere, laconic note acknowledging that the book had been received. I believe Hart Crane's idolatry of jazz, Charles Chaplin, and his mechanolatry, was, in part, the slag of Acheron in his poetry.

There is a doleful chasm between Crane's epistolary comprehension of a mechanized commonwealth and the veneration of brand-new gewgaws which are so apparent in Crane's poems. In one of his letters Crane asserts: "All this talk about being gay...and painfully delighted" with "the telegraph, the wireless, the street-cars and electric lamp posts annoys me." A model T. Ford is more precious to the unshriven up-to-date mind than St. Paul's occiput which was said to have been found in a sheep-cote. We are now near the Last Judgment, making ready for the gaseous declamations of a celestial missile.

The *Letters* have been marvelously arranged by Brom Weber; and though Crane shows lucid knowledge of a society grounded upon money, an opiate phantasy that has no relation to work or the moral values of products, it is necessary to take a fugitive glance at the poetry. Hart Crane desired above all to make an American myth, and notwithstanding his contempt for pessimism, he was a "revolutionary" in the sense that Wyndham Lewis defines it, "a man of the tabula rasa."

The American poet is a nihilist, and because he has no past or any sure, graspable tradition, he starts with nothing and then imagines that is his godhead. Crane's principal faults come from his misuse of language; English is our stepmother language, and we speak, giving the scantiest thought to the reasonable order of words. The music of logic in literature is the sublime use of the metaphor. Crane took swollen and almost deranged risks to make a startling phrase. Crane says: "I now find myself baulked by doubt at the validity of practically every metaphor I coin."

There is no science of literary criticism, and whatever remarks are offered come from countless errors. A man can misread a poem at twenty, fifty, or at my age. The critical faculty is no less splayed than Vulcan's foot. May each one accept as much of this as suits his purpose, and if the reader mislikes what I say let him throw it out of his mind, and stuff himself with lentils, cabbage, and a tithe of Aristotle.

At his best Hart Crane was a Magian of the Logos, but when he felt down he wrote turbid, amorphous doggerel. His work is glutted with neologies, solecisms, and jazz dada locutions which have nothing to do with the sexual feud between his father, a Cleveland candy manufacturer, and his mother, a Christian Scientist. There is no doubt that he was the brunt of bestial, Faustian altercations between his parents. Hart Crane tells his mother: "...my youth has been the rather bloody battleground for yours and father's sex life." "Must every man entomb a withered child?" asks the poet Stanley Burnshaw.

No matter what one's childhood is, a seeming Elysian remembrance or a parental vendetta, the understanding of the afflatus of a poet lies elsewhere. Crane was a neo-American Elizabethan who ran mad for new words. Nor can one assert that his electric shock tropes were the result of a sundered, homosexual nature, for this makes no sense. He could have been drawn to Aphrodite, inflamed by her peplum, and have had no sensibility.

It is too easy at this time to be a canting adorer of Crane's poems; or a pedant who falls upon his work as if he had not eaten a full meal for a week. Crane combines music, color and sound and made of them the "prayer of pariah." His concern with sensations perfectly wrought and gemmed in his mind like the sapphire, emerald, or ruby in Paradise, paradoxically resulted in many of his most turbid lines. Oddly enough he quoted limpid lines from the *Book of Job*, *Tamburlaine the Great*, *The Alchemist*, or a poem from Emily Dickinson, while he himself hurled thundering and forked diction at his auditors. He would have burnt Troy for a memorable stanza and swallowed Hell's sulphur to be laureled a poet. One should allege straightway that his genius was a parcel of the gargantuan follies in *White Buildings* and *The Bridge*. At times there is no grammar in his verse, or he employs, to make an oxymoron, an heroical bathos. I have prowled sundry volumes to understand his poems, which are pages of bedlamite shrieks of a soul sunk like Atlantis, and then there are those green sea cries towering out of the foam. He could be a syntactical zany as is apparent in some of the passages I have culled from *The Bridge*:

Into the bulging bullion, harnessed jelly of the stars

lead-perforated fuselage, escutcheoned wings lift
*   agonized quittance*

Ghoul-mound of man's perversity at balk

And Klondike edelweiss of occult snows!

And white legs waken salads in the brain.

The conscience navelled in the plunging wind,
Umbilical to call—

As a Café Dome expatriate he dropped into rapturous USA jargon:

Stick your patent name on a signboard brother—all
*   over—going west—young man Tintex-Japalac—*

But then who can be the surd adder after these fleshed locutions: "Gongs in white surplices, beshrouded wails..." Or not pity the spirit, thirty years old, only thirty-five months from his Caribbean winding-sheet: "...snow submerges an iron year." Hear this lachrymal expletive: "wounds that we wrap in theorems." And this could have been the magic of a Fletcher or a Tourneur: "Like pearls that whisper through the Doge's hands." Or remain immune, if you can, to this canorous rhetoric:

...take this sheaf of dust upon your tongue.
Ask nothing but this sheath of pallid air.

Be compassionate and drop a tear for this orphan unhoused in Abraham's bosom, with no place to lay his head save on "the pillowed

bay." And though the poet of these states, he was landless: "And fold
your exile on your back again..."

Those who spat upon his identity were not even "dull lips com-
memorating spiritual gates." How many who knew him had that
honeycombed wisdom, his self-knowledge: "Thou sowest doom thou
hast nor time nor chance to reckon..." An acolyte of Keats he wrote,
"I think the sea has thrown itself upon me and been answered." In
"At Melville's Tomb":

> *And wrecks passed without sound of bells,*
> *The calyx of death's bounty giving back*
> *A scattered chapter, livid hieroglyph,*
> *The portent wound in corridors of shells.*

I once saw the portrait of Melville in the house of his granddaughter,
and I wondered how Hart Crane could have known this: "Frosted
eyes there were that lifted, altars..."

A poet is a prisoner of his wounds. One could also attribute some
of his cranial belchings to alcohol, but he wrote to Waldo Frank:
"Lately my continence has brought me nothing in the creative way."
Doubtless the long bouts of penury maimed him. In one of his novels,
Quevedo says the Spanish sharper sprinkled crumbs on his beard so
that it would look as though he has just had a splendid dinner.

His lodgings in New York or Brooklyn Heights was a scabrous
room, which, if one can think of a fugue as a color, was lit by a beige
abscessed electric bulb, the rent for which he often had to borrow
from one of his friends. "I have helped to empty several other pockets
also," said Crane.

Crane had received a hundred dollars as an advance for *White
Buildings*, and Allen Tate, who wrote the Introduction, doubtless
only got desert manna for his work. When a writer can count on as
much for his labors as a charwoman we will have an American El

Dorado. Let anyone tell you that the situation is better now than it was is babbling; there is a great deal of humbug about the Twenties, the Thirties, and the Forties; what difference can one or three decades make? Does anybody really believe that the poet in other centuries was not less hindered than now or forty years ago? Imagine the plight of the poet at the time of the Caesars when Domitian relieved the Roman economy by abating the price of a eunuch. If this sounds bizarre to the doubting Thomases of Philistia, let them ponder the days of hunger of Baudelaire.

Though the writer is reckoned some kind of parasitic Ariel, nothing will prevent him from producing what is absolutely essential to a commonwealth which otherwise exists for millionaires, wastrels, and stupid and immoral articles which nobody needs.

Hart Crane never finished high school, and this seems to trouble his biographer, Philip Horton, who imagines that had he gone to the university he would have been a more cultured poet. A biographer generally is the epicure of a poet's faults. It would be more accurate to describe Crane's lack of formal education as a "blessed dearth," to quote Christian Rossetti. By the time a student can be called a doctor of philosophy, he has very likely never heard of Porphyry, Philostratus, Antisthenes, or the *Rig-Veda*. Crane wrote: "I have been reading the philosophies of the East until I actually dream in terms of the Vedanta scriptures." And "The people I am closest to in English are Keats... and the dear great Elizabethans like Marlowe, Webster, Donne and Drayton."

Nearly all of his canicular days he belonged to the brotherhood of beggars. Both Harriet Monroe and Marianne Moore mangled his verse, and he asked "how much longer will our markets be in the grips of two such hysterical virgins"; the former was the editor of *Poetry* magazine and the latter the arbiter at the *Dial*. He was also assailed because he was not a *whole* man, which, like the Absolute, according to Duns Scotus is *nihil*. Crane was everyman's cully; Waldo

Frank, his steadfast friend, was hemlock to his work. The *Complete Poems* appeared posthumously, and the Introduction by Frank is a masterpiece in astral platitudes. Says Frank in his opening line: "Agrarian America had a common culture, which was both the fruit and the carrier of what I have called 'the great tradition.'"

He had published poems in the *Little Review*, Joseph Kling's *The Pagan*, *The Fugitive*, *Broom*, and had gotten nothing for his jubilant pains. He hoped to buy a pair of shoes for the money he would receive from an article on Sherwood Anderson that had appeared in *The Double Dealer*, a New Orleans literary paper. He had beseeched Thomas Seltzer to publish *White Buildings*, assuring him he had a grandiose audience of five hundred readers, but Seltzer declined to do it. After much pressure from Eugene O'Neill and Waldo Frank, Boni and Liveright brought out the small volume for which he was given one hundred dollars.

Meantime, he was generally looking for "jobs in limbo," his purgatories were the office in which he wrote advertising copy for hot water heaters or in the "bellies and estuaries of warehouses" of his father's candy factories.

Hart Crane had no social creeds, and to Allen Tate he wrote: "Poetry as poetry...isn't worth a second reading any more. Therefore away with Kubla Khan, out with Marlowe, and to hell with Keats." Crane was never baited by the social paroxysms that are the Cain's curse of each generation, be it feminism or Marxist dialectics. Covering a strike in the cotton mills, when I was an extreme advocate for the working class, I slept in the house of a Portuguese laborer; above his bed was a tryptich, on one panel was the Virgin Mary, on the other Shirley Temple, and in the middle Karl Marx. Crane had no inclination, as he averred, to "sum up the universe in one impressive pellet."

Again the letters reveal a comprehension of the perplexities of the American visionary, and despite the influence of the good, gray poet, he says to Tate: "It's true that my rhapsodic address to [Whitman] in

The Bridge exceeds any exact evaluation of the man." Then, scolding his friend, Crane adds: "...you like so many others, never seem to have read his *Democratic Vistas*...decrying materialism, industrialism." Few poets have perused Whitman's *Specimen Days*, but neither of these books will be yeasty pabulum for a good maker of verses. He was far closer to what he hoped to do in expressing his admiration for MacLeish's *Conquistador*, once a renowned poem, as finely wrought as an Aztec lapidary's work on turquoise but now skulled in anthologies.

In Mexico, as a Guggenheim Fellow, he discovered that he could fall into as much of a passion for Venus as he did for "calla lilies, freesia, roses, calendulas, white iris, violets, cannas...geraniums... feverfew, candy tuft." He wrote: "I must admit that I find conjugal life, however unofficial, a great consolation to a loneliness that had about eaten me up."

But the alcoholic frenzies continued, and his flesh ached for Gehenna and the Gates of Jerusalem. "Suffering is a real purification," Crane said. "What is beauty, saith my suffering?" wrote Marlowe, his savant and master. His demise was deliriously close; unable to abide the ignominy of level, average days, he either was ecstatic about the fiesta of Tepozteco, the ancient god of *pulque,* or shuddered with fright as he envisaged himself once more as a penniless urchin in New York. Violence sharpened his intellect; as Plotinus has said: "the... corybantes continue their raptures until *they see what they desire.*" But Crane craved infinite bacchanalian seizures, or the bliss of the shroud and the tomb, and so aboard the *Orizaba,* on his way back to New York, he leaped from the rail of the deck into the sharkish Carib sea.

Exile, wanderer, homeless in all latitudes, strife was his god, and his oracle the sea.

Is the agony or the fury of nonsense any different today? Three decades ago or so, the customs officials insisted that D. H. Lawrence's urned ashes were a work of art and should be taxed; Waldo Frank had to call upon a clergyman to prove to our warders of sexual hygiene that the title of his novel, *The Bridegroom Cometh*, taken from the New Testament, was not obscene.

So we, who cannot conceive the books without sinning, are outcasts and pornographers, our brains void of cassia, ambergris, and camphor until they are dead, and then deemed priceless in the venal agora, a bookstore, a university, ay, a textbook!

Leopardi "saw the world as a vast league of criminals ruthlessly warring against a few virtuous madmen."

—January 20, 1966

4

ROBERT OPPENHEIMER
ON ALBERT EINSTEIN

THOUGH I KNEW Einstein for two or three decades, it was only in the last decade of his life that we were close colleagues and something of friends. But I thought that it might be useful, because I am sure that it is not too soon—and for our generation perhaps almost too late—to start to dispel the clouds of myth and to see the great mountain peak that these clouds hide. As always, the myth has its charms; but the truth is far more beautiful.

Late in his life, in connection with his despair over weapons and wars, Einstein said that if he had to live it over again he would be a plumber. This was a balance of seriousness and jest that no one should now attempt to disturb. Believe me, he had no idea of what it was to be a plumber; least of all in the United States, where we have a joke that the typical behavior of this specialist is that he never brings his tools to the scene of the crisis. Einstein brought his tools to his crises; Einstein was a physicist, a natural philosopher, the greatest of our time.

What we have heard, what you all know, what is the true part of the myth is his extraordinary originality. The discovery of quanta would surely have come one way or another, but he discovered them. Deep understanding of what it means that no signal could travel faster than light would surely have come; the formal equations were already known; but this simple, brilliant understanding of the physics could well have been slow in coming, and blurred, had he not done it for us. The general theory of relativity which, even today, is not well proved experimentally, no one but he would have done for a long, long time. It is in fact only in the last decade, the last years, that one has seen how a pedestrian and hard-working physicist, or many of them, might reach that theory and understand this singular union of geometry and gravitation; and we can do even that today only because some of the *a priori* open possibilities are limited by the confirmation of Einstein's discovery that light would be deflected by gravity.

Yet there is another side besides the originality. Einstein brought to the work of originality deep elements of tradition. It is only possible to discover in part how he came by it, by following his reading, his friendships, the meager record that we have. But of these deep-seated elements of tradition—I will not try to enumerate them all; I do not know them all—at least three were indispensable and stayed with him.

The first is from the rather beautiful but recondite part of physics that is the explanation of the laws of thermodynamics in terms of the mechanics of large numbers of particles, statistical mechanics. This was with Einstein all the time. It was what enabled him from Planck's discovery of the law of black body radiation to conclude that light was not only waves but particles, particles with an energy proportional to their frequency and momentum determined by their wave-number, the famous relations that de Broglie was to extend to all matter, to electrons first and then clearly to all matter.

It was this statistical tradition that led Einstein to the laws governing the emission and absorption of light by atomic systems. It was this that enabled him to see the connection between de Broglie's waves and the statistics of light-quanta proposed by Bose. It was this that kept him an active proponent and discoverer of the new phenomena of quantum physics up to 1925.

The second and equally deep strand—and here I think we do know where it came from—was his total love of the idea of a field: the following of physical phenomena in minute and infinitely subdividable detail in space and in time. This gave him his first great drama of trying to see how Maxwell's equations could be true. They were the first field equations of physics; they are still true today with only very minor and well-understood modifications. It is this tradition which made him know that there had to be a field theory of gravitation, long before the clues to that theory were securely in his hand.

The third tradition was less one of physics than of philosophy. It is a form of the principle of sufficient reason. It was Einstein who asked what do we mean, what can we measure, what elements in physics are conventional? He insisted that those elements that were conventional could have no part in the real predictions of physics. This also had roots: for one the mathematical invention of Riemann, who saw how very limited the geometry of the Greeks had been, how unreasonably limited. But in a more important sense, it followed from the long tradition of European philosophy, you may say starting with Descartes— if you wish you can start it in the Thirteenth Century, because in fact it did start then—and leading through the British empiricists, and very clearly formulated, though probably without influence in Europe, by Charles Pierce: One had to ask how do we do it, what do we mean, is this just something that we can use to help ourselves in calculating, or is it something that we can actually study in nature by physical means? For the point here is that the laws of nature not only describe the results of observations, but the laws of nature delimit the scope of observations. That was the point of Einstein's understanding of the limiting character of the velocity of light; it also was the nature of the resolution in quantum theory, where the quantum of action, Planck's constant, was recognized as limiting the fineness of the transaction between the system studied and the machinery used to study it, limiting this fineness in a form of atomicity quite different from and quite more radical than any that the Greeks had imagined or than was familiar from the atomic theory of chemistry.

In the last years of Einstein's life, the last twenty-five years, his tradition in a certain sense failed him. They were the years he spent at Princeton and this, though a source of sorrow, should not be concealed. He had a right to that failure. He spent those years first in trying to prove that the quantum theory had inconsistencies in it. No one could have been more ingenious in thinking up unexpected and clever examples; but it turned out that the inconsistencies were not there; and often their resolution could be found in earlier work of Einstein himself. When that did not work, after repeated efforts, Einstein had simply to say that he did not like the theory. He did not like the elements of indeterminacy. He did not like the abandonment of continuity or of causality. These were things that he had grown up with, saved by him, and enormously enlarged; and to see them lost, even though he had put the dagger in the hand of their assassin by his own work, was very hard on him. He fought with Bohr in a noble and furious way, and he fought with the theory which he had fathered but which he hated. It was not the first time that this has happened in science.

He also worked with a very ambitious program, to combine the understanding of electricity and gravitation in such a way as to explain what he regarded as the semblance—the illusion—of discreteness, of particles in nature. I think that it was clear then, and believe it to be obviously clear today, that the things that this theory worked with were too meager, left out too much that was known to physicists but had not been known much in Einstein's student days. Thus it looked like a hopelessly limited and historically rather accidentally conditioned approach. Although Einstein commanded the affection, or, more rightly, the love of everyone for his determination to see through his program, he lost most contact with the profession of physics, because there were things that had been learned which came too late in life for him to concern himself with them.

Einstein was indeed one of the friendliest of men. I had the impression that he was also, in an important sense, alone. Many very great men are lonely; yet I had the impression that although he was a deep and loyal friend, the stronger human affection played a not very deep or very central part in his life taken as a whole. He had of course incredibly many disciples, in the sense of people who, reading his work or hearing it taught by him, learned from him and had a new view of physics, of the philosophy of physics, of the nature of the world that we live in. But he did not have, in the technical jargon, a school. He did not have very many students who were his concern as apprentices and disciples. And there was an element of the lone worker in him, in sharp contrast to the teams we see today, and in sharp contrast to the highly cooperative way in which some other parts of science have developed. In later years, he had people working with him. They were typically called assistants and they had a wonderful life. Just being with him was wonderful. His secretary had a wonderful life. The sense of grandeur never left him for a minute, nor his sense of humor. The assistants did one thing which he lacked in his young days. His early papers are paralyzingly beautiful, but there are many errata. Later there were none. I had the impression that, along with its miseries, his fame gave him some pleasures, not only the human pleasure of meeting people but the extreme pleasure of music played not only with Elizabeth of Belgium but more with Adolf Busch, for he was not that good a violinist. He loved the sea and he loved sailing and was always grateful for a ship. I remember walking home with him on his seventy-first birthday. He said, "You know, when it's once been given to a man to do something sensible, afterward life is a little strange."

Einstein is also, and I think rightly, known as a man of very great good will and humanity. Indeed, if I had to think of a single word for his attitude toward human problems, I would pick the Sanscrit word *Ahinsa*, not to hurt, harmlessness. He had a deep distrust of power; he did not have that convenient and natural converse with statesmen and men of power that was quite appropriate to Rutherford and to

Bohr, perhaps the two physicists of this century who most nearly rivaled him in eminence. In 1915, as he made the general theory of relativity, Europe was tearing itself to pieces and half losing its past. He was always a pacifist. Only as the Nazis came into power in Germany did he have some doubts, as his famous and rather deep exchange of letters with Freud showed, and began to understand with melancholy and without true acceptance that, in addition to understanding, man sometimes has a duty to act.

After what you have heard, I need not say how luminous was his intelligence. He was almost wholly without sophistication and wholly without worldliness. I think that in England people would have said that he did not have much "background," and in America that he lacked "education." This may throw some light on how these words are used. I think that this simplicity, this lack of clutter and this lack of cant, had a lot to do with his preservation throughout of a certain pure, rather Spinoza-like, philosophical monism, which of course is hard to maintain if you have been "educated" and have a "background." There was always with him a wonderful purity, at once childlike and profoundly stubborn.

Einstein is often blamed or praised or credited with these miserable bombs. It is not in my opinion true. The special theory of relativity might not have been beautiful without Einstein; but it would have been a tool for physicists, and by 1932 the experimental evidence for the inter-convertibility of matter and energy which he had predicted was overwhelming. The feasibility of doing anything with this in such a massive way was not clear until seven years later, and then almost by accident. This was not what Einstein really was after. His part was that of creating an intellectual revolution, and discovering more than any scientist of our time how profound were the errors made by men before then. He did write a letter to Roosevelt about atomic energy. I think this was in part his agony at the evil of the Nazis, in part not wanting to harm anyone in any way; but I ought to report that that letter had very little effect, and that Einstein himself is really not answerable for all that came later. I believe he so understood it himself.

His was a voice raised with very great weight against violence and cruelty wherever he saw them and, after the war, he spoke with deep emotion and I believe with great weight about the supreme violence of these atomic weapons. He said at once with great simplicity: Now we must make a world government. It was very forthright, it was very abrupt, it was no doubt "uneducated," no doubt without "background"; still all of us in some thoughtful measure must recognize that he was right.

Without power, without calculation, with none of the profoundly political humor that characterized Gandhi, he nevertheless did move the political world. In almost the last act of his life, he joined with Lord Russell in suggesting that men of science get together and see if they could not understand one another and avert the disaster which he foresaw from the arms race. The so-called Pugwash movement, which has a longer name now, was the direct result of this appeal. I know it to be true that it had an essential part to play in the Treaty of Moscow, the limited test-ban treaty, which is a tentative, but to me very precious, declaration that reason might still prevail.

In his last years, as I knew him, Einstein was a twentieth-century Ecclesiastes, saying with unrelenting and indomitable cheerfulness, "Vanity of vanities, all is vanity."

—This was a lecture delivered at UNESCO *House in Paris on December 13, 1965.*

5

DWIGHT MACDONALD
ON DELMORE SCHWARTZ

IN THE FALL of 1937, when *Partisan Review* was about to be revived as a non-Communist literary magazine, a writer with the unlikely name of Delmore Schwartz sent in a short story, "In Dreams Begin Responsibilities," which I and my fellow editors had the sense to recognize as a masterpiece and to print in our first issue. There were also contributions from Wallace Stevens, Edmund Wilson, Agee, Trilling, Picasso, Farrell, Mary McCarthy, and William Troy—we tried to make it a "strong" issue, for obvious tactical reasons—but I think Delmore's story deserved its primacy. It is as good as a story can be, I'd say after reading it again for the fifth or sixth time, comparable with Kafka, Babel, or *Through the Looking Glass*.

> I think it is the year 1909 [it begins]. I feel as if I were in a moving-picture theatre, the long arms of light crossing the darkness and spinning, my eyes fixed on the screen. It is a silent picture, as if an old Biograph one, in which the actors are dressed in ridiculously old-fashioned clothes, and one flash succeeds another with sudden jumps, and the actors, too, seem to jump about, walking too fast. The shots are full of rays and dots, as if it had been raining when the picture is photographed. The light is bad.

The movie is about his parents' courtship, mostly an excursion to Coney Island that ends in a disastrous quarrel, a clash of temperaments, and obstinacies, that is all the more ominous because the causes are so trivial. As he watches this banal home movie that tells more than it means to, the author becomes more and more upset, weeping at first ("There, there young man," an old lady sitting next to him says, patting his shoulder, "all of this is only a movie, only a movie"), and then shouting warnings, to the scandal of the audience, at the images of his parents-to-be as they flicker on their unalterable course across the screen: "Don't do it! It's not too late to change your mind, both of you. Nothing good will come of it, only remorse, hatred, scandal, and two children whose characters are monstrous.... Don't they know what they are doing? Why doesn't my mother go after my father and beg him not to be angry?... Doesn't my father know what he is doing?" The story ends with his being ejected by the usher ("hurrying down the aisle with his flashlight") and his waking up "into the bleak winter morning of my twenty-first birthday, the windowsill shining with its lip of snow, and the morning already begun." An original literary idea that works imaginatively, I think, and that combines the freest, most specific self-revelation with a form that controls the expression of these deep, personal fears partly by "distancing" them in time and medium—a movie is just what suits—and partly by a classical concision—the story is only seven pages long—in which every word counts, as in the opening paragraph quoted above. This unusual combination of expressive candor and tight form is characteristic of Delmore's poetry in general—we were surprised to find, though we shouldn't have been, that he was a poet also, and essentially.

> *What curious dresses all men wear!*
> *The walker you met in a brown study,*
> *The President smug in rotogravure,*
> *The mannequin, the bathing beauty,*

The bubble-dancer, the deep-sea diver,
The bureaucrat, the adulterer,
Hide private parts which I disclose
To those who know what a poem knows.

So he wrote in the copy of his first book (New Directions, 1938) he
gave me—the verses haven't been printed, so far as I know—and so it
was with his work, the private disclosure and the public form, con-
cealment on one level but all the more revealing on another, that of
art, or of "those who know what a poem knows."

Delmore was twenty-four that year, but his open, ardent manner,
and his large, dreaming eyes, sensitive mouth, and proud good looks
as of a newly fledged eaglet made him seem younger. We took to
each other right away. We were alike: New Yorkers by birth and
upbringing, restless, impatient, fond of argument, pushing ideas as
far as they would go, and farther, assuming that talk was not necessarily, or intimately, related to action so that we could say almost
anything to each other without hurt feelings, or bloody noses, and
urban (though not urbane) types to whom "the country" was like the
moon, interesting but alien and a little scary. We also found each
other exotic. Delmore was always ironic about my Yale-gentile
background—we were both middle-class so that wasn't involved
—which struck him as picturesque but slightly primitive; while I
couldn't understand what seemed to me his obsession with his Jewish
childhood. Sometimes I felt like a teacher—I was only seven years
older but that was a big gap at our ages—dealing with a bright student whose affection was greater than his respect. But most of the
time, in the almost thirty years I knew him, we were equals, friends,
and I can't think of anyone who gave himself in friendship more
generously and whose conversation, and companionship, I enjoyed
more.

There was always something doing when Delmore was around. He was a great talker and he never held back, no hedging around with small talk and cautious civilities, unpacking his mind instantly like one of those Armenian peddlers who used to come to our summer house in New Jersey and who would have their enormous cardboard suitcases unstrapped and displaying their treasures of lace and linen before my mother could get the door shut. He was a master of the great American folk art of kidding, an impractical joker—words were his medium —outraging dignity and privacy, present company most definitely not excepted, pressing the attack until it reached a comic grandeur that had even the victim laughing. An intellectual equivalent of the Borsch Circuit *tummler*, or stirrer-upper, his wide mouth grinning, his speedy, raucous New York voice running up and down the scale of sarcasm, invective, desperate rationality, gasping ridicule, his nervous hands clutching his head in despair at the obtuseness of his antagonist or flung wide in triumphant demonstration or stabbing the air with a minatory forefinger. And he could take it as well as dish it out. I can't remember him irritated by the most drastic counterattack; indeed he seemed to welcome direct onslaughts on himself and his ideas like a skillful swordsman who knows he can deflect the thrust. In more placid talk, he was even more impressive, quick on the uptake, bringing to bear on the point a richness of reference and of imagination. He was a conversationalist, not a monologist, his style of discourse being dialectical, depending on the other person, or persons, to stimulate him to his greatest reaches. He was both witty and humorous, the shrewd wisecrack slipped into the interstices of an argument like a quick knife thrust, and also the expansive comic "turn," like one of Mark Twain's leisurely, endlessly climaxing anecdotes, which left us both breathless with laughter as Delmore, with objections or additions from me—he welcomed interruptions, as a clever speaker welcomes hecklers, converting them to his own use and making them part of his improvisation—built up one of his realistic fantasies about an audience with

T. S. Eliot, or the minutely characterized variations in the reactions of mutual friends to the James family plot in Mount Auburn cemetery or some other item in the tour of Cambridge he took them on while he was teaching at Harvard. These set pieces were as detailed as a Dutch genre painting, he seemed to have total recall, and while I suspected many of the details were invented, and sometimes when I had been present knew they were (or was Delmore just a better observer?), the general effect was always so true to life that it was extremely funny.

There was a genial shimmer over Delmore's talk—as the Irish say, he knew how to put a skin on it—generous, easy, and, no matter how outrageously exaggerated, never envious or malicious; like Jove's laughter. He was egoistic without vanity: he was curiously modest, or perhaps "detached" or "objective" might be better words, about himself and his extraordinary talents. Even in his darkening later years, when paranoia was more and more spreading in his mind, his delusions were not of grandeur. He thought he was persecuted but not because of any imagined preeminence on his part; rather did he seem to see himself as the victim, merely, of powerful people—the Rockefellers figured prominently, for reasons as ingeniously complicated as they were tenuous—who were sending out rays from the Empire State Building to damage his poor brain, so superior to those of his fancied persecutors, and yet so vulnerable.

For all the exuberance and even violence with which he expressed himself—an emotional, not a physical violence, it should be noted; even when he came to denounce at last most of his old friends, including me, no blows were struck, so far as I know—Delmore's was a remarkably *reasonable* mind, immune to the passions and prejudices of our period. He was not a joiner. Although he didn't hesitate to throw in with us on *Partisan Review*, first as a contributor, then as an editor, at a time when there was some risk in taking an anti-Communist stand, he seemed to feel no need for any political commitment as a writer, at least I can't recall his signing any of my manifestoes or joining any of my committees. And although he was very conscious of his Jewish family background and returned to it constantly in his work—he was one of the first of the Jewish school that has now succeeded the Southern school—his attitude toward it was sometimes tender and sometimes ironical but never chauvinistic. Even after the war and the death camps he never made me feel uncomfortable as a goy, he could even discuss the Arab refugee question without undue excitement, and if he poked fun at my gentile-ity, he also mocked his own Jewishness, beginning with his name: he used to say he had been named after a Pullman car or a Riverside Drive apartment house, making endless fun of the discrepancy between his first and last names, as in his long narrative poem about a hero named Shenandoah Fish.

In this detachment from ideological fashion, Delmore resembled James Agee, another inspired talker, though tending more toward the monological than the dialectical mode. There are other similarities: both combined, in a way unique in my generation, an extraordinary talent for writing, the sheer gift of technique, in prose and poetry, with an intellectual passion, and a capacity for dealing with ideas, even to the point of writing a good deal of excellent criticism—Agee's movie reviews are now well known; it might be interesting to collect Delmore's reviews, in *The New Republic* and elsewhere, of films, TV, and books—that is not usual in our "creative" writers today. Both died youngish of heart attacks, and both had a positive genius for self-destruction. The gap between what they might have done and what they actually realized in their work is heartbreaking. "Cut is the branch that might have grown full straight/And burned is Apollo's laurel bough/That sometime grew within this learned man."

At Delmore's funeral, M. L. Rosenthal, of New York University, read one of his later poems:

> *All of the fruits had fallen,*
> *The bears had fallen asleep,*

And the pears were useless and soft
Like used hopes, under the starlight's
Small knowledge, scattered aloft
In a glittering senseless drift:
The jackals of remorse in a cage
Drugged beyond mirth and rage.

Then, then, the dark hour flowered!
Under the silence, immense
And empty as far-off seas,
I wished for the innocence
Of my stars and my stones and my trees
All the brutality and inner sense
A dog and a bird possess,
The dog who barked at the moon
As an enemy's white fang,
The bird that thrashed up the bush
And soared to soar as it sang,
A being all present as touch,
Free of the future and past
—Until, in the dim window glass,
The fog or cloud of my face
Showed me my fear at last!

Poetry is a dangerous occupation in this country, as the biographers of too many of our best twentieth-century poets show, from Ezra Pound on, including the recent deaths of Randall Jarrell and Theodore Roethke. This is not a new thing. Writing of our first major poet, Baudelaire often seems to be describing the subject of this memoir:

His conversation deserves particular mention. The first time that I asked an American about it, he laughed a good deal and said: "His talk is *not at all consecutive*." After some explanation I understood that Poe made long digressions in the world of ideas, like a mathematician making demonstrations for advanced students.... It seems that Poe was not at all difficult about his audience. He cared little whether his listeners were able to understand his tenuous abstractions, or to admire the glorious conceptions which incessantly illuminated the dark sky of his mind. He would sit down in a tavern, beside some dirty scapegrace, and would gravely explain to him the grand outlines of his terrible book, *Eureka*.... No man ever freed himself more completely from the rules of society, or bothered himself less about passersby.... In Paris, in Germany, he would have found friends who could easily have understood and comforted him; in America he had to fight for his bread. Thus his drunkenness and his nomadic habits are readily explained. He went through life as if through a Sahara desert, and changed his residence like an Arab.... For Poe the United States was nothing more than a vast prison which he traversed with the feverish agitation of a being made to breathe a sweeter air.

No, the American climate is still not suited for poets. "Dazzling a young and unformed country by his mind," Baudelaire writes, "Poe was fated to become a most unhappy writer. Rancors were aroused, solitude settled around him." Our country is middle-aged but still unformed and, granting that in both poets psychological difficulties were also important, still I cannot but see Delmore, too, as "a being made to breathe a sweeter air." He found it mostly among the young; "Delmore was a regular Pied Piper," one of his students said to me after the funeral, where the attendance was sharply divided between the very young and the very middle-aged, one of the two limousines that went to the cemetery being filled with students who had known him at Syracuse University or in one of the Village bars he frequented.

"I suppose that by the time the war is over, we will be outmoded characters, even such a Yale man as you," he wrote to me in 1942 from
Harvard, groaning about "forty Freshman themes a week to correct,"
but adding: "If you come to one of my classes, you will see how far I
am from the Genteel Tradition and with what shameless gestures I
seek to find the post-war soul." His search continued to the very end;
he was always a good teacher, in or out of the classroom, open to the
young. For what made Delmore—nobody thinks of him as anything
but "Delmore"—precious was his candor, his invincible innocence
(like the Catholics' "invincible ignorance"), his uncalculating generosity of response—all that Meyer Schapiro in his poem finely calls
his "ever-resurgent hopes of light."

—September 8, 1966

6

ALFRED KAZIN
ON JOSEPHINE HERBST

THERE ARE PEOPLE who knew Josie longer than I did, and are better qualified to speak of her, and for her many friends, than I am. I met her early in 1950, a time when she had already endured many disappointments as a writer and as an American radical, and when she was already caught up in the long hard struggle for survival that was to end only in the early hours of January 28th. The nineteen years in which I knew her were years of great poverty, great isolation, often of humiliating frustration and silence. So I cannot speak, as others could directly, of the spunky and brilliantly independent girl from Sioux City who typically enough went off to Berkeley for an A.B. as if college were a romantic adventure—and, the year after, took the lifelong adventure that was already herself to New York, where she read for George Jean Nathan and H. L. Mencken on *The Smart Set* and began to form those friendships with writers for which she had, unlike many writers, a special and enduring genius.

Nor can I speak directly here of her creative beginnings—of how, in 1921 she went to Europe, as so many writers of her marvelous generation did, without quite knowing how she would live, yet typically got right into the heat of things, political and literary, in Weimar Germany. I cannot speak here directly of Josie in the Twenties, when she was so much a part of the new American writing that was emerging in

Paris with her friend Hemingway, or of Josie in the early Thirties, when she found expression for all her burning old-fashioned American idealism in identifying herself with, in being right on the spot as a correspondent to report, what then still seemed the old-fashioned Russian idealism, the Negro boys from Scottsboro, the struggling farmers from her native Iowa. She was with Dreiser and Dos Passos when they went down to investigate the terror against the striking Kentucky miners, with the Cuban peasants during the 1935 general strike, with the first victims of Hitler's terror in those years of the Thirties, before the war, when apparently it took a Socialist experience and imagination to guess the potential horror of what so many bourgeois German Jews could not.

In 1937 Josie was, of course, in Spain to cover the Spanish Civil War—and she was really there, steeped in the life of the frontline villages and, typically enough, getting desperately needed rations for her fellow correspondents in the Hotel Florída from her always well-stocked friend Hemingway, from whose room the smell of frying bacon and other goodies would drive less fortunate writers crazy. And during the Second World War, Josie, who needed the job desperately, was of course fired from the OWI, then busily mobilizing American opinion against Fascism, for having been a premature anti-Fascist.

As I say, I did not know her then—I met her only in 1950, when her books were all out of print, when she was out of a job, out of cash, out of fashion, and might have been out of a home if it hadn't been for that blessed stone house in Erwinna—surely one of the few writers' residences in Bucks County still dependent on an outhouse. Pauline Pfeiffer, Hemingway's second wife, said to me in Key West, talking about Josie's plight with a shudder—"A woman shouldn't be that poor." But she was, and every friend of Josie's knows how tough it was for her up to the end.

Yet—and this is what I have come here to say—I have never known in my life any other writer who was so solid, so joyous, so giving, who was able to take difficulties so much in her stride, and, who even when she was getting pretty old and sick, made you see that flaming girl from Sioux City and Berkeley and New York, Germany and Russia and Cuba and Spain, who was always getting mad about injustice and pompous stupidity, always radiating that marvelous sense of physical space and human possibility that was the gift of the Middle West to so many writers of her generation.

Josie, who could easily get mad and also make you see the fun of getting mad, got mad always in behalf of other people. I was enchanted to read in Carlos Baker's forthcoming biography of Hemingway that one day in that romantic long ago, when Josie and her husband John Herrmann went fishing with Hemingway off the keys, Hemingway lost his temper at John for not getting enough ice to keep their catch fresh, and kept grousing at him until Josie broke in: "Hem, if you don't stop I'll take your pistol and shoot you." Hemingway, who was so fond of Josie that he later gave her one of his manuscripts, was properly impressed.

Josie had many gifts—she was a natural writer, an expressive lyricist of human emotion and of landscape, a firm and canny observer in her novels of every human snare, an extraordinarily warm, loving woman who could express her love for her friends in letters that were as direct and overflowing as the warmth of her voice and the spontaneity of her soul. On Saturday morning, January 25th, she said two sentences that so impressed Dr. Fries that she entered it in Josie's medical chart. "I want you to give a final message to my friends. Tell them that I do not repent, that I love life unto eternity, love and life." When I think of what I loved and valued most in her, as someone in whom the writer and woman were so intermingled, it comes down to this directness, this particular old-fashioned straightness of her every attitude, that exploded out of her, often laughingly, as if Josie Herbst were the shortest distance between two points. This directness was an old-fashioned political attitude in America, it was once our politics, and Josie suffered its loss; it was an old-fashioned morality: you must speak out, now; it was her old-fashioned freedom and her beautiful strength. She was so full of existence, of politics and nature and literature and friendship, that her letters, her incomparable letters, the kind of letters people never even think of writing anymore, were an explosion of directness. You received everything on her mind and heart, and it was the gift of her, direct—

Friday morning, Erwinna, Pa. July 7, 1950—

A tiny yellow duck broke loose from its mother and waddled down the hill to my back door—then began a loud squawk in terror and fearful recognition that it was lost, lost. I got it in my hand and it settled down at once—I could have held it like that forever until we both perished, two ninnies in bliss together while the world fell apart. I called up the farm, they came with a truck as if the duck were a cow to be transported only in a huge affair and took it away. I loved it madly—Russell writes Scribner's may do the Bartram book and that Hastings House are bastards. It will work out. I am glad to think of you with friends away from New York. Here it was divinely cool last night . . . a late big moon and before that a night thick with fireflies. Some stars are pale green. Some icy blue and there are some as red as my barn.

And on she went for a whole solid single-spaced page, ending— "When one wants grapes, one goes to the poor. They will be willing to rob the birds but they will share with you, share and share alike. They will even love you for your need and shelter you in their arms, hasta revista, Josie." But alas, we won't.

This tribute to Josephine Herbst was read at a memorial service held at St. Luke's Chapel in New York on February 18, 1969.

7

JASON EPSTEIN
ON EDMUND WILSON

What they undertook to do
They brought to pass;
All things hang like a drop of dew
Upon a blade of grass.
—W. B. Yeats

OCCASIONALLY, AS HIS death became imminent, I would find myself, most unwillingly, imagining Edmund Wilson's funeral. It would be at a hilltop cemetery in Wellfleet in spring or early fall. The sky would be clear and the sea, through tall grass and bent pines, would be blue in the distant curve of the Truro beaches. There would be a circle of family and friends—about twenty or so—and, as I imagined the scene, I would stand just outside this ring so that I could see the drawn shoulders and bent backs of the mourners. It was a sentimental picture that kept coming to mind, something that a forgotten expressionist might have painted years ago.

Beside the grave someone would be reading, but his text—which Edmund himself would surely have chosen—was more than I could guess, though no doubt it would be something very humane, very unyielding, a text that would put death in its correct, inevitable, not very terrible place. The residual emotion would be less a sense of loss than of continuity. The spirit of the occasion would be that we must get together and do this again soon.

Except for minor topographical differences, this was pretty much how it happened. It was a bright day in June, clear, humid, and windy. I could feel the wind bend the pine that I was leaning against. We were not on a hilltop, as I had imagined, but in a sort of sandy clearing amid sparse trees, slightly below the main part of the tiny Wellfleet cemetery, and well out of sight of the sea. There were moments of humor that I had not anticipated: the young Orleans curate, like a scrubbed Beatle, shyly adjusting his lacy canonicals beside his blue Volkswagen in the Wilsons' driveway, as if he were hanging curtains; Edmund's daughters, Rosalind and Helen, his son, Reuel, and Elena's son, Henry, smiling as they took turns shoveling sand back into the grave where Edmund's ashes had been placed, like children playing at the beach. Death seemed incidental to the occasion, and compared with the life that Edmund had led and the work he did, his death really was only an incident, a detail of no great moment, except for those who had known him well enough to love him.

In his last years Edmund was often in great pain. Once last summer when I visited him in Wellfleet for what I assumed would be the last time, he asked me to help him out of his chair. Though he was fully alert to the end of his life, there were days when he lacked the strength to dress himself and could hardly move from room to room without help. I took him by the elbow, but as I began to lift him as gently as I could he fell back into his chair and cried out, as when one stubs a toe. By this time he had moved permanently downstairs, accompanied by two alarming green iron bottles of oxygen, to his study in the beautiful frail old Wellfleet house. Actually he had settled himself in the most recent annex to this study, since this part of the building, for the past ten years or so, has been regularly expanded by the addition of ells and wings to accommodate his proliferating collections of

Russian, Hebrew, Hungarian, and the usual Western literatures, collections that grew and spread through the house as if they were alive.

A year ago I noticed on one of his shelves a set of Scott. Since I had never seen these books in his study before, I asked him what he planned to do with them. I suppose I meant to find out whether he was thinking of writing about this subject, but as I asked the question I realized how rude it must have seemed. Edmund was plainly close to death and the set must have contained forty volumes. "I am going to read them," he said, a snapping turtle's gaze of unruffled malevolence momentarily crossing his face.

After the funeral, when we sat in the blue and white living room, Elena showed me a volume of Balzac, opened and folded back, a large silver magnifier resting on it. "He was reading that last week," she told me, "and he asked me such hard questions about those old-fashioned agricultural words that Balzac used." Last winter in Naples, Florida, he read through nearly all of Balzac and I learned from his old friend Morley Callaghan, who had come down from Toronto for the funeral, that on the advice of the Naples librarian he had also taken an interest in Robertson Davies, the Canadian writer, whose books he then proceeded to read and with whom he began to exchange letters.

During this same winter he finished his book on the 1920s, put together a collection of his Russian pieces, and finished his revision of *To the Finland Station*. In April, when I saw him in New York on his way up from Florida to Wellfleet, he seemed surprisingly more vigorous than he had been the summer before on Cape Cod. Even so he remained, during my brief visit, propped up in his bed in the Plaza Hotel and he seemed to have more than his usual difficulty understanding what I said to him. "Tell me what he said," he would demand of Elena. "I can't hear what he's saying." I swallow my words, and this difficulty had plagued my recent meetings with Edmund, whose hearing had begun to go, so that Elena, in her mélange of accents, had to interpret for me. Yet Edmund refused to use a hearing device and, more seriously, would not let his doctors install a pacemaker, which might have kept his heart going a while longer.

He was a Darwinian fundamentalist in this respect and at an earlier time in his life had even held out against vaccination because it interfered with nature's superior wisdom in matters of selection and survival. He had, he told me some years ago as we walked along Forty-third Street on a rainy winter day, no interest in abstract ideas. This was in answer to my effort to interest him in Thomas Mann, a writer he claimed, with some pride, never to have read, but whose vaporous metaphysics seemed to me, at the time, just fine.

No abstract ideas. No pacemaker. No vaccination. The point was not to tamper with the marvelous arrangements worked out at such length by nature and history, but to try to understand them well enough to live in their midst without presumptuously violating them. Edmund was very much an Old Testament man, for whom the concreteness of things was sacred. In politics it was the same. Large power units, as he called such countries as the United States and the Soviet Union, were like metaphysical propositions. They blocked true comprehension and led to deadly error. To put one's trust in them was as much an intellectual fault as to accept as true the ontological propositions of formal religion.

Even the American Civil War was fought, he believed, in the name of a mystical proposition—the abstract idea of Union. But why Union? he asked in his masterpiece *Patriotic Gore*. Was it worth that terrible struggle so that the United States could become still another large power unit, along with Russia, Britain, and Germany? So that Lincoln, like Bismarck and later Lenin, could contrive an empire whose fate was inevitably to collide with those other empires that were monstrously growing in the world, like great biological malformations? Wasn't the idea of Union yet another of those religious frenzies that, at various times, sweep across history and by which political leaders justify their aggrandizements and their need for power, while the lives of ordinary people are needlessly disrupted or destroyed?

It was this old republican skepticism that led Wilson, in his later years, back into what he called a pocket of the past, to the old Talcottville house in upstate New York, that Transylvanian fastness where he was sometimes able to imagine that the presumed virtues of the old republic may once have prevailed, though in fact he knew better than to take such myths literally. But his reclusiveness, to those who knew him, was half-hearted. As eagerly as he would retreat to Talcottville, he would restlessly emerge from it, and even when he was in residence there he would coax his friends to visit him with literary news and gossip. His interest in the world was broad and passionate. For the last month, Elena told me, he had been wearing a McGovern button.

That this stubborn old republican should once have considered himself a Marxist must seem puzzling, but the Marxism was an aberration, a plausible, but false, inference from the optimistic rationality of those writers of the last century whom he admired in his youth— Anatole France, Ernest Renan, Hippolyte Taine, Sainte-Beuve. Occasionally in his last years he would say how fortunate he was to have been born in the 1890s, a time of relative optimism when the human condition still seemed something of an adventure and when sensible men believed that through their enlightened efforts the social world could be improved upon. He disliked Kafka for inventing heroes who were mainly victims and who never seemed to find the energy to defend themselves against—much less to understand—the outrageous things that were happening to them.

One of Edmund's gambits was to impute to his friends knowledge that, in fact, they did not have. What he wanted was an opportunity to explain something that currently interested him to a competent listener or, if he really had an expert in his grasp, to learn something from him. In my own case, he never accepted the fact that I knew nothing about Hebrew. "You know Hebrew, don't you?" he would ask whenever I visited him, and when I said that I didn't his face would fall. "Oh, I thought you did," he would reply in surprise. With less recondite subjects, he risked no such disappointments. "Have I told you about Swinburne?" he would ask as he proceeded toward his study. "Well go on in there and let me tell you," and for an hour or more the lecture would go on in his high, somewhat breathless, exquisitely articulated voice, until after much whisky it eventually subsided.

Edmund was shy and impatient with small talk. These lectures were his chief way of communicating, even with close friends. One New Year's Eve we were together on the old *Ile-de-France*. At the ship's gala we found ourselves at a table with Buster Keaton, who was on his way to Paris to perform in the Medrano Circus. The swirl of the gala surrounded us, music, streamers, dancing couples. There was a wild storm that night to enhance the occasion. But at our table no one could think of what to say. Keaton in real life turned out to be as taciturn as he appears in his films.

Soon, however, he began to fidget with a couple of those little cotton balls—the size of golf balls—that ships supply for the merriment of their passengers, who are supposed to throw them at each other. Eventually Keaton began to juggle his, silently, his gaze straight ahead, the corners of his mouth turned down. No sooner had he begun, however, than Edmund found three such balls of his own and, in the same expressionless way, began juggling too. My memory of the occasion, after so many years, is imprecise, but I seem to recall that before they abandoned this odd dialogue they may each have had as many as four or five balls in the air at a time. It wasn't much, but it was as good a conversation on the subject of Keaton's expertise as Edmund could manage. On the following day Edmund, who was on his way to Israel to work on his study of the Dead Sea Scrolls, met an Israeli businessman and for the rest of the trip could not be found.

Edmund's interest in Hebrew came partly from his Talcottville ancestors, among whom there had been some Protestant divines for whom Hebrew was a sacred and living language. One of these, I believe, actually wrote a Hebrew grammar. Partly too it came from his preoccupation generally with languages, which supplied him with abundant opportunities for the kind of investigation and discovery that he thrived on. But his main interest in the Dead Sea Scrolls, I suspect, was to see if he couldn't proceed from where Renan left off: to get to the bottom of the scriptural mysteries. Who, in fact, was Jesus and what, once the mystifications are stripped away, had he been up to? That these mystifications may not have been incidental to the life of Jesus but some of its essential data was a possibility that could hardly have occurred to a mind as practical as Wilson's. I have always suspected that his interest—often tedious to those who were subjected to it—in performing magical tricks was less to mystify his friends than to show them how easily they could be taken in by deliberately falsified appearances; and, of course, there was always his own interest in learning how these appearances could be contrived.

He put his poems together in much the same way, through the studied application of prosodic tricks—backward rhymes, multilingual puns—that once assembled were meant to create a certain illusion. But these poems, I have always felt, were intended less to be read than to be disassembled. Edmund's capacities were not especially of the synthetic kind; the author of *Axel's Castle* was not much of a symbolist. His gift was in taking things apart to see what made them work. Yet at the end of this dismantling, something whole, and wholly original, would accumulate.

This was his critical technique and his genius, this uncanny power to apprehend the components of a literary or historical process and, in the act of explaining them piece by piece, recreate the work of art or the event so that the reader could see for himself how it worked. It was the way Fromentin described pictures, detail by detail, so that the description itself became a work of art often more intelligible, if less spectacular, than the original. It was only his magical performances that he refused to explicate. On these occasions, and only these, he was content to leave his audience in the dark, as he stagily smirked, brows raised over widened eyes, his hand delicately frozen over the silver tube which clearly had held no string of silken handkerchiefs a moment before. In his journalism and his critical writing he was a passionate expositor of "man's ideas and imaginings in the setting of the conditions which have shaped them."

In 1930 Edmund wrote an account of the old Coronado Beach Hotel in San Diego. This vast and elegant place was opened, he explained, in 1877, the year Geronimo was defeated and the last of the Apaches were put away on reservations; when Standard Oil was "already well embarked on the final stage of its progress; and Edward Bellamy had a huge and unexpected success with his socialist novel, *Looking Backward*, which prefigures an industrial utopia."

But in the Coronado Beach Hotel Wilson felt that he could "still enjoy here a taste of the last luscious moment just before the power of American money, swollen with sudden growth, had turned its back altogether on the more human comforts and arrangements of the old non-mechanical world." This "lovely delirium of superb red conical cupolas, of red roofs with white lace crenellations, of a fine clothlike texture of shingles," where in the "pavement of the principle entrance have been inlaid brass compass points and brass edges mark the broad white stairs which, between turned banister-rungs, lead up to the white doors of bedrooms embellished with bright brass knobs" and from whose higher galleries "you look out at the tops of exotic tame palms and at the little red ventilators spinning in the sun"; this hotel, "with its five tiers of white railinged porches like decks, its long steep flights of stairs, like companionways, its red ladders and brass-tipped fire hoses kept on hand on red wheeled carts around corners, the slight endearing list of its warped floors," all of this he describes with something like the passionate curiosity of Proust at Combray and with the same sympathetic accumulation of detail that one finds in his own critical writing about literature.

Though in the last few years Wilson came to be known in the popular press as "the dean of American letters," he was not much read. As far as I know he had no disciples or even any imitators. His exquisite prose, with its echoes of Sainte-Beuve and Saintsbury, was no longer fashionable and perhaps, for many readers, no longer intelligible. Nor were the subjects that interested him in much favor. An obituarist writing in *Time* found him "ponderous" and quoted a professor who complained that Wilson avoided "all the really disturbing and aberrant writers of our own time." What bothers these people, I suppose, is that Wilson, for the last twenty years or so, came to write more and more as if he still lived in the old republic of his imagination, and lately he had come to live there pretty much alone.

Just before we left for the funeral I was sitting in the kitchen of the Wellfleet house remembering how when Edmund laughed he would raise his fist to the side of his mouth and puff and jiggle like an old steam engine starting up. Elena interrupted this reflection to ask if I knew Hebrew. It was only when we got to the grave that I understood why she had asked. I should have known that it was Edmund's idea to have the language of the prophets spoken at the end. As it turned out, my ignorance didn't much matter, for Charlie Walker, who had known Edmund for more than fifty years, made a little speech and when he was done took a step toward the grave, flung his arms wide, and said in his bold, quivering, old Yale-man's voice, "*Shalom*, old friend."

—July 20, 1972

8

SUSAN SONTAG
ON PAUL GOODMAN

I AM WRITING this in Paris, in a room about 4' by 10', sitting on a wicker chair at a typing table in front of a window which looks onto a garden; at my back is a cot and a night table; on the floor and under the table are manuscripts, notebooks, and two or three paperback books. That I have been living and working for more than a year in such small bare quarters, though not at the beginning planned or thought out, undoubtedly answers to some need to strip down while finding a new space inside my head. Here where I have no books, where I spend too many hours writing to have time to talk to anyone, I am trying to make a new start with as little capital as possible to fall back on.

In this Paris in which I live now, which has as little to do with the Paris of today as the Paris of today has to do with the great Paris, capital of the nineteenth century and seedbed of art and ideas until the late 1960s, America is the closest of all the faraway places. Even during periods when I don't go out at all—and in the last months there have been many blessed days and nights when I have no desire to leave the typewriter except to sleep—each morning someone brings me the Paris *Herald-Tribune* with its monstrous collage of "news" of America, encapsulated, distorted, stranger than ever from this distance: the B-52s raining mega-ecodeath on Vietnam, the repulsive martyrdom of Thomas Eagleton, the paranoia of Bobby Fischer, the irresistible ascension of Woody Allen, excerpts from the diary of Arthur Bremer—and, last week, the death of Paul Goodman.

I find that I can't write just his first name. Of course, we called each other "Paul" and "Susan" whenever we met, but both in my head and in conversation with other people he was never "Paul" or ever "Goodman" but always "Paul Goodman"—the whole name, with all the ambiguity of feeling and familiarity which that usage implies.

The grief I feel at Paul Goodman's death is sharper because we were not friends, though we coinhabited several of the same worlds. We first met twenty years ago. I was nineteen, a graduate student at Harvard, dreaming of living in New York, and on a weekend trip to the city someone I knew at the time who was a friend of his brought me to the loft on Twenty-third Street where Paul Goodman and his wife were celebrating his fortieth birthday. He was drunk, he boasted raucously to everyone about his sexual exploits, he talked to me just long enough to be mildly rude. The second time we met was four years later at a party on Riverside Drive, where he seemed more subdued but just as cold and self-absorbed.

In 1959 I moved to New York, and from then on through the late 1960s we met often, though always in public—at parties given by mutual friends, at panel discussions and Vietnam teach-ins, on marches, in demonstrations. I usually made a shy effort to talk to him each time we met, hoping to be able to tell him, directly or indirectly, how much his books mattered to me and how much I had learned from him. Each time he rebuffed me and I retreated. I was told by mutual friends that he didn't really like women as people—though he made an exception for a few particular women, of course. I resisted that hypothesis as long as I could (it seemed to me cheap), then finally gave in. After all, I had sensed just that in his writings: for instance, the major defect of *Growing Up Absurd*, which purports to treat the problems of American youth, is that it talks about youth as if it consists only of adolescent boys and young men. My attitude when we met ceased being open.

Last year another mutual friend, Ivan Illich, invited me to Cuernavaca at the same time that Paul Goodman was there giving a seminar, and I told Ivan that I preferred to come after Paul Goodman had left. Ivan knew, through many conversations, how much I admired Paul Goodman's work. But the intense pleasure I felt each time at the thought that he was alive and well and writing in the United States of America made an ordeal out of every situation in which I actually found myself in the same room with him and sensed my inability to make the slightest contact with him.

In that quite technical sense, then, not only were Paul Goodman and I not friends, but I disliked him—the reason being, as I often explained plaintively during his lifetime, that I felt he didn't like me. How pathetic and merely formal that dislike was I always knew. It is not Paul Goodman's death that has suddenly brought this home to me.

He had been a hero of mine for so long that I was not in the least surprised when he became famous, and always a little surprised that people seemed to take him for granted. The first book of his I ever read—I was sixteen—was a collection of stories called *The Break-up of Our Camp*, published by New Directions. Within a year I had read everything he'd written, and from then on started keeping up. There is no living American writer for whom I have felt the same simple curiosity to read as quickly as possible *anything* he wrote, on any subject. That I mostly agreed with what he thought was not the main reason; there are other writers I agree with to whom I am not so loyal. It was that voice of his that seduced me—that direct, cranky, egotistical, generous American voice.

Many writers in English insist on saturating their writing with an idiosyncratic voice. If Norman Mailer is the most brilliant writer of his generation, it is surely by reason of the authority and eccentricity of his voice; and yet I for one have always found that voice too

69

baroque, somehow fabricated. I admire Mailer as a writer, but I don't really believe in his voice. Paul Goodman's voice is the real thing. There has not been such a convincing, genuine, singular voice in our language since D. H. Lawrence. Paul Goodman's voice touched everything he wrote about with intensity, interest, and his own terribly appealing sureness and awkwardness. What he wrote was a nervy mixture of syntactical stiffness and verbal felicity; he was capable of writing sentences of a wonderful purity of style and vivacity of language, and also capable of writing so sloppily and clumsily that one imagined he must be doing it on purpose. But it never mattered. It was his voice, that is to say, his intelligence and the poetry of his intelligence incarnated, which kept me a loyal and passionate addict. Though he was not often graceful as a writer, his writing and his mind were touched with grace.

There is a terrible, mean American resentment toward someone who tries to do a lot of things. The fact that Paul Goodman wrote poetry and plays and novels as well as social criticism, that he wrote books on intellectual specialties guarded by academic and professional dragons, such as city planning, education, literary criticism, and psychiatry, was held against him. His being an academic freeloader and an outlaw psychiatrist, while also being so smart about universities and human nature, outraged many people. That ingratitude is and always was astonishing to me. I know that Paul Goodman often complained of it. Perhaps the most poignant expression was in the journal he kept between 1955 and 1960, published as *Five Years*, in which he laments the fact that he is not famous, not recognized and rewarded for what he is.

That journal was written at the end of his long obscurity, for with the publication of *Growing Up Absurd* in 1960 he did become famous, and from then on his books had a wide circulation and, one imagines, were even widely read—if the extent to which Paul Goodman's ideas were repeated (without his being given any credit) is any proof of being widely read. From 1960 on, he started making money through being taken more seriously—and he was listened to by the young. All that seems to have pleased him, though he still complained that he was not famous enough, not read enough, not appreciated enough.

Far from being an egomaniac who could never get enough, Paul Goodman was quite right in thinking that he never had the attention he deserved. That comes out clearly enough in the obituaries I have read since his death in the half-dozen American newspapers and magazines that I get here in Paris. In these obituaries he is no more than that maverick interesting writer who spread himself too thin, who published *Growing Up Absurd*, who influenced the rebellious American youth of the 1960s, who was indiscreet about his sexual life. Ned Rorem's touching obituary, the only one I have read that gives any sense of Paul Goodman's importance, appeared in the *Village Voice*, a paper read by a large part of Paul Goodman's constituency, only on page 17. As the assessments come in now that he is dead, he is being treated as a marginal figure.

I would hardly have wished for Paul Goodman the kind of media stardom awarded to McLuhan or even Marcuse—which has little to do with actual influence or even tells one anything about how much a writer is being read. What I am complaining about is that Paul Goodman was often taken for granted even by his admirers. It has never been clear to most people, I think, what an extraordinary figure he was. He could do almost anything, and tried to do almost everything a writer can do. Though his fiction became increasingly didactic and unpoetic, he continued to grow as a poet of considerable and entirely unfashionable sensibility; one day people will discover what good poetry he wrote. Most of what he said in his essays about people, cities, and the feel of life is true. His so-called amateurism is identical with his genius: that amateurism enabled him to bring to the questions of schooling, psychiatry, and citizenship an extraordinary, curmudgeonly accuracy of insight and freedom to envisage practical change.

It is difficult to name all the ways in which I feel indebted to him. For twenty years he has been to me quite simply the most important American writer. He was our Sartre, our Cocteau. He did not have the first-class theoretical intelligence of Sartre; he never touched the mad, opaque source of genuine fantasy that Cocteau had at his disposal in practicing so many arts. But he had gifts that neither Sartre nor Cocteau ever had: a genuine feeling for what human life is about, a fastidiousness and breadth of moral passion. His voice on the printed page is real to me as the voices of few writers have ever been—familiar, endearing, exasperating. I suspect there was a nobler human being in his books than in his life, something that happens often in "literature." (Sometimes it is the other way around, and the person in real life is nobler than the person in the books. Sometimes, as in the case of Sade, there is hardly any relationship between the person in the books and the person in real life.

I always got energy from reading Paul Goodman. He was one of that small company of writers, living and dead, who established for me the value of being a writer and from whose work I drew the standards by which I measured my own. There have been some living European writers in that diverse and very personal pantheon, but no living American writer apart from him.

Everything he did on paper pleased me. I liked it when he was pig-headed, awkward, wistful, even wrong. His egotism touched me rather than put me off (as Mailer's often does when I read him). I admired his diligence, his willingness to serve. I admired his courage, which showed itself in so many ways—one of the most admirable being his honesty about his homosexuality in *Five Years*, for which he was much criticized by his straight friends in the New York intellectual world; that was six years ago, before the advent of Gay Liberation made coming out of the closet chic. I liked it when he talked about himself and when he mingled his own sad sexual desires with his desire for the polity. Like André Breton, to whom he could be compared in many ways, Paul Goodman was a connoisseur of freedom, joy, pleasure. I learned a lot about those three things from reading him.

This morning, starting to write this, I reached under the table by the window to get some paper for the typewriter and saw that one of the two or three paperback books buried under the manuscripts is *New Reformation*. Although I am trying to live for a year without books, a few manage to creep in somehow. It seems fitting that even here, in this tiny room where books are forbidden, where I try better to hear my own voice and discover what I really think and really feel, there is still at least one book by Paul Goodman around, for there has not been an apartment in which I have lived for the last twenty-two years that has not contained most of his books.

With or without his books, I shall go on being marked by him. I shall go on grieving that he is no longer alive to talk in new books, and that now we all have to go on in our fumbling attempts to help each other and to say what is true and to release what poetry we have and to respect each other's madness and right to be wrong and to cultivate our sense of citizenliness without Paul's hectoring, without Paul's patient meandering explanations of everything, without the grace of Paul's example.

—September 21, 1972

9

ANNA AKHMATOVA
ON AMEDEO MODIGLIANI

I BELIEVE THOSE who describe him didn't know him as I did, and here's why. First, I could know only one side of his being—the radiant side. After all I was just a stranger, probably a not easily understood twenty-year-old woman, a foreigner. Secondly, I myself noticed a big change in him when we met in 1911. Somehow, he had grown dark and haggard.

In 1910 I saw him extremely seldom: only a few times. Nevertheless he wrote to me all winter long.[1] He didn't tell me that he composed verses.

As I understand it now, what he must have found astonishing in me was my ability to guess rightly his thoughts, to know his dreams and other small things—others who knew me had become accustomed to this a long time before. He kept repeating: "*On communique.*" Often he said: "*Il n'y a que vous pour réaliser cela.*"

Probably, we both did not understand one important thing: everything that happened was for both of us a prehistory of our future lives: his very short one, my very long one. The breathing of art still had not charred or transformed the two existences; this must have been the light, radiant hour before dawn.

---

1. I remember a few sentences from his letters. Here is one of them: "*Vous êtes en moi comme une hantise.*"

But the future, which as we know throws its shadow long before it enters, knocked at the window, hid itself behind lanterns, crossed dreams, and frightened us with horrible Baudelairean Paris, which concealed itself someplace near by.

And everything divine in Modigliani only sparkled through a kind of darkness. He was different from any other person in the world. His voice somehow always remained in my memory. I knew him as a beggar and it was impossible to understand how he existed—as an artist he didn't have a shadow of recognition.

At that time (1911) he lived at Impasse Falguière. He was so poor that when we sat in the Luxembourg Gardens we always sat on the bench, not on the paid chairs, as was the custom. On the whole he did not complain, not about his completely evident indigence, nor about his equally evident nonrecognition.

Only once in 1911 did he say that during the last winter he felt so bad that he couldn't even think about the thing most precious to him.

He seemed to me encircled with a dense ring of loneliness. I don't remember him exchanging greetings in the Luxembourg Gardens or in the Latin Quarter where everybody more or less knows each other. I never heard him tell a joke. I never saw him drunk nor did I smell wine on him. Apparently, he started to drink later, but hashish already somehow figured in his stories. He didn't seem to have a *special* girlfriend at that time. He never told stories about previous romances (as, alas, everybody does). With me he didn't talk about anything that was worldly. He was courteous, but this wasn't a result of his upbringing but the result of his elevated spirit.

At that time he was occupied with sculpture; he worked in a little courtyard near his studio. One heard the knock of his small hammer in a deserted blind alley. The walls of his studio were hung with portraits of fantastic length (as it seems to me now—from the floor to the ceiling). I never saw their reproductions—did they survive? He called his sculpture "*la chose*"—it was exhibited, I believe, at the Salon des

Indépendants in 1911. He asked me to look at it, but did not approach me at the exhibition, because I was not alone, but with friends. During my great losses, a photograph of this work, which he gave to me, disappeared also.

At this time Modigliani was crazy about Egypt. He took me to the Louvre to look at the Egyptian section; he assured me that everything else, *"tout le reste,"* didn't deserve any attention. He drew my head in the attire of Egyptian queens and dancers, and he seemed completely carried away by the great Egyptian art. Obviously Egypt was his last passion. Very soon after that he became so original that looking at his canvases you didn't care to remember anything. This period of Modigliani's is now called *la période nègre.*

* * *

He used to say: *"les bijoux doivent être sauvages"* (in regard to my African beads), and he would draw me with them on.

He led me to look at *le vieux Paris derrière le Panthéon* at night, by moonlight. He knew the city well, but still we lost our way once. He said: *"J'ai oublié qu'il y a une île au milieu [l'île St-Louis]."* It was he who showed me the real Paris.

Of the Venus of Milo he said that the beautifully built women who are worth being sculptured and painted always look awkward in dresses.

When it was drizzling (it very often rains in Paris), Modigliani walked with an enormous and very old black umbrella. We sat sometimes under this umbrella on the bench in the Luxembourg Gardens. There was a warm summer rain; nearby dozed *le vieux palais à l'italien,* while we in two voices recited from Verlaine, whom we knew well by heart, and we rejoiced that we both remembered the same work of his.

I have read in some American monograph that Beatrice X may have exerted a big influence upon Modigliani—she is the one who called him *"perle et pourceau."* I can testify, and I consider it necessary that

I do so, that Modigliani was exactly the same enlightened man long before his acquaintance with Beatrice X—that is, in 1910. And a lady who calls a great painter a suckling pig can hardly enlighten anyone.

People who were older than we were would point out on which avenue of the Luxembourg Gardens Verlaine used to walk—with a crowd of admirers—when he went from "his café," where he made orations every day, to "his restaurant" to dine. But in 1911 it was not Verlaine going along this avenue, but a tall gentleman in an impeccable frock coat wearing a top hat, with a Legion of Honor ribbon—and the neighbors whispered: "*Henri de Régnier.*" This name meant nothing to us. Modigliani didn't want to hear about Anatole France (nor, incidentally, did other enlightened Parisians). He was glad that I didn't like him either. As for Verlaine he existed in the Luxembourg Gardens only in the form of a monument which was unveiled in the same year. Yes. About Hugo, Modigliani said simply: "*Mais Hugo c'est déclamatoire.*"

* * *

One day there was a misunderstanding about our appointment and when I called for Modigliani, I found him out—but I decided to wait for him for a few minutes. I held an armful of red roses. The window, which was above the locked gates of the studio, was open. To while away the time, I started to throw the flowers into the studio. Modigliani didn't come and I left.

When I met him, he expressed his surprise about my getting into the locked room while he had the key. I explained how it happened. "It's impossible—they lay so beautifully."

Modigliani liked to wander about Paris at night and often when I heard his steps in the sleepy silence of the streets, I came to the window and through the blinds watched his shadow, which lingered under my windows. . . .

The Paris of that time was already in the early Twenties being called "*vieux Paris et Paris d'avant guerre.*" Fiacres still flourished in great numbers. The coachmen had their taverns, which were called *"Rendez-vous des cochers."* My young contemporaries were still alive—shortly afterward they were killed on the Marne and at Verdun. All the left-wing artists, except Modigliani, were called up. Picasso was as famous then as he is now, but then the people said: "Picasso and Braque." Ida Rubinstein acted Salome. Diaghilev's Ballet Russe grew to become a cultural tradition (Stravinsky, Nijinsky, Pavlova, Karsavina, Bakst).

We now know that Stravinsky's destiny also didn't remain chained to the 1910s, that his work became the highest expression of the twentieth century's spirit. We didn't know this then. On June 20, 1911, *The Firebird* was produced. *Petrushka* was staged by Fokine for Diaghilev on July 13, 1911.

The building of the new boulevards on the living body of Paris (which was described by Zola) was not yet completely finished (Boulevard Raspail). In the Taverne de Panthéon, Verner, who was Edison's friend, showed me two tables and told me: "These are your social-democrats, here Bolsheviks and there Mensheviks." With varying success women sometimes tried to wear trousers (*jupes-culottes*), sometimes they almost swaddled their legs (*jupes entravées*). Verse was in complete desolation at that time, and poems were purchased only because of vignettes which were done by more or less well known painters. At that time, I already understood that Parisian painting was devouring French poetry.

René Gille preached "scientific poetry" and his so-called pupils visited their maître with a very great reluctance. The Catholic church canonized Jeanne d'Arc.

> *Où est Jeanne la bonne Lorraine*
> *Qu'Anglais brulèrent à Rouen?*
>
> —Villon

I remembered these lines of the immortal ballad when I was looking at the statuettes of the new saint. They were in very questionable taste. They started to be sold in the same shops where church plates were sold.

* * *

An Italian worker had stolen Leonardo's Gioconda to return her to her homeland, and it seemed to me later, when I was back in Russia, that I was the last one to see her.

Modigliani was very sorry that he couldn't understand my poetry. He suspected that some miracles were concealed in it, but these were only my first timid attempts. (For example in *Apollo*, 1911). As for the reproductions of the paintings which appeared in *Apollo* ("The World of Art") Modigliani laughed openly at them.

I was surprised when Modigliani found a man, who was definitely unattractive, to be handsome. He persisted in his opinion. I was thinking then: he probably sees everything differently from the way we see things. In any case, that which in Paris was said to be in vogue, and which was described with splendid epithets, Modigliani didn't notice at all.

He drew me not in his studio, from nature, but at his home, from memory. He gave these drawings to me—there were sixteen of them. He asked me to frame them in *passe-partout* and hang them in my room at Tsarskoye Selo. In the first years of revolution they perished in that house at Tsarskoye Selo. Only one survived, in which there was less presentiment of his future "*nu*" than in the others.

Most of all we used to talk about poetry. We both knew a great many French verses: by Verlaine, Laforgue, Mallarmé, Baudelaire.

I noticed that in general painters don't like poetry and even somehow are afraid of it.

He never read Dante to me, possibly because at that time I didn't yet know Italian.

Once he told me: "*J'ai oublié de vous dire que je suis Juif.*" That he was born in the environs of Livorno and that he was twenty-four years old he told me immediately—but at that time he really was twenty-six.

Once he told me that he was interested in aviators (nowadays we say pilots) but once, when he met one of them, he was disappointed: they turned out to be simply sportsmen (what did he expect?).

At this time light airplanes (which were—as everybody knows—like shelves) were circling around over my rusty and somewhat curved contemporary (1889) Eiffel Tower. It seemed to me to resemble a gigantic candlestick, which was lost by a giant in the middle of a city of dwarfs. But that's something Gulliverish.

* * *

And all around raged the newly triumphant cubism, which remained alien to Modigliani.

Marc Chagall had already brought his magic Vitebsk to Paris and Charlie Chaplin—not yet a rising luminary, but an unknown young man—roamed the Parisian boulevards ("The Great Mute"—as cinematography then was called—still remained eloquently silent).

* * *

"And a great distance away in the north..." in Russia died Leo Tolstoy, Vrubel', Vera Komissarzhevskaia; symbolists declared themselves in a state of crisis and Aleksandr Blok prophesied:

> *Oh, if You children only knew*
> *About coldness and darkness*
> *Of the days to come....*

The three whales, on which the Twenties now rest—Proust, Joyce, and Kafka—didn't yet exist as myths, though they were alive as people.

* * *

I was firmly convinced that such a man as Modigliani would start to shine, but when in coming years I asked people who came from Paris about him, the reply was always the same: we don't know, never heard of him.[2]

Only once N. S. Gumilev, when we went together for the last time to see our son in Bezhetsk (in May 1918), and I mentioned the name Modigliani, called him "a drunken monster" or something of the kind. He told me that they had had a clash because Gumilev had spoken in some company in Russian; Modigliani protested this. Only about three years remained for both of them and a great posthumous fame awaited both.

Modigliani regarded travelers with disdain. He considered journeys as a substitute for real action. He always had *Les chants de Maldoror* in his pocket; this book at that time was a bibliographical rarity. He told me that once he went to a Russian church to the Easter matins—he went to see the religious procession with cross and banners—he liked magnificent ceremonies—and that "probably a very important gentleman" (I should think from the embassy) came up to him and kissed him three times. It seems to me Modigliani didn't clearly understand the meaning of this.

For a long time I thought that I would never hear anything about him. But I did and quite a lot.

* * *

In the beginning of NEP,[3] when I was on the board of the Writer's Union of those days, we usually had our meetings in A. N. Tikhonov's office.[4] At that time correspondence with foreign countries began to return to normal, and Tikhonov used to receive many books and periodicals. It happened that once during the conference someone

---

2. He was not known to A. Ekster (the artist, from whose school came all Kiev's left-wing artists), or to Anrep (well-known mosaic artist), or to N. Al'tman, who in the years 1914–1915 painted my portrait.

3. The New Economic Policy.

4. At the World Literature Publishing House, 36 Mokhovaia Street, Leningrad.

passed an issue of a French art magazine to me. I opened it—a photograph of Modigliani.... Small cross.... There was a big article—a kind of obituary—and from this article I learned that Modigliani was a great artist of the twentieth century (as I remember he was compared with Botticelli) and that there were already monographs about him in English and in Italian. Later on in the Thirties Ehrenburg, who dedicated his verses[5] to Modigliani and who knew him in Paris later than I did, told me much about him. I also read about Modigliani in a book, *From Montmartre to the Latin Quarter*, by Carco, and in a cheap novel, whose author coupled him with Utrillo. I can say firmly that the hybrid, which is pictured in this book, does not bear any resemblance to Modigliani in 1910–1911, and that what the author did belongs to the category of the impermissible.

And even quite recently Modigliani became a hero of a pretty vulgar French film, *Montparnasse 19*. That's extremely distressing!

—Bol'shevo 1958–Moscow 1964;
translated by Djemma Bider

—July 17, 1975

---

5. They were printed in a book, *The Poetry About Eves*.

10

ROBERT CRAFT
ON IGOR STRAVINSKY

THE FOLLOWING REMARKS are more personal than they might have been had I not made so many "stand-in" conducting appearances for Stravinsky this year and not also begun to go through my mementos, most of which had been stored away in the decade since his death. Looking through these again, I was engulfed by a wave of affection, surprising in view of the estrangement I had felt of late as a result of annotating his 1930s correspondence, in which he sometimes scarcely resembles the man I knew. Seeing the memorabilia, however, I was transported back to the events and emotions of our first years together.

Of course I did not save everything. No one could have been thinking constantly of Stravinsky's immortality while living with him— sharing three meals a day, spending most evenings together, and traveling all over the planet in automobiles, trains, ships, and airplanes. But in pursuing the contents of these old packing cases, I was more poignantly touched by his mortality than at any time since April 6, 1971. Here were those neatly typed letters—some with drawings: a heart in red ink, a California desertscape in spring—and the calligraphically addressed postcards sent during later separations. (He kept *my* cards, too, even pasting some of them in a music sketchbook—not for their contents, but as exhibits of engineering skill in cramming 200 words into a three-by-four-inch space!) Here, too, were those sheets of my questions with his answers, later destined for books; on one page that I had asked him to return in a hurry, he wrote: "You cannot complain."

I was particularly moved to find again the manuscript copies that he made for me of a canon by Mozart and three pieces by Lasso, and gave to me on special occasions, as well as published scores of his own music, always with original dedications: on the first page of *Monumentum*, for instance, he wrote: "To Bob, who forced me to do it and I did it"—a statement that might have been inscribed on *The Flood* and the *Canticles* as well, and that could serve as an *apologia pro vita mea*. The boxes also contained lists of passages in scores to be rehearsed; scraps of paper with messages, passed across the aisles of airplanes or from adjoining seats in concert halls; and menus, paper napkins, backs of envelopes on which he had jotted down bits of music. What disturbed me enough to make me stop this nostalgic rummaging was the sight of my baggage tags filled out by him in July 1951 before we left California for Venice and the premiere of *The Rake's Progress*—these and bottles of pills that he had given me for pre-concert nerves. As I said, my deepest feelings for Stravinsky have returned and have inevitably influenced these observations about him.

Our present view of Stravinsky is almost exactly the opposite of what it was when I met him in 1948. In the 1940s, it often seemed that rather than pursuing an inner-directed course, Stravinsky was allowing himself to be led by circumstances, composing music that diverged widely in subject and form from what was thought to be his proper genus. The man who during the late 1920s and early 1930s had been inspired by the Psalmists, Homer (*Perséphone*), Sophocles (*Oedipus Rex*), Virgil (*Duo concertant*), and Petrarch (*Dialogue Between Reason and Joy*) was now writing a cabaret vocalise (the 1940 Tango), reharmonizing our sprawling national anthem, fulfilling commissions for the big bands of Paul Whiteman and Woody Herman, providing a polka for pachyderms, and composing music for the cinema (none of it used, but converted into concert pieces, in the *Ode*, Norwegian Moods, *Scherzo à la Russe*, Sonata for Two Pianos). Stravinsky was also writing for the symphony orchestras of Chicago, Boston, New York, for Balanchine's ballet, and for the Church (though not the one to which he belonged). But it is the extravagant variety of these other works that bewildered even his most faithful followers.

Only now do we see how these diverse creations both fit together and integrate with Stravinsky's earlier and later music. Thus a passage in the 1965 Variations (measure 103) might have come from a sketch for the *Ebony Concerto* of twenty years earlier, the two-note dirge-rhythm in the Interlude of the *Requiem Canticles* had already appeared in the *Symphonies of Wind Instruments*, while the "Te Deum" in *The Flood* (1962) recalls *Les Noces*, the flute-and-piano figures at the beginning and end of the storm, *Petrushka*. The Flood, moreover, is best described by the subtitle "to be read, played, and danced" introduced in 1918 for *Histoire du soldat*. These random examples—they can be multiplied a hundredfold—help to demonstrate that continuing threads as well as new departures, evident in Stravinsky's music of all periods, are the secret of its unity.

A change came about in the 1950s; Stravinsky was finally conceded to have found a path—or vehicle—when he jumped on the twelve-tone bandwagon. Few people accepted this new music as the real Stravinsky, and even fewer liked it, but by 1956, with the *Canticum Sacrum*, his use of series was clearly no mere experiment but here to stay. At this point I must emphasize that Stravinsky's *modus vivendi* in the first half of the 1950s differed in almost every respect from that of the monumentalized Master of today—though, paradoxically, even if he had died in June 1913 (or anytime thereafter), he would have ranked, with Schoenberg, as one of the century's two great composers. In the early 1950s his music was comparatively rarely performed and only sparsely represented on records, while his new pieces of whatever kind met with open hostility. If the popular audience were aware of him at all, it was as the composer—probably dead—of *Firebird*. Having been with him through this period of trial, watching him struggle to support his family—which he had to do by conducting, not composing—yet steadily advancing from the Septet (1952) to *In Memoriam Dylan Thomas* (1954), the *Canticum*, and *Agon* (1957), I believe that this last was the turning point in Stravinsky's later life and art.

Ironically, *Agon*'s success came about through Balanchine's smash-hit ballet, and not through concert performances of the score. Today, according to publishers' figures, the piece in either form is one of Stravinsky's most popular, and no one seems to notice a Webern influence, though this was a principal objection at the first audition. In 1982, we recognize Stravinsky's characteristic gestures, temperament, and energy on every page of the score. Most of it was written during a period of recovery from a near-fatal stroke, and the first performance took place on the composer's seventy-fifth birthday. Nevertheless, the music, from beginning to end, especially in its fleetness, is that of a young man. The rhythms (changing meters, syncopations, jazz patterns), sonorities (new but inimitably Stravinskyan), harmonic structure and canonic games, contrasts (of speed, dynamics, and everything else), and the shapes of individual dances and the work as a whole link *Agon* to *Histoire du soldat*—to name only one predecessor: I am thinking of the parallel function between the castanet part in "Bransle gai" and the string-bass part in the "Marche du soldat."

As could be expected, the audience at the concert premiere grasped none of this, while today the piece is regarded as a comfortable classic. With *Agon*, other composers began to fellow-travel with Stravinsky in his idiosyncratic use of tone rows, for it is true that he did not keep abreast of developments in academic serial theory, simply borrowing what he required in order to write masterpieces.

Stravinsky's eightieth year was marked by another turning point, the return of the native to Russia, for the first time since 1914. That deep-freeze in which his music had been stored since the early days of Stalin began to thaw. It did not matter that while Stravinsky was being welcomed by Khrushchev in the Kremlin, the fifty-one-volume Soviet Encyclopedia (1958 edition) did not even contain the composer's name, or make any difference that he was not permitted to play any of his post-*Agon* music—which by then included *Movements* and *The Flood*—since audiences were not prepared for it anyway. But now, in 1982, belatedly recognizing their greatest son in the arts of this century, the Russians are performing not only *The Rake's Progress* (in their own language) but also the *Requiem Canticles*, and are publishing more studies of his music than any other country in the world.

I am often asked what Stravinsky believed to be his place in the history of music, in the sense that Schoenberg viewed himself as the bridge into atonality and saw his twelve-tone row as ensuring the supremacy of German music for another hundred years. In relation to Stravinsky the question is more complex, first because his notion of what constituted music history was so very much larger than Schoenberg's, extending not only backward to Machaut and earlier (music that Schoenberg regarded as of no more than antiquarian interest) but also outward to Oriental and ethnic art. Stravinsky maintained that the motets of Josquin should be heard at least as frequently as Brahms lieder, Monteverdi madrigals, rather more often than anything by Dvořák. But Stravinsky's affinities, technical and aesthetic, *are* closer to the composers of the Renaissance than to those of the late nineteenth century, although in old age his catholicity expanded to include that period as well: finally, he gave up referring to himself as Wagner's Antichrist and even learned to appreciate Mahler's Ninth Symphony.

Whatever Stravinsky thought of Schoenberg before 1950, after that date the Russian-American regarded the Austro-American not as the embodiment of an antithesis but as a great colleague from whom he could and did learn. (It is important to remember that Stravinsky was always a student, never a teacher, and that, of the great composers, he had the most perpetually acquisitive mind, the keenest antennae.) If Stravinsky is the center of excitement in twentieth-century music, it is not only by virtue of his innovations and all the other qualities of his music including its power of personality, but also because he captured more of the whole contemporary world, American as well as European, than did his counterpart. When I speak of synthesis, therefore, I am not referring to any merger with the school of Schoenberg, but rather to the assimilation of a vast range of elements filling the sound waves of the last seventy-five years from Ukrainian folk music to Broadway variety shows, ragtime to Kabuki. I realize that I have not answered the question, but I cannot, and when I once asked it of Stravinsky himself, he replied, curtly: "That is for history to decide."

Nevertheless, Stravinsky clearly saw his place in his own time. In Munich, February 1, 1933, he told an interviewer:

> Audiences want the familiar, that to which they are accustomed.... People feel confident in putting the great masters of the past against a musician of today, against a "cultural Bolshevik," as I am called. Perhaps in twenty-five years, my works, which will then have become familiar, will be held up as examples of *real* music to younger composers.

A week later, when a reporter in Milan addressed him as "the recognized leader of modern music," he responded, "Perhaps, but there are *good* and *bad* modern musicians. I am Stravinsky and that is enough." Although some would attribute this remark to conceit, I would not, believing it to be the honest statement of a man with rare self-knowledge. Stravinsky knew the value of what he was doing and was simply asserting that his music would endure. The retort was also a way of refusing the crown and scepter of a school or movement. To these characteristic rejoinders, one should be added from the rehearsal record in CBS's thirty-one-disc Stravinsky album, where he can be heard correcting a musician, then saying, "Excuse me, please, but I *like* my music."

Looking backward from the 1980s, we can also see that Stravinsky's music interacts more organically with architecture, choreography, painting, and poetry (in three languages) than does any other composer's. This is a subject for another essay, and little more can be said here than that he was at the hub of the arts, both bestowing and receiving inspiration thereby. It is well known that the five domes of St. Mark's suggested the five-movement form of the *Canticum Sacrum*. But Palladian principles, such as surrounding a central axis with rooms of sequentially different sizes, also influenced Stravinsky, who was familiar with many of the great architect's villas, as well as with the Venetian churches. (The *Canticum* even has a portico.) Besides the *Canticum*, with its "Trinity of Virtues" as the centerpiece, *Agon* has an axial movement (the Pas de deux), as does *Requiem Canticles* (Interlude). Fewer listener-viewers are aware that the orthogonal style of *Sacre* and the falcated one of *Apollo* determined the choreographic postures that Nijinsky and Balanchine created for these works. It should also be mentioned that at least one painter has testified that his Cubism owed more to *Les Noces* than to Picasso.

Poetry and its relation to Stravinsky's music is a still larger subject and, because both are formed with sounds, more closely connected. Some musicians—the composer Leon Kirchner is one—have even detected an intuited comprehension of Chomsky's deep-language structures in Stravinsky's use of words in parts of *The Rake's Progress*; but however that may be, Stravinsky did borrow technical concepts from verse patterns and poetic forms. The first examples to come to mind are of Pushkin and Boileau in *Apollo*, of Gide's Alexandrines that the music of *Perséphone* sometimes duplicates, and of Auden's haiku. Moreover, the changing meters, unequal time intervals, and shifting accents in Stravinsky's music are devices comparable to the rhythmic innovations of the poets of the time, Americans as well as Russians, though no modern writer, including Pound, understood Stravinsky's techniques to the degree that he had understood theirs. Still another parallel could be mentioned between Stravinsky's pilferings from the past and Eliot's chrestomathy in *The Waste Land*.

What are some of the principal reasons for Stravinsky's preeminence? First, he continued to grow, as minor artists do not. The *Requiem Canticles*, written at the end of a sixty-five-year evolution, is a no less astonishing epiphany from a man of eighty-four than that of *Firebird* by one of twenty-seven. The *Requiem* combines a new Stravinsky—in, for one example, the melodic intensity of the music for four solo flutes—with such of his older though mutated devices as the verse and response in the "Lacrymosa," the ostinato with concertante upper parts in the Prelude, and the apotheosis of bells in the Postlude. When the *Requiem* was first given by the Los Angeles Philharmonic, Harris Goldsmith remarked that Stravinsky chose the minatory rather than the consolatory portions of the text.[1] In fact, I chose them, not Stravinsky, as the libretto, containing his marks and mine, reveals; but this does not change the observation, since I was guided by the conviction that he was becoming more defiant and less mellow with age—as well as by the realization that the octogenarian was naturally somewhat short-winded.

Another reason why Stravinsky is one of the dominating artists of his century is that he introduced a new medium as Haydn did in his century and Wagner in his. True, Stravinsky composed, in Mozartian variety, operas, oratorios, cantatas, melodramas, symphonies, concertos, overtures, sonatas, incidental music, divertimentos, songs,

1. *Performing Arts Magazine*, March 1970.

string quartet pieces. Yet his epochal creations were originally ballets, or choreodramas, as he called them. It cannot be coincidental that he is also music's greatest revolutionary in rhythm, in which dimension, but not only, he irrevocably altered our lives.

Finally, Stravinsky was a great artist because he knew that depth of allusion can be attained only by using the past, and that creation depends as much on the old as on the new.

To turn to the forward view from 1982, what should be placed on the Stravinsky agenda for future generations of music lovers? First, his published music is in an unspeakable condition. The example that comes to mind is the 1919 *Firebird*, with its more than three hundred errors; but this is not atypical, since every Stravinsky score has quantities of them. To some extent the Russian Revolution is to be blamed, having deprived the composer of copyright protection in much of the world and exposed his music to legalized piracy. Despite his American citizenship and the new US–USSR copyright agreement, the abuse continues; in their original versions, all of his pre-1931 compositions are permanently in the public domain in this country. Even so, a "complete works" must be begun, the variorum edition his publishers promised him (in November 1968, in Paris). A small body of compositions, including Stravinsky's arrangements of his own and other people's music, has never been published at all, while some pieces that were in print have long been unavailable, which explains the absence of an accurate catalog, let alone a corrigenda.

The first step in correcting this situation would be a search for markings, traceable to him, in the scores of vocalists, instrumentalists, and such conductors as Monteux and Ansermet, Malko and Rosbaud, Desormière and Dorati, Goossens, Collaer, Molinari, and others whose names are less well known but whose libraries should be examined for the possible information. For example, Stravinsky rewrote some of the harpsichord part in *The Rake's Progress* for piano, in Santa Fe in July 1957. The pianist understandably kept the manuscript, which, for that reason, surely still exists and can be found. Detective scholars should embark on an all-out search.

Stravinsky's recordings are both a help and a hindrance to the improvement of performances of his music. Norman del Mar's book *Orchestral Variations* demonstrates how the composer's recordings of *Apollo*, the Etudes for Orchestra, and *Danses concertantes* not only correct, but also supplement the published scores. What Mr. del Mar overlooks are the obstacles that arise when Stravinsky's recordings of the same work contradict each other. For a time, Stravinsky believed that he could establish performance traditions through his recordings. But he did not tell us which tempo we are to follow for the final section of the *Symphony of Psalms*, whether that of the recording he made closest to the time of composition, the twice-as-fast version released in March 1949, the still different tempo of the suppressed recording, made in Los Angeles in June 1962, or of that of the one taped in Toronto in the spring of 1963, after he had had the most experience conducting the piece (*mutatis mutandis* concerning the advancement of technological influence and the dangerously enlarged co-conductor role of the recording supervisor).

The aforementioned CBS album credits me as the conductor of ten or so pieces under the composer's supervision, though in some cases the supervising was remote indeed. Naturally I tried to carry out what I believed Stravinsky wanted, but who knows how differently his performances might have been if he had broken ground with them and done all of the conducting himself (i.e., if I had not rehearsed them and inevitably suggested tempos and other questions of interpretation)? The facts are that when Stravinsky *wanted* to record, in the early 1950s, CBS would not support his project, and in the 1960s, when the money was offered him, he no longer believed in the recording process.

The next item on the Stravinsky agenda should be the completion of the oral history. When London Weekend Television began its

Stravinsky documentary[2] only three survivors with pre–World War I connections could be located and, since then, one has died. Some seventy interviews were taped with people who had known the composer in various degrees of intimacy; but seventy is far below the actual number of those who might have contributed, and this quotient excludes some valuable witnesses, a Dominican Sister living in Wisconsin, for instance, and a violist living in California, both in their nineties, both compos mentis, and both directly involved with Stravinsky premieres. To judge from the London videotapes, this now-popular method for producing history should be reclassified as a branch of autobiography instead, since the participants really only recount incidents in their own lives that may have little bearing on Stravinsky's.

What struck me is that certain apocryphal stories revealed more significant truths about his character than some of the readily verifiable material. Thus Kyra Nijinsky, daughter of the dancer and an incontinent reminiscer, first saw Stravinsky when she was two, and only once or twice after that in later life. This does not prevent her from describing an encounter with him in Venice in September 1937, walking between his actual wife Catherine, and his common-law wife Vera, both of whom he introduced as if such public threesomes were the foundation of respectability. But in truth Catherine was in a tuberculosis sanitarium at the time, and though she and Vera were friends and did take walks together, it is highly doubtful that Stravinsky ever promenaded with both women at once.

Nonetheless, the anecdote is not without value, since it describes behavior that anyone who knew Stravinsky would agree to be characteristic of him and of his logical, as opposed to psychological, mind. The concocted story was based on well-known true ones. In 1920, at the beginning of his affair with Chanel, he immediately told his wife, because, as he said, she was the person most concerned. A few months

---

2. *Stravinsky*, directed by Tony Palmer.

later, he again fell in love, this time with Vera Sudeikina. He again told his wife, and for the same indisputably logical reason. Soon after, he brought the two women together, insisting that since they were the people he most cared for, they really had to know each other.[3] The logic is still consistent, yet something seems to be wrong!

The last item on my Stravinsky agenda concerns publications, musicological, analytical, and—most difficult of all—biographical. Such technical work as Richard Taruskin's study of folk music sources, and Allen Forte's of the chord structure in *Sacre*, sets new and high standards. But a comprehensive biography is still far from being a possibility, for the reason that the crucial information about Stravinsky's formative years through the period of the *Firebird* is lacking. Perhaps the diary of Stravinsky's father, which covers Igor's life until age twenty in great detail, will provide the essential clues. But until now, only a few Russian musicologists have had access to this volume, and none of these employs an approach to the biographical material about the infant and the young child that is even remotely psychoanalytical.

This, I submit, is central for a man who was extremely anal, exhibitionistic, narcissistic, hypochondriacal, compulsive, and deeply superstitious. He was also quarrelsome and vindictive, which is stated not as moral judgment but merely as description of behavior. The probable cause of all this goes back to the cradle, and the deprivation of the mother. But we do not have the evidence: no observation of the infant Igor has so far surfaced, or, if so, been made available in the West. The combative relationship existing between the young boy and his parents extended throughout his life to others in authority,

---

3. Even so, Stravinsky went extremely far in his demands on Catherine, as is evident in a letter from her to him, December 29, 1934:

> I gave Vera 6300F yesterday, as you asked me to do. I asked her to come to the bank and we sat in the car for a little while and talked. In a day or so, we will set a time for me to come and visit her.

most prominently music teachers and orchestra conductors. He repeatedly said that he wrote *Le Sacre du printemps* in order to send everyone in his Russian past, tsar, family, instructors, to hell—in other words, everyone who failed to recognize his genius. The *Sacre*, after all, is music's masterpiece of iconoclasm.

Finally, who is qualified to write Stravinsky's biography? To the suggestion that I might be, let me answer with an analogy to the obstacles encountered by Flaubert's niece in describing the initial inaptitude of the future author of *Madame Bovary* in his attempt to master the alphabet and consequent backwardness in learning to read. First, her main source was Flaubert himself, and, second, she had to find an objective and unobtrusive way of presenting herself. My difficulty is of the same order, since I play a very large part in the narrative from which, to achieve perspective, I must detach myself. I was too close to Stravinsky to do this, and I do not yet understand the real relationship between us, personal, professional, psychological, cultural, not to mention the irrational, such as "karma"—or, for that matter, Hamlet's "there's a divinity that shapes our ends."

Why Stravinsky in my life, and why me in his? The question paralyzes me now more than it did while he was alive. After all, we came from the ends of the earth, had entirely different backgrounds, and were forty-two years apart in age—though this last was a factor only very near the end, for generation gaps did not exist with Stravinsky. (The poet Eugenio Montale, describing the dress rehearsal for *Threni* in Venice, September 24, 1958, wrote: "The frequent interruptions showed that the good preparatory work done by the young Craft in pulling it all together was thrown to the winds by the still younger Stravinsky, always unsure. . . ."[4]) But in many ways we were also alike. A biochemist at MIT, the late Max Reinkel, one-time physician to us both and a man of uncommon insight, noted that our nervous systems

---

4. *Prime alla Scala* (Milan: Mondadori, 1980).

and temperaments were virtually the same. We were similarly ironic, hypercritical, perfectionist (in our unequal ways), intransigent, and our eupeptic-dyspeptic cycles usually coincided. Moreover, our tastes in people, as well as in music, art, literature, and cuisine, were amazingly compatible.

Stravinsky's personality was overwhelming and dominating, of course, and I had to seek refuge from it in order to preserve my identity. Yet my personality—whose features, as I see them, were my certainty about musical values and my crippling Libran indecisiveness and procrastination in most other things—must actively have contributed to the relationship. It goes without saying that Stravinsky shared the first of these qualities but not the second (did anyone ever act so positively and immediately?), which probably promoted our friendship. As it flourished, Stravinsky discovered that I was more independent than he had initially supposed, and markedly unlike his children and the numerous acolytes schooled by Nadia Boulanger. Yet I think that, after an initial shock, he welcomed this difference in me. No one before seems ever to have contradicted him, or questioned a patently foolish statement (of which he was as capable as anyone else). No doubt my bad manners were to blame when I talked back, as much as the feeling that disagreements should not always be swallowed. But we did adjust to each other.

What was the magnet that brought us together? Our letters immediately before and after we met reveal conscious and unconscious motives on both sides that helped to establish the basis of the twenty-three-year symbiosis. But Stravinsky's correspondence also exposes a prescience concerning me, at least to my hindsight, that goes far deeper. Was I looking for vicarious or reflected glory? I don't think so, and certainly I succeeded in avoiding it in the formative period to which I am referring, that of the private, even hermetic three years during which Stravinsky composed the *Rake* and began the Cantata, years interrupted by only rare forays for conducting engagements.

The only observer present then, when we stayed home together, and crossed the continent together five times by automobile, and took innumerable other trips exploring the Western states, was Mrs. Stravinsky, and she alone understood our relationship. From the first, she believed that I, or someone like me, was essential to her husband if he were to remain in the midstream of new music. She sensed—as she had done in the early 1920s, when she introduced Arthur Lourié to Stravinsky—that he needed a musical confidant and sounding board, which is not to say that my role was comparable to that of Lourié, who had a family life of his own and was near to Stravinsky in age and cultural background. In any case, and as their correspondence shows, Lourié was never as close to Stravinsky as I was from the beginning.

When I met Stravinsky, in the spring of 1948, his fortunes were at low ebb. Most of his music was not in print, he was not recording, and concert organizations wanted him to conduct only *Firebird* and *Petrushka*. More important, he was becoming increasingly isolated from the developments that extended from Arnold Schoenberg and had attracted the young. Stravinsky was aware of this, despite the acclaim for *Orpheus*, his latest composition, and he wanted to understand this other, unfamiliar music, but did not know how to go about it. Perhaps the time has come for me to say, as I have not done before, that I provided the path and that I do not believe Stravinsky would ever have taken the direction that he did without me. The music that he would otherwise have written is difficult to imagine.

The 1948 meeting occurred at a propitious time and place—a crossroads—in other ways as well. Until then, the Stravinskys had lived largely in a world of non-English-speaking refugees, most of whom were returning to Europe. On the very day that we met, Stravinsky received the English libretto of his next work, thus automatically making me useful to him. Interactions began to take place, and, inevitably, he was Americanized through this exposure—to the extent that this transmogrification can be said to have taken place. Finally, though it is scarcely believable today, Stravinsky in 1948 lacked performing champions of his music, and was himself its only specialist conductor. He saw me, at first and increasingly in later years, as an interpreter of his works.

I dread to contemplate the prurient hypotheses and tendentious projections of music historians concerning the nature of the glue that held us together. What I can say with certainty is that my friendship with Igor Stravinsky endured because of continuing exchange; because of an ever-increasing mutual dependency; and, above all, because of an affection, which, though not always visible to others, was abiding and profound.

—June 10, 1982

II

SAUL BELLOW
ON JOHN CHEEVER

JOHN AND I met at irregular intervals all over the US. I gave him lunch in Cambridge, he bought me a drink in Palo Alto; he came to Chicago, I went to New York. Our friendship, a sort of hydroponic plant, flourished in the air. It was, however, healthy, fed by good elements, and it was a true friendship. Because we met in transit, as it were, we lost no time in getting down to basics. On both sides there was instant candor. The speed at which necessary information was exchanged was wonderfully amusing. Each of us knew what the other was. We worked at the same trade which, in America, is a singularly odd and difficult one practiced by difficult people who are not always pleased by the talents of their contemporaries. (Think of that wicked wizard, the late Nabokov, who coined terms like "ethnopsychic novelists," dismissing us by the platoon.) John was not in the least grudging or rivalrous. Like the late John Berryman he was fabulously generous with other writers. Yes, an odd lot, poets and writers of fiction, and to those who write novels about it the country, too, is singularly paradoxical, very different from the "normal" America that businessmen, politicians, journalists and trade unionists, advertising men and scientists, engineers and farmers live in.

I think that the differences between John and me endeared us more to each other than the affinities. He was a Yankee; I, from Chicago, was the son of Jewish immigrants. His voice, his style, his humor were different from mine. His manner was reticent, mine was—something else. It fell to John to resolve these differences. He did this without the slightest difficulty, simply by putting human essences in first place: first the persons—himself, myself—and after that the other stuff, class origins, social history. A fairly experienced observer, I have never seen the thing done as he did it—done, I mean, as if it were not done at all but flowed directly from his nature. And although his manner was reticent there was nothing that John would not say about himself. When he seemed to hesitate he was actually condensing his judgments, his opinions, his estimates of his own accomplishments in order to give them greater force. He spoke of himself as he would speak of anybody else, disinterestedly and concisely. He preferred short views and practiced the same economy in speech as in writing. He might have said, as Pushkin did, "I live as I write; I write as I live."

Miss Kakutani of *The New York Times* used excellent judgment in choosing the quotation with which she began John's obituary. "The constants that I look for," he once wrote, "are a love of light and a determination to trace some moral chain of being." I'm sure that John didn't relish making statements about morals and being, that wasn't his style. I see it as a reluctant assertion, something he had at last to say to correct distortion by careless readers, book reviewers, and academic category makers. I suppose that he felt it necessary at last to try to say what he had been doing with himself for some fifty years.

There are writers whose last novels are very like the first. Having learned their trade, mastered it once and for all, they practice it with little variation to the very end. They can be very good novelists. Think of Somerset Maugham or Arnold Bennett (you can supply American names of your own), exceedingly proficient and dependable servants of the reading public. What they lack is the impulse to expand. They do not develop, they seldom surprise. John Cheever was a writer of another sort, altogether. He was one of the self-transformers. The reader of his collected stories witnesses a dramatic metamorphosis. The second half of the collection is quite different from the first. Rereading him, as I have recently done, it became apparent to me, and will certainly be evident to anyone who reads him attentively, how much of his energy went into self-enlargement and transformation and how passionate the investment was. It is extraordinarily moving to find the inmost track of a man's life and to decipher the signs he has left us. Although the subjects and themes of his stories did not change much, he wrote with deepening power and feeling.

With characteristic brevity and diffidence he only tells us, toward the end, that he loved the light and that he was determined to trace some moral chain of being—no simple matter in a world which, in his own words, lies "spread out around us like a bewildering and stupendous dream." His intention was, however, not only to find evidence of a moral life in a disorderly society but also to give us the poetry of the bewildering and stupendously dreamlike world in which we find ourselves. There are few people around who set themselves such a task, who put their souls to work in such a way. "Normal America" might ask, if it were inclined to formulate such a question, "What sense does that actually make?" Perhaps not much, as "sense" is commonly defined. But there are other definitions. For me no one makes more sense, no one is so interesting as a man who engages his soul in an enterprise of this kind. I find myself, as I grow older, increasingly drawn to those who live as John did. Those who choose such an enterprise, who engage in such a struggle, make all the interest of life for us. The life John led leaves us in his debt, we are his debtors, and we are indebted to him even for the quality of the pain we feel at his death.

John Cheever died on June 18, 1982. The preceding was read at the annual meeting of the American Academy of Arts and Letters in December.

—February 17, 1983

12

MARY MCCARTHY
ON F. W. DUPEE

"I HAVE LIKED being miscellaneous," Dupee roundly declares in the foreword to *The King of the Cats* (1965), sounding a note of defiance, of boyish stubbornness, where to the ear of a different author an apology might have been called for. "Fred" was taking his stand as a literary journalist, a *flâneur*, a stroller, an idle saunterer, in an age of academic criticism, of "field" specialists on the one hand and fanatic "close readers" on the other. The shorter pieces of *The King of the Cats*, originally written for magazines, seem at first to bear out the confession: he turns from the letters of Dickens to a life of Sir Richard Burton, to Behrman's reminiscences of Max Beerbohm, to "the secret life of Edward Windsor," to the letters of Yeats, to Kafka's letters to a Czech woman he was going to bed with, to Chaplin's autobiography. Quite a variety.

Yet Dupee was no butterfly, no moth singeing his wings at the flame of letters, no boulevardier. Or, rather, all that random sensuous delectation was both real and a masquerade. *The King of the Cats* was less miscellaneous than it appeared. It was not a series of peeps into literary shop windows where the mannequins were being undressed—stately Henry James, naughty Nabokov, Charlie the Tramp. In all its diversity that collection had a remarkable unity, which may or may not have been intentional—a unity of matter as well as of manner and style. Even the most fugitive of those essays (and there is always something fugitive, some touch of "light housekeeping" in Dupee's approach) is pinned down by slender ties to its fellows like Gulliver stoutly bound by the Lilliputians. The point in common, the *trait d'union*, is that Dupee's "remarks," as he called them, tended to be about letters of authors, biographies of authors (La Rochefoucauld, Sir Richard Burton), autobiographies of non-authors (Chaplin, the Duke of Windsor), late works of authors (Thomas Mann, James Agee), rather than about the primary work of authors. The big exceptions were Gertrude Stein, Proust, Nabokov, and Robert Lowell's *Life Studies*, which fitted, however, into the overall Dupee pattern by being, itself, a prose-verse hybrid of autobiography and self-portraiture.

No doubt the unity I speak of was partly imposed by editors, who "typed" Dupee as they do any regular contributor. He was the right man to send a volume of Casanova to, a posthumous work of Jim Agee's (he *knew* him; they were at Yale at the same time), anything marginally to do with James, Proust, or Kafka, and, above all, any curio coming to light in the collector's corners of literature, e.g., a new, unexpurgated translation of Petronius' *Satyricon*. The only misfit (from that point of view) I find in *The King of the Cats* is a review of J. F. Powers's *Morte d'Urban*. Had I been an editor at *Partisan Review* then, I would not have thought of Powers as Dupee material. The Middle West, a golf-playing, Chevrolet-driving, go-getter of a Catholic priest?—I would have sent it to James T. Farrell or myself. But maybe Dupee *asked* for the book, seeing Powers as a *writer* rather than as a chronicler of Catholic rectories. Nevertheless the piece, even more so than its companion, a review of Bernard Malamud's *Idiots First*, seems a bit out of place in a collection so unconcerned with grading current fiction. Malamud, too, would hardly have been a "natural" for Dupee were it not for a curious resemblance noticed by him (and by no one else, surely) between *The Assistant* and *The Golden Bowl*. But there was something else: in the Chagall-like,

Orthodox Malamud, Dupee had found an intriguing quality that he had already sensed in the Roman Catholic Powers—that of being *by choice* an outsider, a marginal figure, a minority, in the contemporary republic of letters, whose insiders at the moment of writing were Heller, Burroughs, Pynchon.

The essential art of Dupee is defined by himself in the foreword to *The King of the Cats* as literary portraiture. His models for that, he tells us, were Sainte-Beuve and Macaulay. More generally as influences he cites Gide, Mencken, the early T. S. Eliot, and Edmund Wilson. That is clear; it shines through his work with a wonderful perspicuity, and the visible line of descent going back to a vanishing point is a beauty of his criticism: every debt is gladly acknowledged, and if he with his favorites occupies a slightly larger space than his masters lined up behind, that is only the law of perspective, which requires the present to come forward.

Modesty is one of his critical traits, and he is mannerly, too: in the new collection of his work[1] there is only one unfavorable review ("Leavis and Lawrence"); it advances the mild, sidelong suggestion that Leavis is a philistine. "What arrogant nonsense, one is tempted to say, while at the same time remarking on the amazing persistence and tortuous transformations of the philistine spirit in English letters."

The virtual absence of adverse comment is no sign of laxity. Luckily, too, his reviews are not free of mischief, even of delicate malice, as when he observes of Robert Lowell that Boston became "his Lake Country" and that the prose of *Life Studies* is "malign and dazzling." I am not sure whether it was mischief or malice that led him to say that there was something of the eternal bachelor in Yeats (and how true that was of Lady Gregory's star boarder!). Certainly a gleeful mischief dictated the following: "There are old photographs of Burton—dark, beetle-browed, his left cheek deeply scarred where a Somali

---

1. University of Chicago Press, 1984; this essay appeared as the introduction.

warrior had put a spear through it, his gaze intensified by what is surely the Evil Eye, his mustaches six inches long and good for twirling. Such photographs suggest those sometimes reproduced on the jackets of books by our scarier contemporaries, Fiedler or Mailer." Blunter and less characteristic is: "*New Poets of England and America* [an anthology] assists us in penetrating the apparent anonymity, not to say nonentity, of the youthful band of men and women who make verse under these circumstances."

"He's French, you see," Edmund Wilson used to emphasize in his roaring voice, meaning, I suppose, that continental sophistication ran in the Dupee blood, making him suaver than his fellow PR editors—Rahv and Phillips and Dwight Macdonald. I don't know how much French blood Fred really had—perhaps a quarter or an eighth, certainly not as much as Wilson liked to imagine. In the distant past, Fred thought, the name had been "Dupuis." A true Middlewesterner, from Joliet, Illinois, he had no more command of spoken French than Wilson and probably less of the written language. I doubt that it was his major field at Yale. Yet he was almost fatally attracted to French literature, starting with Stendhal. (I never heard him speak of the old authors, not even the likely ones—Montaigne, Louise Labé, Maurice Scève.... The exception was Rousseau, maybe not surprisingly in view of the *Confessions*. And there was also, I suddenly remember, Chateaubriand: *Mémoires d'outre-tombe*.) For PR in the early days, his undisputed "field" was French culture and politics.

Our interest in Gide was spurred mainly by him. At least it was at his urging that we published Gide's second thoughts on his trip to the Soviet Union, which I translated. And he was very much aware of Sartre—the Sartre of *Le Mur* and *La Nausée* in preference to the philosopher. When existentialism came in, after the war, our French specialist turned into William Barrett, who knew philosophy, the modern kind, and was able to read *L'Être et le néant*. But Dupee remained the magazine's authority on Malraux and the aesthetics of action; I remember a very long article, in several parts, I think, that he was writing on Malraux and could not seem to finish. Composition was hard for him then. There was no question with him of a "writing block," like the one Dwight Macdonald got when the wind of radicalism went out of his sails, but the act of writing was painful, and Malraux was his most agonizing subject. He did finally finish that study, shortly after we had despaired. But he did not choose to reprint it in *The King of the Cats* or schedule it for inclusion in the present collection.

The truth was, he wrote extremely well. I do not think that we on PR were fully conscious of that. Knowing the pain he suffered over those pieces, we were conscious of the process rather than of the result. Only now, reading the essays over, I see how brilliant they are in what appears to be an effortless way. He is amusing, observant, nonchalant. The tone is that of conversation. The continuing flashes of insight appear almost casually, like heat lightning. There are many offhand lines, let drop as it were negligently, in an undertone. Kafka's letters are reminders of "the lost art of being unhappy." James Baldwin's sentences "suggest the ideal prose of an ideal literary community, some aristocratic France of one's dreams." Writing of *Pale Fire*, he lightly observes that Nabokov has made a "team" of the poet and the novelist in himself. Recalling James Agee, he mentions the Luce connection and lets fall the dreadful phrase "captive genius," without stress, without follow-up. In his essay on "difficulty" (a theme that recently took George Steiner a whole book to deal with), he calmly wonders whether "a high degree of difficulty is not an aspect of the modern poetic style just as a peculiarly brilliant and aggressive clarity was a stylistic aspect of the school of Pope." And, of Flaubert, very simply: "He lived amid a clutter of dormant manuscripts."

He has a wonderful gift for quotation; bearing witness to a memory stuffed with luscious plums, which he pulls out one by one for our benefit. He gets his title for the 1965 collection from words Yeats is supposed to have spoken on hearing from his sister that Swinburne was dead: "I know, and now I am king of the cats." The quotations he pulls out often have juicy traces of anecdote clinging to them, e.g., the following, drawn from Burton's "Terminal Essay" to his translation of *The Arabian Nights*: "How is it possible for a sodomite Moslem prince to force a Christian missionary against his will and the strong resistance instinctively put up by his sphincter muscle? Burton could tell us: by the judicious use of a tent peg."

Dupee's criticism, in fact, is strongly anecdotal throughout. That is what gives it worldliness—both kinds, the terrestrial and the social. As he came to understand this of himself as a literary artist, we can watch his work grow. In his unsurpassed essay on *L'Éducation sentimentale*—one of the last pieces he published—he asserts the sovereignty of the anecdote for a kind of new and modern epic, whose nature is "mock" or comic. The enthronement of the anecdotal means that the work affirming it will be flooded with irony. Flaubert's feat in *L'Éducation* was "to have made an epic novel out of an accumulation of anecdotes." It follows that "each episode extracts from the situation a maximum of irony and then, having made its point with a precision consonant with its brevity, is caught up in the furious current of the enveloping narrative." This accords with the mood of drift, so terribly modern, so twentieth-century, that pervades *L'Éducation*, which might have been subtitled "The Story of a Drifter," just as well as "The Story of a Young Man." No doubt it means something that our first glimpse of Frédéric Moreau is on a river boat that is bringing him home from Paris to Nogent-sur-Seine; he is susceptible to tidal currents, the ebb and flow of the age, the eddies of art and politics, and the net effect of the novel is of a general purposelessness. Dupee likens it to Joyce in its rigorous impersonality but distinguishes it from Joyce by the coldness Flaubert shows toward his characters, in comparison to which Joyce is "warm."

In this late and splendidly written essay, we seem to see Dupee at last finding himself. Always brilliant, succinct, intelligent, informative, "French," in Wilson's word, here he is decidedly more—emotionally moving, electric. I had often suspected, fancifully, that Fred identified himself with Frédéric Moreau, a bit because of the name and a bit because he, too, in his younger years, had known "the melancholy of steamboats," if not in the most literal sense. But this penetrating essay is an act of total self-recognition (if Frédéric is Flaubert, he is also, transparently, Fred); it is the apotheosis of a wry, self-observing nature, and, as always happens at such moments of confrontation, the reader feels caught in the mirror too.

There is little left here of his faithful old models, Macaulay, Mencken, and the others. In some respect, even before this, he had left Wilson, his immediate mentor, behind: in the Gertrude Stein essay (cf. the *Axel's Castle* handling of her); in the several essays on Nabokov and *Lolita*; in the Samuel Butler foreword ("In Butler, the man and the writer were entangled as the drowning man is entangled with his rescuer"), which, after the Flaubert, is my favorite and shows a fineness of intuition of which Wilson with his wounds and bows was incapable; finally in his sympathetic short book on James (cf. Wilson on "The Turn of the Screw"). The difference, as I see it, is that Wilson took on himself the "heavy," huffing-and-puffing role of educator to his readers while Dupee made himself into a teacher in real life, first at Bard, then at Columbia, and in his writings did not seek to instruct but instead learned from his subject with a jaunty grace. The result was the sense of a mind and personality growing that buoys us up as we reach the end of this volume, knowing regretfully there will be no more. And it is perhaps not complete chance that the visible growth of Dupee coincides with the birth of *The New York Review* (1963) where he had not only a more amused, appreciative, in short more sympathetic audience in Barbara Epstein and Robert Silvers and also more space. The earliest essay in the new collection that seems unmistakably his is the Burton portrait—"Sir Richard and Ruffian Dick." Moreover, it was in *The New York Review* that the final, Flaubert essay appeared.

One aspect of Dupee I miss in what I have been saying is the side that—after Yale, after a short-lived little magazine called *The Miscellany* he and Dwight Macdonald edited with another friend, after a year of semi-slumming in Mexico—became an organizer for the Communist Party on the New York waterfront and concurrently literary editor of the *New Masses*. I do not see where a CP "streak" in him fits, unless he got it from the *Zeitgeist*, like a Thirties Frédéric Moreau. He was always against authority, but that fails to explain it—the Party was authority incarnate. It was at some *good* urging, I now feel, that he joined and bravely passed out leaflets. He wanted to be helpful to our poor, foolish, grotesque old society. Could that have had something to do with coming from Joliet, which after all is a prison town? Prison towns are sinister and hateful, and in Marxism he may have seen a set of burglar's tools to smuggle past the guards to the inmates. You cannot grow up in the shadow of prison walls without a few generous daydreams of escape for those inside.

Maybe so, but I wonder where the boyish idealism *went* when the Party let him down. Stalinism, now advertising itself as twentieth-century Americanism, had shown its colors in the Moscow trials and the Spanish betrayal and it was not too hard for Macdonald to convince him to leave the Party and the *New Masses*, taking the correspondence files with him. He appeared blithe about it; indeed, nobody breaking with Stalinism ever seemed to suffer regrets. And his sojourn there with Trachtenberg's "boys" had not been long: I first met him, just back from Mexico, at a party for the sharecroppers, given by Macdonald in 1935; by 1937, at the second congress of the League of American Writers, he was on our side. And I don't think he lost his idealism in the course of that adventure. It must have turned into an underground stream, making his teaching (he was very popular) fertile. Was it out of pure nonconformity that he never got his Ph.D.? I cannot find the idealism, as such, in his later writing. But it may be its long-term effects I notice in the growth indicators exuberantly branching and swelling in his later work. In 1968, anyway, at Columbia during the student strike, he risked some brandnew dentistry to join a line of faculty drawn up to protect another group of "boyish idealists" from the forces of order and got a black eye for doing so.

—October 27, 1983

13

DEREK WALCOTT
ON ROBERT LOWELL

And we are put on earth a little space,
That we may learn to bear the beams of love...
                                    —Blake

I

BIOGRAPHIES OF POETS are hard to believe. The moment they are published they become fiction, subject to the same symmetry of plot, incident, dialogue as the novel. The inarticulate wisdom of really knowing another person is not in the broad sweep of that other person's life, but in its gestures; and when the biography is about a poet the duty of giving his life a plot makes the poetry a subplot. So we read from the comfort of a mold. The book becomes an extension of the armchair, the life becomes the shadow cast by the reader.

Inevitably the biographies of poets, no matter how different, become a series of ovals in frontispieces. Robert Lowell has become one of these ovals, his dates now closed, the hyphen completed.

> *We are poor passing facts,*
> *warned by that to give*
> *each figure in the photograph*
> *his living name.*

The life itself is shattering. Lowell died at sixty. Most of that life had been spent recovering from, and dreading, mental attacks, of having to say early "my mind's not right," but more than drugs restored him. The force that is the making of poetry, while it took its toll of his mind, also saved him. His heroism is primal, his servitude to it savage. Bedlam, asylum, hospital, his bouts of mania never left him, but they also never left him mad. Clinically, they can be listed in depressing records of collapse and release, but what cannot be described in prose is their titanic bursting out of manacles.

All that cold sweat now congealed into an epoch, on the marble forehead of a bust! We look at the face on the book jackets, the brow shielding the eyes from the glare of pain, and we complete it as we dared not when he was alive. To use the past tense about him, not Lowell so much as "Cal," is almost unendurable. The present is the tense of his poetry. The eyes, with their look of controlled suffering, still hurt. We wince and look away.

In life we looked at that large head, heard his soft jokes, watched his circling hands, knowing that he would become one of the great dead. The jolt that we get now is reading the work as part of the past. His industry was frightening. The head was square and noble, but it was also an ordinary American head, and it was this unrelenting ordinariness that denied itself any sort of halo. He was a man of enormous pride and fanatical humility. He softened objects around him, blurred their outlines, made the everyday myopic, saw political systems as played out. History lived in his nerves, not as a subject but as irrational repetition.

If modern suffering cannot achieve sublime tragedy but ends in breakdown, no poet before Lowell has written so close to his own nerves. The poems of his middle age recoil to the touch, raw as a fresh cut. Their progression is supposed to form a scar, exposure forcing a healing. But often, in the Notebooks, or *History*, the wound of the poem is left raw. All of his writing is about writing, all of his poetry is about the pain of making poems. The physical labor. He doesn't sweep the fragments off the floor of his study, or studio, and show you only the finished sculpture. In *History* you see the armature, the failed fragments, the revisions, the compulsions. He could have settled into a fix, but every new book was an upheaval that had his critics scuttling. They settled and watched from a distance. Then his mind heaved again, with deliberate, wide cracks in his technique. Criticism of Lowell is more seismographic than aesthetic.

His apprenticeship was a fury. In youth every phrase was compacted with the vehemence of ambition. Rhymes were wrenched to fit the hurtling meter. He could not manage an ambulatory pace. Sometimes the wheels whirred groundlessly in air; even when they gripped, the reader shared the groan of effort, the load. In *Lord Weary's Castle* couplets barrel past the senses like boxcars, too fast to read their symbols, and leave a stunned, pumping vacancy behind them. "Time runs," he cites Marlowe, but here it lurches:

> *Time runs, the windshield runs with stars. The past*
> *Is cities from a train, until at last*
> *Its escalating and black-windowed blocks*
> *Recoil against a Gothic church. The clocks*
> *Are tolling. I am dying. The shocked stones*
> *Are falling like a ton of bricks and bones*
> *That snap and splinter and descend in glass*
> *Before a priest who mumbles through his Mass....*

The detonating phrases are more than just noise, although the poem is after "the big bang," but Lowell, like any other good poet in youth, does not care for lessons in thrift. That is natural, but here the prodigality is maneuvered, and we have, instead of excess, a strategy so forceful it repels. What sounds like passion is not heat but cold. The effects are overcalculated. Every phrase has been worked on separately to look like ease. Some layers are erased, but you can feel the vehemence of the erasures. Their basis is the pun, a brutal name for ambiguity. The windshield runs with tears as well as stars. The tears slide down the glazed iris as stars slide down the glass window of the train in the night. There is a poem in each phrase, but the pace does not match the meter. The first two lines should have had the leisure of recollection. Instead the tears hurtle in pentameter, and the couplets increase the speed. The "at last" does not go inward, like memory, but elevates itself into address. The speed is imitated from Hart Crane, but we can see where the phrases are joined by an iron chain, whereas in Crane at his best the links are invisible:

> *How many dawns, chill from his rippling rest,*
> *The sea-gull's wings shall dip and pivot him.*

In Crane, there is one shot, one action, on which the stanza pivots, the gull's flight.

Lowell is a long distance from it:

> *We are like a lot of wild*
> *spiders crying together,*
> *but without tears . . .*

not only in the casual intimacy of the lower-case beginning (it was he who made me drop capitals from my lines), but also in the technical poignancy of this other train poem, the slackened-tie assurance of "The Mouth of the Hudson."

> *A single man stands like a bird-watcher,*
> *and scuffles the pepper and salt snow*
> *from a discarded, gray*

Westinghouse Electric cable drum.
He cannot discover America by counting
the chains of condemned freight-trains
from thirty states. They jolt and jar
and junk in the siding below him.

In the earlier poem, from *Lord Weary's Castle*, the train, like time, is racing. In the later poem the cars of the freight train are clanking and trundling to a halt.

His eyes drop,
and he drifts with the wild ice
ticking seaward down the Hudson,
like the blank sides of a jig-saw puzzle.

The years that brought this difference, this reconciliation with ambition, lie in the prose word "ticking." It is the sound of cracking ice, of a bomb, of wheels, of a clock, of the floe, fated to melt as it gets near the ocean, and every word around it is ordinary. That is, it is ordinary at first, then it is wonderful.

By the time he did his translation of the Oresteia, an achievement in modern dramatic verse, which critics have ignored, Lowell understood technical serenity. He had blent Williams with Aeschylus. He saw the light on the brick opposite his apartment in New York not as the radiance in Shelley, or the marble light of Yeats, or the ineffable light of Wordsworth, but as light in New York, on modern brick.

Style sits easily on good poets, even in conversation. In intimacy, their perceptions go by so rapidly that a few drinks with them are worth a book on poetics.

In his apartment about to go out somewhere with him, I fix the knot of Cal's tie. He returns the knot to its loose tilt. "Casual elegance," he said, his hands too large to be those of a *boulevardier*. The correction was technical, one moment's revelation of style. His verse, in that period of two close books, *Near the Ocean* and *For the Union Dead*, had the casual symmetry of a jacket draped on a chair, genius in shirt sleeves. He has written about the stiffness that had paralyzed his meter, how he found its rigidities unbearable to recite, skipping words when he read in public to contract them like asides. He had learned this from Beat poetry and William Carlos Williams. Still, his free verse was not a tieless meter. Debt to ancestry, to the poets who had been his masters, went too deep for that. The "Fords in search of a tradition" could dress in the striped vests of "new money," he would wear his meter loosely with ancestral hauteur.

On another occasion, and the reader must not think that I have a fetish about poets' ties, I admired, with casualness, a pale orange and brown figured tie he wore. He took it off and gave it to me. I did not fawn on Lowell the poet. I did not collect bits of his clothing like his valet. Yet he once made a terrible accusation as if I were. "You use people," he told me. It was a night when he was "going off." Darkness hadn't yet come but the light was dimming. I didn't know, as his older friends knew, how to recognize the spark that meant that, like Hieronymo, he would be mad again.

The insult went deep. Did he think that I had cultivated his friendship to advance my career? I was not an American poet. I did not think in those terms. For there to be a career there has to be a tradition, and my new literature had none. A career, like that of any explorer's, was instantaneous. Did I feed off his verse like a parasite to fatten my own? *That* I would have confessed to, because his influence was irresistible, yet what imagination was more omnivorous than his? Yes, I said to myself, above the pain, I had used him. But only as I had used other masters, ancient or modern.

In mania veritas. Sing to me, Muse, the mania of Achilles, not the "rage," he had written, updating Homer. I had never confronted the grotesque Lowell, who struck the terror of pity in those who loved him. If Cal was drowning in the darkness at the back of his mind, it was still an illumination.

My style had been, perhaps still is, that of the magpie. A bit here, a bit there, hopping from one poet to another, but it wasn't that of the buzzard. I had practiced Imitations all my life, and I had given up hope of not sounding like Lowell. At Stanley Kunitz's apartment in the Village one afternoon, Anthony Hecht, Stanley, Lowell, Henry Rago, who was then editor of *Poetry*, and I had been reading. We had not come there to read, but Cal liked reading among friends. I read a poem called "A Letter to Brooklyn." Rago said, "It's like a female Lowell." This was a little new. Talk of a cleaning maid would have been better, but too many American writers did not know the art of the insult. They undertook epigrams and it came out gossip.

I've described the sundering that put me off Lowell for a long time —during which he went into a hospital and I cursed and told everyone, yes, I too was tired of his turmoil. But I want to record, tears edging my eyes when he invited me years later to his apartment on West Sixty-seventh Street, the dissolving sweetness of reconciliation. He opened the door, hunched, gentle, soft voiced, while he muttered his apology, I gave him a hard hug, and the old love deepened. The eyes were still restless, haunted. A phantom paced behind the fanlight of the irises. He reached into the inside pocket of his jacket. I knew why. For a snapshot of his daughter and my son, who are the same age, that had been taken at a beach house in Trinidad.

During the breach I had asked his friends, how badly had he treated them? Violently. Unutterably. Forgivably. I never heard any stories. I did not probe. Their shock, the trauma of awful memory protected him. "Pity the monsters," he had written.

We think of the sanity of John Clare, a brightness between demonic clouds, of Poe staggering through hell in Baltimore, of Crane's or Berryman's drunkenness, but the clear and ordinary Lowell—he could recover rapidly—often showed no scar of the recent agony. The mania of elation is a kind of despair, but what biographer could catch the heartbreaking smile, his wit, his solicitude, his shyness?

It is this that has made things so difficult for his biographers. They settle for the easier thing, plot the manic bouts, the devastating attacks, and the agonized recovery. It is the old nineteenth-century diagnosis of the poet as madman. And how easy it is to fit Lowell into that tradition, some would say the natural inheritance of damned genius, of which Poe is the high priest. Lowell was not a madman, or a *poète maudit*; he was a great poet who had devastating bouts of mental illness. Clouds covered him, but when they went, he was extraordinarily gentle. He had that masculine sweetness that draws a deep love from men.

It is its unrelenting fierceness that makes one want to ask of the poetry, as one did of the man, why it drives itself so hard. Why can't it forgive itself? The answer is that Lowell did not lie. There was no Byzantium for him, as there was for Yeats, a gold-hammered and artificial paradise which became true because need had created faith. There was no white rose in which all substances cohere at the end, as for Dante. Once I asked him what he thought of Hopkins's "Wreck of the Deutschland." He smiled: "All those nuns." He had written in his youth about nuns, demented, passion starved, but faith had gone. He could have mourned the loss of faith with a ripened, elegiac softness, with melody. But he had no heaven left. He had no symbol to seal his torment, like Yeats's singing mechanical bird, or the rose of Eliot. American heraldry provided only "the sharp-shinned hawk in the bird-book there."

What this says about the whole quivering body of Lowell's poetry, strapped down, drugged, or domestically blissful, is what has to be said about poetry written in English from Caedmon to this minute. No other poetry I can think of is as tender, as vulnerable, in which a pitiless intelligence records its own suffering. The closest parallel is Meredith's *Modern Love*. "To live a life," Pasternak wrote, "is not to cross a field." Lowell refuses to let go of himself. It is not masochistic, this refusal, but a process of watching how poetry works, to learn if it can heal; and if poetry is a beak that plucks at the liver, like Villon, or Prometheus, then Prometheus becomes Aeschylus, the victim is his own subject, the vulture becomes a companion. He never took time "off" as a poet, like some American writers who like to say that they do other things apart from writing: farm, fish.

> *No help from his body, the whale's*
> *warm-hearted blubber, foundering down*
> *leagues of ocean, gasping whiteness.*
> *The barbed hooks fester. The lines snap tight.*
> . . . . .
> *We asked to be obsessed with writing,*
> *and we were.*

Once I told him how much I admired that line of his in which the ice floes are compared to the blank sides of a jigsaw puzzle, and asked him how long it took him to see that. He said, "It was like pulling teeth." But the line from the same poem, "Westinghouse Electric cable drum," he had gotten from his daughter, who had been skipping along repeating it. It was Harriet, too, who had given him the line, "We are like a lot of wild spiders crying together, but without tears."

A writer worries and works away from his fate, and he becomes it. Lowell has joined the "long-haired sages breezing through the Universe," the transcendentalists, Emerson, Hawthorne. The New England sanity, married to the Southern, the Gothic, the sounds of the sane Atlantic wind in the southern cypress are blended in the soft prose lilt of the later poetry, the triple adjectives that became a signature of Lowell's and of his second wife, Elizabeth Hardwick. But he has also joined those sepia ovals of New England. In his youth they drove him south in search of a more fragrant soil, more calming fragrance than rank salt, but their magnet pulled him back to his ancestry in the Notebooks, and *History*. He judged the politics of the world in the only way he could, with a puritanical harshness as fierce as his ancestors'.

Poetry is not the redemption of conduct. Anyone standing on the opposite side of this commemoration of mine, without knowing Lowell, could contradict it from the cruel litany that biography must provide. The row at the writers' colony at Yaddo, where he hounded a woman for what he thought were her Communist politics, is horribly degrading; the shambles of his marriages are a feminist's battlefield, the first, to Jean Stafford, full of drunken violence. Nor does a penitential or remorseful poem absolve the past by its music. But we have all done awful things, and most biographies that show the frightening side of their subjects have a way of turning us into moral hypocrites. Lowell, in his ranting mania, a full Caligula, when, to use a West Indian phrase, "the power had gone to his head," fantasized dictatorship. To me these fantasies are not merely paranoia, but a way of absorbing universal guilt as a child comforts himself by becoming the demon that he imagines in the dark. When Lowell's sanity broke the evils of our century flooded his brain with horrors. Original sin or the political ingenuousness of democracy were not enough. The tortured blended with their torturer, and his brain was one arena for both. Besides, his delusions were both demonic and angelic. Like Faust, he could mutter "I myself am hell," but he turned one aspect of paranoia into serenity with *Imitations*, making honey from the bile of his illness.

In taking on the voices of poets he loved and unashamedly envied, he could, in rewriting them, inhabit each statue down the pantheon of the dead and move his hand in theirs. It was high fun. But it is also benign possession. He did it with living poets too: Montale, Ungaretti. He becomes Sappho, Rilke, Pasternak, and writes some of his finest poetry through them, particularly Rilke. His imitation of "Orpheus and Eurydice," to me, is more electric than its original. This shocks scholars. They think that Lowell thought himself superior to these poets. He was only doing what was a convention for the Elizabethans, often improving certain lines by imitation, heightening his own gift. The ambition that saw itself as Milton when he wrote "The Quaker Graveyard in Nantucket," and the derangement that once believed it was the author of "Lycidas," both gave us the sunlit sanity of his "Imitations." Some of them, for me, fail: Rimbaud seems too sanitized, the Villon ballade, thanks to Williams, too flat for a remorseful echo. Still, he had the honesty to know his greatness, to make the great his colleagues.

"I have known three great poets," Auden said, "and each one was a prime son-of-a-bitch." In *History*, Lowell says this of himself. There are no secret passages. Many of them open, fetid with remorse. Like Meredith, Lowell is a poet of modern marriage. In *Modern Love*, as in "To Speak of Woe That Is in Marriage" from *Life Studies* and in much of the Notebooks, a flat, frightening chill comes off the lines, like the look of a kitchen knife. Knife, or legendary sword dividing lovers, "deep questioning," it "probes to endless dole" (*Modern Love*). And there is much that is Victorian in Lowell: divorce as death, guilt, the lines used to lash the mind to penitence. Meredith used the word "modern" with moral sarcasm. Lowell's morals aren't modern. The guilt of his adulteries, even if he thought his heart had gone cold and was only ashes, was still seen by the dance of hellfire; the woe that is in marriage was not merely modern neurosis as anatomized by Updike, but a burning pit.

Without faith, without a belief in absolution and therefore of forgiveness, yet also without the remorseful terror of damnation, he talks through the grille of his lines like a confessional, a poet confessing not to religion but to poetry, the life of errors that he has committed for its sake. "My eyes have seen what my hand did." Unlike Villon, he had lost the Virgin.

Disturbing as they are in their domestic intimacies, the moral of the Notebooks is forgiveness. Lowell preempted the task of his biographers. The poems are there not to justify conduct or excuse the brutalities of betrayal, but to make whatever would be said of him and those whom he had hurt audible and open to accusation, even disgust and censure while he lived. In this he went even further than Meredith, or Hardy, whom he admired. What his biographers would have revealed about him, in his collected letters, his official "life" as a postmortem, was made as open as a collection of his posthumous papers.

In some ways the Notebooks are like an index to Dante. We are in a dark wood. But the light at the end of the tunnel, as he wrote, is an oncoming train, and there is no paradise but domestic bliss.

2

All autumn, the chafe and jar
of nuclear war;
we have talked our extinction to death.

In the large, squat glasses of golden whiskey, of smoky bourbon, the ice kept tinkling like literary gossip. If there were two or three too many in their apartment on Sixty-seventh Street, I felt like an intruding shadow when the Lowells had guests. The couches and the books in their high bookcases, the highest of which had to be reached by a sliding ladder, were comforting, but not the portrait of some ancestor on the wall, a face with a frogged, pert authority that looked like the British prime minister Hugh Gaitskell. I remember something vague and golden about this ancestor and his horse, but that lineage did not interest me. Nor, for that matter, the friendly malice with which the work of colleagues was dismissed by the guests. Whole reputations crunched out like butts. It was just New York, but with others there, it was a casual salon. It was inescapably a salon, since Elizabeth Hardwick and Robert Lowell, a brilliant prose writer and the best poet in America, were married. It was midtown Manhattan, but it was also a fact of literary history, like the Brownings or the Carlyles. This is not meant as a violation of intimacy. It is as much a setting for some of the poems in *Life Studies* and *History*.

This was when he looked happiest, I thought, in those dusks at the apartment. Also, this was the end of a day of hard work, hours on hours put in in his study, one flight up. Lowell went to work like an artisan, putting in a full day on his lines. Like all great poets he did not believe in "inspiration" but in labor. We know his working methods. They brought on cold sweats, but at the end of the day, usually, exhaustion had him a little high, and the golden, iced drinks had been earned.

I cherish those visits. They are ticking ice and amber. They have the casual and comforting depth of sofas, with Cal's voice as soft as a fire, Elizabeth's curly golden hair and her high, rocking screech, and her habit of reaching out to pat your hands with a smile. "Honey," she'd smile, with a voice as sweet and slow as that substance, and they were honeyed evenings all right. The Lowells made me feel comfortable in New York. Then things darkened. We lost touch, as they say, and then he was in England.

In the darker passages of the Notebooks, a low ground mist, like English weather, came off the lines and obscured the figure of Lowell. He does not break clear of it, or wait for weather to lift, for the clouds that scud across the page to pass and the white to reemerge. It is not willfulness. The syntax of the Notebooks, its disconnectedness, asides, may look perverse, and with each new line we hope for the light to break. We would like the figure of the poet to step closer, to stand still in a pool or shaft of revelation. In poets who know, either in themselves, or by their fame, that they have become great, that, for whatever it means, they have achieved immortality alive, we can sense the

marble hardening in their poems, the casual mannerism of every gesture immobilizing itself. A lazy or calculating Lowell could have
earned that soundless applause readers give a famous poet's emblematic postures. Yeats, cloaked, striding in the great storm that is in his
mind (applause), the canonical Eliot (applause), Frost in his freckled
light in the fall woods (applause). The Notebooks, instead, refuse to
become heraldic, they keep refusing to be poetry.

Turner and Whistler did the same thing in painting, refusing the
summary of the canvas as an idea, scumbling, chafing the strokes till
the solidity and known outlines of its subjects blended into the
coarseness of the surface. Lowell would love to have been Constable
or Vermeer. I asked him what painter he imagined to be his comple-
ment, and he said Vermeer. But in his late work, the light comes not
from one but from all directions, and it is dim and shifting. We squint
through the thicket.

It is important to try to assess this work not as confession or psy-
chology, not even as poetry that proves the chaos of his life, or our
own, but as technique. Poets take on enormous challenges of technique,
first of all in fun. His friend Berryman's "Dream Songs" prompted that
competition, the way athletes challenge one another without envy.
Once caught in this race he could not stop. Berryman had devised a
stanza form that was just right for his snarls of self-abuse, his alcoholic asides, self-insults, elations. Shambling, shaggy, yelping or muttering, the stanzas have the jagged shape of a manic graph. Lowell
heard his mind talk and directed it gently, but without bending it into
a formal structure of rhyme, or the conclusive homilies of a couplet.
He simply lopped it off when he knew its length was right. It is the
instinct of the stonemason, the instinct that knows the weight and fit
of each block, rough-edged, and fitting into a structure whose ultimate
shape is unclear, not drawn in advance. The style is Gothic. It keeps
going till it becomes cathedral, tapestry. Only death stops it. His last
book, *Day by Day*, is filled with this exhaustion, after *History*.

Lowell wrote little prose, few critical essays. He did some reviewing, short pieces, and there is "Revere Street" in *Life Studies*, in which the poems themselves break from prose. Compared to Graves, Pound, Williams, Eliot, Yeats, he did not buttress his poetry with polemics, with the politics of his literary platform. Eliot fortified his direction with essays that supported his campaign, his essays were as much warnings about a change in style as they were self-endorsements. Pound, who was hardly ever wrong about poetry, wrote like a defrocked professor. For Lowell, living in America, prose must have seemed like another aspect of show business. It is the one form that is really respected because it is accessible, democratic, a thing everyone can be invited to share. It can drive the poet who only wants to use words in verse, not in explication, into loneliness or to arrogance.

This is putting it too simply, of course, but it accounts for that sense of public responsibility which American poetry has, its manic alternatives of an isolated madness or the common sense of day by day. It divides American poetry as surely as it divided Lowell's psyche, into the sane (not the Apollonian, just plain American common sense) and the crazy (not the Dionysian, just the disturbed, the misfit). On the one side are the sane poets like Williams, Bishop, Frost, Stevens (a didactic aesthete), on the other, Crane, Poe, Weldon Kees, Berryman. Lowell did not veer maniacally between those states. He did not fear wildness as his good friend Randall Jarrell did who kept his verse as sane as his criticism; he was not as wild as Roethke or Berryman. The wildness, wrestled into a taut hysteria, tight-lipped control, took its toll of Plath, Sexton: it led to "confessional" poetry, to the compulsion to conform. Ginsberg, to save himself from derangement, loosened all the valves, and his scream, *Howl*, gushes like scalding steam.

Instead, Lowell had a sense of structure, of technical order that was so strong it saved his mind and his work. It could look down on himself as a subject. To have destroyed himself would have been to interrupt his work. He made his madness a subject. The moral strength of this is astonishing. Waves wash and batter him, and he never falls overboard. Even when he ditched orthodoxy he had faith. In poetry. This was the New Englander in him.

The last time I saw him he was elated but tired. He had just published *Day by Day*. *Day by Day* is really the Notebooks truncated. The exhalations, the short, tired intakes of his last lines are a commentary on the labor, the turmoil of the preceding books. It peers at the light, no longer interested in great subjects.

History, the title with which he renamed the Notebooks, had been attacked by Geoffrey Grigson for having everything thrown in. That was the point. The poet who never relented in his undertaking to be, even in private, the conscience of America, of the twentieth-century mind, did not, could not, repeat the collage of beached fragments that is *The Waste Land*. The shards, rubble, waste, were not the subject of the poem but in the mind of the poet itself. The meter of the poem has potholes, the step is irregular. It rushes, rests, gets up again, labors on. It follows Donne's injunction that the poem itself reproduces the action of its journey, and "about it and about must go."

Once we are used to heraldic, anthologized poems, we demand of poetry something more than merely loving it. We rummage in the unread, difficult, even failed poems of those whose great labors have grown dust. The real Browning, the real Donne, the real Ben Jonson are not in their lyrics but in their verse letters, book-long mono-dramas, elegies, and speeches in dead plays. *Notebook*, as I wrote to Lowell when I read Grigson's jeer, will remain a mine for hardworking poets. Jaded sometimes by the music of poetry, we look for something else, something hard, complex, embedded: the ore itself. It was this search that turned Keats inward away from sweetness and bombast and that Lowell pursued further and further in each new book. Those who were irritated that he did not stick to a known path, his own path, however brambled and thick, but had turned off again into something even more complicated and lonely, were angry that he seemed to want to get lost. The poems can be infuriating, they are simply "too hard." But if one, as their reader, learns how to listen, they are, for technique, masterful. And is this not the quality that Lowell brought to twentieth-century verse, the gift required from the reader, of not just reciting along with the poet, be it Hart Crane, or Stevens, or Williams, but of listening? The utter refining of the ear, the supreme compliment to our intelligence?

Lowell blessed others before he blessed himself. The benediction, wild as this sounds, is like Blake's. Everything is holy, but everything suffers. Light itself is a burden.

In Trinidad, in a stone house by the sea at night, a place where we spent vacations, we lit pressure lamps because there was no electricity. The house was on a small cliff above the white noise of the Atlantic, and once the salty darkness had set in and the trees went into the night, the hiss of the gas lanterns was like a far surf. The light from the hung lanterns made a wide ring of huge shadows, dividing our faces sharply into bright and dark like old paintings. The night air was salt, damp, and full of the steady noise of the sea; and when I think of my family there, our cook, Lizzie and Harriet, my son Peter and my wife Margaret, it is always by the light of a phrase in Pasternak's poem about women sewing. "Two women, by a Svetlan lamp's reflection/ among its heavy burdens beam and gleam." In such windy places the light made by fuel lamps is both a burden and a benediction.

We had invited the Lowells to spend a weekend there with us. They were going to Brazil. Lowell had just published *Imitations*. When I think of his book I think of the sea, the night, the gas lamp, my family, then, near the ocean. He showed me the poems and asked me my opinion of them. The honor I felt before his humility remains. He did this with many people. I admired his adaptation of Rilke's poem "Homecomings"—"The terrible Egyptian mater-familias" sitting like Madame Recamier on her tomb lid, the substitution of a sarcophagus for a sofa, and the daring phrase, "her breasts spread apart like ox-horns." "Are these Rilke?" I asked him. "No," he said, "two stanzas in there are mine." He looked pleased by my question.

To purists or scholars the "Imitations" were insolence, violation, pride. But after *Imitations* Lowell had reached a happiness in his work in which all poetry was his. He had made the body of literature his body, all styles his style, every varying voice his own. The "Imitations" were not appropriations, but simply a rereading of literature in his own soft accent. I remember him watching me in the half-darkness, in one of the used-up armchairs of the beach house. I remember feeling that he had given me them to read not for my admiration, but for a pleasure as soft, as dim, as companionable as the darkness.

I was at the Chelsea Hotel in September 1977 when a friend called to say that Cal had died. I felt more irritation than shock. Death felt like an interruption, an impudence. The voice was immortal in the poems and others after me would hear it. In his last book, *Day by Day*, he had made exhaustion inspiration. He had married often but his muse was not widowed. He had been faithful to her in sickness and in health that was generally convalescence. To the last he refused to be embalmed by fame:

> *Those blessèd structures, plot and rhyme—*
> *why are they no help to me now*
> *I want to make*
> *Something imagined, not recalled?*
> *. . .*
> *All's misalliance.*
> *Yet why not say what happened?*
> *Pray for the grace of accuracy*
> *Vermeer gave to the sun's illumination. . . .*

—March 1, 1984

14

DARRYL PINCKNEY
ON DJUNA BARNES

MANHATTAN WAS BURNING up that Bicentennial summer, and those without air conditioners, those who could not buy refuge in the cinemas or bars, were driven into the streets. Far into the spangled night, welling up from the muggy cross streets and streaming avenues, came the noise of tape-deck anthems, revving motorcycles, breaking bottles, dogs, horns, cats in heat, bag ladies getting holy, and children going off the deep end.

I was beginning a new life. I was still on the Upper West Side, but every change of address within the twenty-two square miles of Manhattan was, back then, before I knew better, a hymn to starting over. So, two rooms with splintered, softwood floors and walls the dingy, off-white color of a boy's jockey shorts after scout camp; two rooms at 2— West 95th Street in a small, shaggy building of only two apartments, rooms sanctified by rent stabilization.

The old brick held the mean heat, sun streaked through the windows and lit up the smoky dust that hung in the air. The pipes leaked, the doors were warped, spider webs formed intricate designs in the corners. The oven and refrigerator refused to work on days that were not prime numbers. In the mornings paint dropped from the ceiling like debris idly flung into traffic from an overpass. The bathroom tiles had buckled and the cracks in the plaster resembled outlines of fiords in a map of Norway. Roaches? O yes, the totemic guerrillas of urban homesteading were there.

None of this mattered. I was unpacking boxes of secondhand and overdue library books, fondling dirty envelopes of tattered letters, hitting my shins on milk crates of blackened pots, tarnished flatware, and chipped Limoges plates. In the new ascetic life I imagined I would not need much. I was not made for keeping up the perfect kitchen for the right sort of dinner party, not equal to the task of digging up that intriguing print for the gleaming, glossy-white vestibule. I was through with telephone madness at 5 PM—that calling and calling to find someone home while a tray of ice melts on the thrift store table. And the nights of the wide bed, of the mattress large enough to hold the combat of two, were definitely over. The seediness into which I had slid held the promise of a cleansing, monastic routine.

My rear window looked out on a mews, on Pomander Walk, a strand of two-story row houses done in a mock-Tudor style. The shutters and doors were painted blue, green, or red. The hedges were prim and tidy. Boxes of morning glories completed the scene. An odd sight, unexpected, anachronistic, I thought of it as a pocket of subversion against the tyranny of the grid and the tower. But Pomander Walk's claims were modest, as were its proportions—a mere sideshow of a lane that ran north and south, from 95th Street to 94th Street. Its survival probably had something to do with its being in the middle of the block, not taking up too much room, and that it was family property.

A little street in the London suburb of Chiswick was celebrated in the play *Pomander Walk*, first produced in 1911. I was told that an Irish-American restaurateur was so charmed by it that he brought the designer over to help build a replica of the set. That is what he got— a set. It was built in 1921, a rather late, unhistorical-sounding date. When Pomander Walk was finished the land immediately west of it was virginal, undeveloped. Residents had a clear view of thick treetops down to the Hudson River. Perhaps then it was close in mood to the ideals of the City Beautiful period, to the harmony of Hampstead Way or Bedford Park. Perhaps not. This was a mirage inspired by haphazard Chiswick, not by an architect's vision of a utopian commuter village.

I was disappointed to learn that Pomander Walk had always been apartments. I thought each structure had originally been a house and, like those of Belgravia, then had been violated, cut up, humbled by the high cost of living well. Pomander Walk harbored high-ceilinged efficiencies "intended for and first occupied by theatrical people," the WPA *Guide to New York City* reported in 1939. In the Twenties, so the lore went, it was a pied-à-terre for the likes of the Gish sisters, Katharine Hepburn, and Dutch Schultz. Bootleggers threw scandalous parties at which guests refused to remove their homburgs.

Pomander Walk had seen better days. The sentry boxes were empty. The caretaking staff had been reduced to two elusive Poles, the apartments themselves were in various stages of decay, and behind the valiant façades, in the passageways between the tombs of West End Avenue and the cheap clothing stores of Broadway, were fire escapes grim as scaffolds and mounds of garbage through which chalk-white rats scurried. These were the days before gentrification—where is the gentry?—before the ruthless renovations that would turn entire neighborhoods into a maze of glass, chrome, exposed brick, polished blond oak, and greedy ferns.

Pomander Walk had become a kind of fortress, as it had to be, surrounded as it was, like the enclaves of early Christian merchants in the Muslim ports of the Levant. Pomander Walk struggled against the tone of the blocks swarming around it. High iron gates at either end of the lane, at the steps that led down to the streets, spoke of a different order. "Do Not Enter." "Private Property." A peeling red rooster kept vigil over the main entrance. The fields sloping down to the Hudson were long gone. Sandwiched between dour, conventional buildings, Pomander Walk seemed an insertion of incredible whimsy and brought to mind Rem Koolhaas's phrase in *Delirious New York*, "Reality Shortage."

During my vacant hours I fed my curiosity about the inhabitants of that pastoral, pretentious, Anglophile fantasy. The tenants were mostly women. I imagined that they were widows surviving on pensions or on what their husbands had managed to put aside, and that there were a few divorcées sprinkled among them, the sort not anxious to define themselves by respectable jobs with obscure art galleries. Their custom, on those hot afternoons, before, as I supposed, trips to married sons at the Jersey Shore, was to leave their electric fans and gather on the stoops. They sat on newspapers, pillows, or lawn chairs for cocktails. Sometimes large, festive deck umbrellas appeared.

The women got along well with the blond or near-blond actors and dancers who lived in warring pairs in some of the smaller apartments. The artists, when they came out in tight shorts for a little sun, joined with the women in discouraging intruders from looking around. No, they said, there were no flats available and the waiting list was as long as your arm. Defenders of the faith. I kept the frayed curtain over my rear window drawn after some tourists, as nonleaseholders were called, stepped up to the bars and, seeing me, a black fellow struggling with a can of tuna fish, asked, "Are you the super?"

Once upon a time I was morbidly sensitive about the impertinence born of sociology. Taxi drivers would not stop for me after dark, white girls jogged to keep ahead of my shadow thrown at their heels by the amber street lamps. Part of me didn't blame them, but most of me was hurt. I carried props into the subway—the latest *Semiotext(e)*, a hefty volume of the Frankfurt School—so that the employed would not get the wrong idea or, more to the point, the usual idea about me. I did not want them to take me for yet another young black prole, though I was exactly that, one in need of a haircut and patches for my jeans. That Bicentennial summer I got over it. I remembered a gentleman of the old school who, after Johns Hopkins and Columbia, said his only ambition had been to sink into the lower classes. By the time I knew him he had succeeded and this gentle antique lived out his last days among harmless drunkards at a railroad yard in Norfolk, Virginia. I resolved to do the same, as if, away from Mama and Papa, I had been anywhere else.

As a matter of fact I had been sinking for some time. First stop downward: a bookshop. Not the supermarket variety where women phoned in orders for two yards of books, repeating specifications of height and color, completely indifferent to title. Not one of the new boutiques where edgy Parisian slang skipped over the routine murmur. But a "used" bookshop, one of those holes in the wall where solitude and dust took a toll on the ancient proprietor's mental well-being, much like the health risks veins of coal posed to miners. That summer, unable to pay the rising rent, the owner gave up, wept openly at the auction of his stock. Next stop: office temp (let go). Waiter (fired). Telephone salesman (mission impossible). Then I found my calling— handyman. The anonymity of domestic service went well with the paranoid vanity of having a new and unlisted phone number.

I should have advertised my services in *The Westsider*. Even so, I lucked into a few appointments. Among my clients was an exalted bohemian on the upper reaches of Riverside Drive. I spent most of the day cleaning up after her impromptu séances. Two mornings a week I worked for a feminist psychologist who lived in one of the hives overlooking Lincoln Center. I walked her nasty Afghan hound, which was often woozy from pet tranquilizers; stripped the huge roll-top desk she hauled in not from the country but from Amsterdam Avenue. I was not allowed to play the radio and, in retaliation, I did not touch the lunch of tofu and carrot juice she left for me on the Formica counter. Then to Chelsea where I picked up dry cleaning for a furtive, youngish businessman. His mail consisted mostly of final notices from Con Ed, Ma Bell, and collection agencies in other states. I was certain that I was being tailed whenever I delivered one of his packages to the dubious factory outlets with which he had dealings. I made him pay me in cash.

One glaring morning someone I knew in publishing called to say that she knew of a woman who was getting on in years and in need of some help. The only thing Djuna Barnes required of her helper was that he not have a beard. I shaved, cut my hair, and fished out jacket and tie in spite of the heat, having been brought up to believe that I was not properly dressed unless I was extremely uncomfortable. I was so distracted that my socks did not match.

Miss Barnes lived in the West Village, just north of the old Women's House of Detention, in a blind alley called Patchin Place. Shaded by ailanthus, a city tree first grown in India that in the days of the pestilence was believed to absorb "bad air," the lime-green dwellings of Patchin Place had once been home to Dreiser, John Reed, E. E. Cummings, Jane Bowles, and John Mayfield. Through the inter- com at no. 5 came a deep, melodious voice and after an anxiety- producing interrogation, I was buzzed in. I found the chartreuse door with its "Do Not Disturb" sign and, after another interrogation, it slowly opened.

The home of this "genius with little talent," as T. S. Eliot said of Miss Barnes, was brutally cramped—one tiny, robin's egg–blue room with white molding. The kitchen was such a closet that the refrigera- tor hummed behind French doors in a little pantry packed with iron- ing board, vacuum, boxes of faded *cartes d'identité*, linen, and, so my covetousness led me to think, hoarded Tchelitchew costume sketches. Great adventures, I was sure, awaited me in the clutter—bibelots on the mantel and side tables, picture frames on the floor turned toward the wall, shoeboxes under the fat wing chair. On either side of the fire- place were bookcases. Her low, narrow bed was flush against one of them. Two plain wooden desks dominated the dark room. Stacks of letters and papers had accumulated on them like stalagmites. Meticu- lously labeled envelopes warning "Notes on Mr. Eliot," "Notes on

Mr. Joyce" rested near a portable typewriter. The blank page in the Olivetti manual had browned.

The booming voice was deceptive. Miss Barnes was shrunken, frail. The Lazy Susan of medicines on the night table was so large that there was scarcely room for the radio, spectacles, and telephone. Her introductory remarks were brief. She came down hard on the point of my being there. "See that you don't grow old. The longer you're around the more trouble you're in." Miss Barnes had been old for so long that she looked upon herself as a cautionary tale. The first day of my employ I was told to see to it that I never married, never went blind, was never operated on, never found myself forbidden salt, sugar, tea, or sherry, and, above all, that I was never such a fool as to write a book.

Yet there was a hypnotic liveliness to her, moments when the embers of flirtatiousness flared. The thin white hair was swept back and held by two delicate combs. She wore a Moroccan robe trimmed in gold, opaque white stockings, and red patent-leather heels. Her eyes glistened like opals in a shallow pond and her skin was pale as moonlight. Her mouth was painted a moist pink, her jaw jutted forward, her bearing was defiant, angrily inquisitive. The tall, stylish eccentric of the Berenice Abbott and Man Ray photographs lived on somewhere inside the proud recluse who cursed her magnifying glass, her swollen ankles, overworked lungs, hardened arteries, and faulty short-term memory. "Damn, damn, damn," she muttered.

My inaugural chore was to refill the humidifier. Under her scrutiny this task was far from simple. Her hands flew to her ears. "That's too much water. We can't have that." Next Miss Barnes wanted me to excavate an unmarked copy of "Creatures in an Alphabet." Stray pages were tucked here and there, none clean enough for her. She settled on one version of the poem, retreated to the bed, and set about crossing out the dedication. "Can't have that. He ruined my picture." The explanation of how some well-meaning soul had smudged a portrait when he tried to wash it gave way abruptly to a denunciation of modern pens, how they were not made to last. I gave her my Bic, told her to keep it. "Why thank you. Would you like to support me?" She sank into the pillows and laughed, dryly, ruefully, as one would at a private joke.

By some sorcery the laugh became a racking cough. She clutched a wad of tissues and coughed, coughed. I tried to help—water? A pill? She held up her hand for silence. The barking subsided. She sat for some time with head lowered, fists in her lap. Then she looked around, as if disappointed to find herself still in the same place. Fearing dizziness, she asked me to fetch her black handbag. She found the leather coin purse, from which she slowly extracted five one-dollar bills. She laid them on the bed in a fan shape and commanded me to "run along." She pushed the pages of "Creatures in an Alphabet" away, like a patient trying to shove a tray of Jello and thin sandwiches from view. Miss Barnes was tired. Asking for a fresh copy of that poem was a symbolic gesture—she was no longer a writer at work. At least she had an air conditioner, I thought, as I closed the warm gate to the street and put a match to the cigarette I was not permitted to smoke in her presence.

I learned not to call and volunteer: Miss Barnes turned me aside with mandarin courtesy. I went when summoned, which was not often. If I arrived early she implied that the zeal of the young was inelegant, and if I came late, panting, she stated flatly that the young were hopelessly self-absorbed. Miss Barnes thought my given name, with its contemporary dixie-cup quality, ridiculous, and my surname, with its antebellum echo, only barely acceptable. I had to admit that it had the goofiness of a made-up name. Delmore Schwartz, what a beautiful name! Delmore Schwartz is said to have exclaimed.

I went to the market—"What's an old woman to eat, I ask you"— for bananas, ginger ale, coffee ice cream, hard rolls, and plums. "Not the red ones, the black ones. When they're good, they've white specks on them." I rushed out to the hardware store for pesticide and back again to exchange it for a brand to which she was not allergic. I went to the shoe repair and back again to have her black heels stretched even more. "I forgot. You're young. Don't mind running up and down the steps, do you?" And, of course, I stood on line at the pharmacy.

"I haven't been out of this room in five years. You'd think I'd be climbing the walls, wouldn't you?"

"Yes."

"I am."

Miss Barnes was not above a little drama and I believed she exaggerated the extent of her isolation. She had a brother in Pennsylvania, a nephew or some such in Hoboken. Regularly her devoted "boy," an East European in his sixties, came to wash the floors and walls. I had heard that two elderly gentlemen, her doctor and her lawyer, still climbed the stairs to pay their respects. There were romantic rumors —one had it that an heiress to the company that supplied paper to the US mint sometimes stepped from a great car to call on the friend of her expatriate youth. I hoped the radio was a comfort, that it filled her room with music, voices, but it was never on in my presence, during business hours, as it were.

She was reasonably informed about large events, seemed up on literary gossip. The TLS was stored in a basket like kindling, the light-blue wrappers unbroken. If she did not have much to say about the outside world, well, she had lived a long time. The ways in which most of us burned up daily life were, to her, pure folly. "What fools are the young." I am sure Miss Barnes managed to do a great deal of wrangling by telephone. She had a combative, litigious streak, an outgrowth, perhaps, of the yearning to take hold, to fend for herself. Rights and permissions had become an obsession that filled the place once occupied by composition. She dismissed me before she dialed the number of some unsuspecting publisher.

It was bad manners to be too curious. Many had been banished. She spoke of one former helper as being "stupid as a telephone pole." She fumed against one enterprising character who had insinuated himself into her confidence, gotten into her will "with both feet," and then packed up cartons of treasure. She claimed to have been relentlessly ripped off, down to the monogrammed spoons, but I wondered about that since, evidently, she regarded the sale of her papers as a kind of theft. As for admirers, those pilgrims and would-be biographers who brought her "one bent rose from somebody's grave," she declared that they wanted her on 42nd Street standing on her head with her underwear showing. Some acolytes, she said, had taken advantage of her failing eyesight to smuggle out a souvenir or two. She complained that a bookstore in the vicinity had, without her consent, used the name her father had conjured up for *her*, and that when she called to protest the manager hung up on her.

Pessimism Miss Barnes wore as regally as a tweed suit and perhaps an early career as a reporter had taught her not to expect too much of the "hard, capricious star." Everything and everyone came down to the lowest common denominator in the end. "Love is the first lie; wisdom the last." The one time I was foolish enough to quote from her work she looked at me as if I had lost my mind. "Am I hard of hearing," she screamed, "or do you mumble?" That was a break, the possibility she hadn't heard. "You're shy, aren't you? Pretend that you aren't." I wanted to be different, to be one who did not ask about the cafés, the parties, Peggy Guggenheim, or her portrait of Alice Rohrer over the fireplace.

Her seclusion was a form of self-protection as much as it was a consequence of age. Even if she had been temperamentally capable of going off, like Mina Loy, and leaving everything to scavengers, it was too late. When Miss Barnes was on a roll, launched on a tirade fueled by grievance, her tiny figure seemed to expand and take up the whole room. The bold voice forced me into a corner, words came like darts.

I had the feeling that the locksmith's clumsy work stood for some-thing larger, that it was simply an occasion for the release of fury. I nodded and nodded as she pointed to the scratches around the new cylinder in the door. "You mustn't say 'Oh really' again." Then the inevitable deflation, that rasping cough. I stood very still, like an animal waiting for a hunter to pass.

The temper had its source in the underground fire of physical pain. Once I was sent away minutes after slipping through the door because clearly she was having a rough day. Though Miss Barnes, like most old people, talked of her ailments—"I can't breathe and I'm going blind. Damn."—she did not want a stranger to witness her private struggles. She arranged five dollars on the bed and apologized for having ruined my Sunday. I told her that I admired her work, that coming to see her was one of my few joys. "You're mad. You're abso-lutely mad. Well, there's nothing we can do about that." I refused the money. Miss Barnes did not part with cash easily. In her life she had been broke and stranded more than once. My wage she regarded as wildly generous, a gift to, say, the United Negro College Fund, because she thought of dollars in terms of a prewar exchange rate. She insisted, gave me a bill to mail so that I would feel I had earned my pay. "I used to be like you. Not taking the money. It didn't matter." She wagged an index finger. "Make money. Stuff it in your boots, as Shakespeare said." Behind me I heard the bolts slide across her door.

The summer unfolded like a soggy sheet and, except for Miss Barnes, my clients casually drifted away. I lived on an early birthday present from home but, somehow, I managed to get behind in the rent. I assured my parents that I was knocking on doors, sending out résumés, proving once again that if you nag your children they will lie to you. Days evaporated like spilled water on sizzling pave-ment. Rock bottom was not so bad and if sinking had not turned out to be as liberating as I had hoped, it was not without some con-solations. The afternoons I traveled in humid subway cars from

Pomander Walk to Patchin Place lifted me out of my torpor. The chance to see Miss Barnes struck me as an omen—but of what?

Fame was not much of a consolation to her. She was not rich, could not trade her name for much, and so reputation she treated as a joke—on herself mostly. "You may like the book but not the old girl." Being a character, a survivor, made her one who had evacuated a large portion of her life, mindful of the clues carelessly left behind for detectives. "Would you believe I lived in Paris nine years and never learned a word of French?" Her memories, those she shared, had the quality of set pieces. Even when she talked of intimate matters there was something impersonal about it, and I wondered how many visitors had heard her say that she was never a lesbian, could never abide "those wet muscles" one had to love to love women; or that she was too much of a coward to take her own life.

A joke, yes, but not entirely. "No, don't move those. I'm a vain woman. I want them near me." Miss Barnes meant the translations, the various editions of *Nightwood* and *Ryder*. I was putting the bookshelf in order, not that it was needed. She was resistant to change: the autographed copy of Dag Hammarskjold's *Markings* had to remain where it had been for ages, a red pocket edition of Dante was also happy where it was. "Mr. Eliot learned Italian just to read this poem. He must have liked it, don't you think?"

I rescued a paperback, a biography of Natalie Barney, from under the bed. "Let me see that. Remy de Gourmont called her 'the Amazon of love' and she never got over it. That's what you get, that's what you end up looking like," she, peering through her magnifying glass, said to a photograph showing Barney in later life. I broke my promise to myself and asked about Colette. "Yes, I knew that silly, blue-haired lady." I got carried away and told Miss Barnes about a night at the opera when I, an undergraduate, just off the boat, was introduced to Janet Flanner. I mentioned to Miss Flanner that I too was from Indiana and she, taking in my costume of tan polyester suit, red, shiny tie, and platform shoes, answered: "I haven't been back since 1921—and I would advise you to do the same." Miss Barnes didn't crack a smile: "Often she knew whereof she spoke." I found yet another copy of *Nightwood*. "Sometimes I wonder, 'Did I write this? How did I do it?' Do it while you're young. Put all of your passion in it." She smiled.

But that was enough, not a syllable more. The shelves had to be swabbed down, and then the windows. So there I was, clinging to the fire escape, with Miss Barnes telling me over and over what a mess I was making. She leaned on the windowsill, handed out bouquets of paper towels, pointed to the lint and suds left in the corners. She absolutely refused to hear my thoughts on investing in a sponge. "Don't tumble into that Judas tree." She groped her way back to the bed to prepare for another onslaught of coughing.

In the shelves of the bookcases were mysterious little phials solemn as votive candles. She said that they contained oxygen. They looked like cloudy, empty bottles to me. I had to wash them, all twenty-four of them. One lid got trapped in the drain. "Now you've done it." I worked with a pair of scissors to pull it out. "Oh, you've done it now," she repeated, swaying against the bathroom door, fretting with the collar of a pink, satinlike dressing gown. "Take down the trash and you may go." The sad thing was realizing that there was really nothing I could do for her.

When I got the bright idea of devising a flow chart for her flotilla of pills—often she complained of headaches, of not knowing what to take when—she was offended. I argued that many of the prescriptions had been voided, that some of the tubes were empty, that it was amazing she could find anything in the jumble. We had a tug of war over a box of opium suppositories on which she depended for whatever peace she had. I made a little speech on obstruction, in the way one sometimes talks down to the elderly, on not being able to help if she didn't let me. "I know what I'm about, thank you very much!"

Miss Barnes ordered me to wash out a silk blouse in the sink. I said no. She started to say that she didn't understand why blacks had become so touchy, caught herself, and said that she didn't know why young men had such silly notions about what they considered women's work. But I knew what she meant, knew it from the way she had swallowed the "knee" of "Negroes," that despised word of her generation, knew it from the soft blush that spread like ink across the folds of her face. I don't remember what I said, but I can still see the five dollars on the blue coverlet, Miss Barnes hunched over, her dressing gown slightly hitched up, she hitting her palms together slowly. I paused at the door—for an apology?—but she was too old to take anything back. She met my gaze with a look of her own, a flicker of bewilderment, then hard as a stone tablet. I walked out.

I went back to living in steerage at the edge of Pomander Walk. Families were staking out territory along the oily river to watch ships, couples were hiking with blankets and beer to fireworks, but I had other things on my mind. By nightfall, when bagpipes started up within Pomander Walk to commemorate the Queen's walk down Wall Street to Trinity Church, the misunderstanding with Miss Barnes had assumed, to me, the magnitude of an incident.

In a punitive, self-righteous mood, I decided to "get" them all, to expose, as I termed it, the sins of Western literature. I set out the pens dipped in venom, the crisp, militant index cards. I turned up the flame under the pot of bitter Bustelo and started off, like a vigilante or a bounty hunter, in search of *them*. I was going to make Hemingway pay for the nigger boxer in Vienna in *The Sun Also Rises*. Fitzgerald was going to be called out for the Cadillac of niggers who rolled their eyes when they pulled up on the highway next to Gatsby.

I was going to get Dashiell Hammett for "darkie town," and Evelyn Waugh, Ronald Firbank, even Carl Van Vechten. This was serious—no Julia Peterkin, Fannie Hurst, or Dubose Heyward. I was going to stick to the Dilseys and Joe Christmases. If Conrad had to go, so be it, Céline too for his scenes in Little Togo. Sweat dripped from my nose onto the index cards. The laughter boiling in the streets added to my sense of lonely mission.

I woke in my clothes determined to beat up poor Hart Crane for "Black Tambourine." Not even William Carlos Williams was going to get off easy. Poe, Defoe. The jig was up for Rimbaud's sham niggers. Sins were everywhere: Katherine Mansfield in a letter spoke of one woman as "the sort to go with negroes." I was going to let Shaw have it, show Sartre a thing or two about the aura of the text of *Black Orpheus*. How dare Daniel Deronda condescend to defend Caliban.

But by noon, thanks to hypoglycemia, I wasn't sure that it mattered that in 1925 Virginia Woolf had come across a black man, spiffy in swallow tails and bowler, whose hands reminded her of a monkey's. How far back would I have to go, to Pushkin's Ibrahim or to the black ram tupping the white ewe? And to what purpose? Roussel's *Impressions d'Afrique* didn't even take place on earth, not really. Dinesen's farm was real, but so what? What was done was done, though most of the "gothic horror" was far from over. "Let them talk. You know your name," my grandfather used to say. I threw out the index cards. The motive for my note taking was pretty sorry: after leaving Miss Barnes I had fallen into the pit of trying to prove that there was more to me than she thought.

There was more to sinking, to being a handyman, to becoming a part of the streets around me, than I had thought. I had only to approach the surface of things, like a child coming too near the heat of a kitchen range, to discover that. Being in arrears made me afraid to meet anyone from Pomander Walk. I didn't have the nerve to ask the caretakers to fix a faucet. I sold off some big books to keep the lights on. The curtain over my rear window stayed down. What companionship of the outside I had was provided by the view of 95th Street from my front windows. It was there that I sat on those penniless summer nights, watching the elderly across the street scrutinize me from their prisons. There was a parking lot belonging to a Salvation Army residence. Daily the employees dragged themselves to their horrible duties and in the evenings they exchanged gossip with the night shift before hurrying away. Sometimes, on Sundays, guilty families came to wheel their begetters into sleek sedans for useless outings.

It was a street on which anything could happen and a lot did happen. Sometimes the angry voices after midnight terrified me, as if a wife or a whore were being beaten at the foot of my bed. I gave up calling the police and got used to it. That accounted for Pomander Walk's general fear of invasion. Between Riverside Drive and Central Park West, 95th Street was a no man's land, a zone of foreign tongues and welfare tenements. There were enough stories of ivy being torn from the walls by vandals, or someone who had had her purse ripped from her arm by a fleet-footed phantom who could not have been more than fifteen. The chilling cry of *"Motherfuckers! All y'all motherfuckers is gonna die!"* was enough to send every light on Pomander Walk blazing, as if a whistle had been blown to alert the local militia.

The building directly across from me had the most unsavory of reputations. It was an SRO, a very dark, benighted affair embedded in a slope. I noticed that pedestrians crossed the street to my side rather than risk the building's contagions that waited in ambush. A check-cashing joint occupied one of the rooms on the first floor and from the number of men coming in and out in their undershirts, wielding soiled paper bags from which the tops of wine or beer bottles were visible, I guessed that there was also a bookie joint somewhere inside. These men with missing teeth and shimmering hair who paced back and forth on the street, discussing their chances in that snapping, high-wire Spanish, made a strange tableau with the drag queens who also congregated outside the SRO.

The drag queens were impossible to miss, impossible not to hear. Hour on hour they milled around the entrance, dancing intricate steps to snatches of music that came from automobile radios. Most of them were in "low drag"—cutoffs, clogs, improvised halter tops, hair slicked straight back. Some appeared in wigs, curlers, black bathrobes, golden house slippers. They held cigarettes, long, brown More menthols or Kools, which they rationed scrupulously. They gossiped, waited, and played whist, "Nigger Bridge." They taunted young mothers who pushed baby carriages and balanced Zabar's bags and helium balloons; they hissed at broad-backed boys who sauntered up the street in Harvard or Columbia Crew T-shirts. "Honey, you need to go home and take off that outfit. That green gon' make yo' husband run away from you." Or: "Come over here, sugar, and let me show you somethin'."

Sometimes, for no apparent reason, just standing there, one of them would let out a long, loud, high scream—"Owwwwwww"— and then look around with everyone else on the street. This was particularly unnerving to the people who lined up with ice cream cones in front of the film revival house to see Fassbinder or Fellini. Equally unsettling to the neighborhood was their booby-trapped friendliness: "How ya doin' baby? Okay. Be that way. Don't speak, Miss Thing. You ain't gettin' none noway."

I watched the people of the SRO every day as the buds on the gingko that grew at a slant toward my window failed one by one and the pigeons pushed through the litter of frankfurter buns, hamburger wrappers, and pizza crusts. I recognized some of the SRO inmates at the Cuban tobacconist, the Puerto Rican laundromat, the Korean deli, at the Yemenite bodega, the hippie pot store, the Sikh newsstand. I watched them with a kind of envy. I loitered on the corner one night but everyone stayed clear of me. Perhaps they took me for a narc. But it was perfectly natural to cross the street to get the instant replay after a Checker had slammed into a station wagon or a fire been put out three blocks away.

Of course I did not find friendship, no matter how swiftly some of the drag queens and youths stepped off into the personal. Raps about the doings on Broadway or in the park inevitably shifted to breathless, coercive pleas for loans, though I told them I had had to break open my Snoopy bank for cigarettes. The soft-spoken owner of Pomander Bookshop took me aside to give me a warning. More than one innocent had fled that SRO without watch, wallet, or trousers. Three "bloods" invited me up to discuss a deal. An alarm went off in my head. I remembered how, as a child, three classmates had invited me to join their club. They escorted me to a garage and kicked the shit out of me. Remembering that, I got as far as the lobby, made some excuse, and split. I had always been uncomfortable with their questions about Pomander Walk.

It is hard to recall the murky, inchoate thinking that led me to make those inept gestures toward infiltrating what I saw as the underside of life, hard to camouflage the fatuity of my cautious hoverings. One night, late, a young woman was attacked by two kids. I heard her scream, saw her throw herself to the ground and thrash about. The kids couldn't get to her purse. By the time I got across the street others had come running. That was it, she moaned, she was going home to Baton Rouge. One grinding dawn I stumbled out into the haze with loose change for a doughnut. The intersection of Broadway and 95th Street was clogged with squad cars. Flashing lights whipped over the faces of the somber onlookers. There had been a shooting. A handsome Hispanic man in handcuffs was pulled over to the ambulance, presumably to be identified by the victim. His shirttails flapped like signal flags. A policeman cupped "the perpetrator's" head as he pushed him into the rear of a squad car at the curb. The man's head sagged on his smooth chest and shook slowly, rhythmically. Who was it that said the man who committed the crime was not the same man as the one in the witness box?

The violence was arbitrary. I was in a crowd that watched in horror as the policemen who had been summoned to defuse a fight beat a black teenager until coils of dark blood gushed from his head, his mouth, and drenched his shantung shirt. To my shame it was a black cop who used his stick with the most abandon. We were ordered to disperse, didn't, were rushed, and the voltage of fear that seized us was nothing like that of the political demonstrations in another time.

Shortly afterward, I called home. It seemed that I packed more than clothes. I carried to the corner all the baggage of my youth. I thought, as a taxi driver slowed to look me over, that I could leave those weights behind, like tagless pieces chugging round and round on a conveyor belt. Pollution made the sunset arresting, peach and mauve like the melancholy seascapes of The Hague School. On the way to La Guardia, stalled somewhere near the toll booth, I, looking forward to my prepaid ticket, to the balm of the attendants' professional civility, felt a wind. It came like forgiveness, that sweet, evening breeze, the first promissory caress of the high summer. The storm that followed delayed the departure of my flight.

—1984

15

MAURICE GROSSER ON
GERTRUDE STEIN AND ALICE TOKLAS

GERTRUDE STEIN'S APARTMENT on the rue de Fleurus was on the ground floor of an undistinguished building which had none of the grandeur of the seventeenth-century hotel on the rue Christine that she subsequently occupied. From the courtyard, a tiny entrance hall opened onto a large, square, high-ceilinged drawing room, actually a painter's studio. To the right of the fireplace hung Picasso's celebrated portrait of Gertrude looking rather hard and stern. To the left was a portrait of Mme Cézanne, perhaps the most beautiful work of that painter I have seen. The puce-colored walls of the studio were completely covered with unframed canvases. There was one small André Masson and two or three Juan Grises, including a lovely picture of a vase of flowers, the bright-colored flowers having been cut out of a seed catalog and pasted on.

The remaining works were practically all pre-Cubist Picassos of his blue and rose and early Negro periods. There was the little pink girl (whether nude or in long pink underwear I never could make out) standing and holding a basket of flowers; the mysterious woman depicted in profile with a half-closed fan; some early night landscapes in tones of dark Prussian blue; a series of beautiful tiny canvases in his early Negro style, heads and studies for the—in my opinion—quite unsuccessful *Les Demoiselles d'Avignon*. There were indeed some

Cubist works but I do not remember any of his classic Cubist period, those done in straight lines, arcs of circles, and tones of gray, which are so difficult to tell from Braque's. By the time Picasso arrived at this style, Gertrude, I believe, had stopped collecting.

The furniture was of dark oak and walnut—Louis XIII and Spanish, and there were lots of little prickly baroque-style objects of a vaguely ecclesiastical nature, like polychrome saints and candlesticks. Alice presided over the tea table or occupied herself at an embroidery frame, executing in petit point the backs and seats for a pair of little eighteenth-century chairs after designs Picasso had made for her, all the while telling stories with a mordant and entertaining wit, a wit sharpened by her skill in knowing exactly what to leave out. (Like this from her book, *What Is Remembered*: "Mrs. Luce came to lunch. She was convinced that her husband would be the next president." That was all, but it probably accounts for the outrageous review the book received in Luce's magazine *Time*.) Gertrude's *Autobiography of Alice B. Toklas* is made up word for word of the stories I have heard Alice tell. In fact, the autobiography presents an exact rendition of Alice's conversation, of the rhythm of her speech and of the prose style of her acknowledged works. It is such a brilliant and accurate pastiche that I am unable to believe that Gertrude with all her genius could have composed it and I remain convinced that the book is entirely Alice's work, and published under Gertrude's name only because hers was the more famous.

Gertrude would sit on the other side of the room and talk and question. She was short, thickset, and remarkably attractive, her close-cropped gray curls giving her something of the look of a Roman portrait head. She had great forthrightness and a wonderful deep belly laugh. She was not at all the gracious and ingratiating hostess she is usually pictured to be. To the contrary, she was brusque, self-assured, and jolly. Virgil Thomson said that she and he got along like two old Harvard men. When she hit on a phrase or idea that pleased her, she would repeat and repeat it, exactly as she did in her writing. Actually, her writing was not too different from her speech. For example, take her "Conversation as Explanation," a lecture she delivered at Oxford. If one reads it out loud supplying the punctuation which the text omits, one will have the exact manner and cadence of her conversation.

Alice was indeed ingratiating. She was more of the conventional hostess, but she was not at all the subservient companion she is sometimes pictured as being. She helped in household matters and typed Gertrude's manuscripts from devotion, not because she was a dependent—her income, I believe, being considerably larger than Gertrude's.

Gertrude's remarks were penetrating, laconic, memorable, and full of common sense. Examples: "Young painters do not need criticism. What they need is praise. They know well enough what is wrong with their work. What they don't know is what is right with it." And "I am I because my little dog knows me." The same earthy wit appears in her answers to a questionnaire submitted by the *Little Review* (May 1929) to the artistic and literary personalities of the quarter—the sort of large, general questions fated to receive pretentious answers: "What was the greatest moment of your life?" "What do you expect of the future?" "What is your attitude toward modern art?" and so on.

According to answers received, the greatest moment of Margaret Anderson's life was when she met Jane Heap, and Jane Heap's greatest moment was when she met Margaret Anderson. The Italian futurist painter Enrico Prampolini kidded the questions. His greatest moment was "one of simultaneous creation, artistic and sexual. At the moment of possessing a woman I loved to madness, I drew on her back the design for my greatest masterpiece." In what, I wonder.

Gertrude's answers were straightforward and somewhat wry. Her greatest moment was "birthday." To "What do you expect of the future?" she wrote, "More of the same." And to "What is your attitude toward modern art?" she answered: "I like to look at it."

She did indeed, both to look and to buy. At least she liked to buy in the earlier days when the Steins, Michael and his wife Sarah, Leo and Gertrude, turned up in Paris fresh from San Francisco. This was in 1903 when Mike, the eldest and the businessman, had sold a railroad spur they had inherited and made enough money out of the deal for them all to retire, made them rich enough also to be able to invest in the works of the new, young painters. Mike specialized in Matisse. Gertrude and Leo went straight to Picasso. (There is a story of how Leo locked the terrified painter in a room and refused to let him out until he had explained Cubism.)

Gertrude and Leo must have formed a very united couple, and I believe that it was Leo's eye rather than Gertrude's that guided their brilliant early foraging. Alice arrived from San Francisco in 1906 and moved in with them. They all lived together until 1912 when Leo moved out. The break must have been complete. As far as I know, Gertrude never saw him again. At any rate, I myself never heard either Gertrude or Alice speak his name. After his departure, Gertrude stopped buying pictures. Her explanation was that she had acquired a Ford and that there was not enough money both to run a car and to collect art. Whatever the reason, after her separation from Leo, she did not interest herself seriously in any painter—though she flirted with a great many of them—until in the late Thirties she encountered Sir Francis Rose and, according to rumor, purchased some four hundred of his works.

Francis was a well-to-do and vastly irresponsible young Englishman, quite pleasant looking but with a rather childish speech defect of spitting. He had been brought up by his mother and uncle in Villefranche-sur-Mer—until 1928 the home port of our Mediterranean fleet and a fashionable resort for that very reason—and was a protégé of Bérard and Cocteau from whom he had derived whatever training in painting and drawing he received. Nobody took his painting seriously then and no one takes it seriously now. Indeed, in the exhibition held in 1971 at the Museum of Modern Art in New York of pictures that had passed through the hands of the Stein family, not one of Gertrude's four hundred Francis Roses was shown. To explain Gertrude's faith in him, I must suppose that she was less interested in painting than in personality; that she was not looking for more pictures but for another great man, another Picasso marked with genius, and the tumultuous excesses of Sir Francis's life and his undisciplined facility convinced her that she had found one. Alice's several published cookbooks contain illustrations by Francis which well exhibit his amateurish and untrained vigor.

In the fall of 1929 when I first met her she had been looking over the new young painters, who at the time were Christian Bérard, Kristians Tonny, and Pavel Tchelitchew, and had decided against them all. Bérard was the first actually French painter of the School of Paris since Braque, all the others being foreigners, and he had already acquired a body of enthusiastic admirers. Tonny was a handsome young Dutchman, a contemporary Brueghel, and his depictions of a fantastic insect world executed in a linear form of monotype were much admired. Gertrude owned an oil portrait he had done of her dog Basket and a painted fire screen. Tchelitchew was a White Russian of aristocratic family, a rival to Bérard, and a draughtsman every bit as good as Ingres. Gertrude kept him around for some time without making any serious commitment and ended by turning him over to the Sitwells who took him to London and prepared his English success.

Gertrude asked Virgil if he had heard of any other interesting new painters. This was in the spring of 1930. He suggested Léonid's younger brother, Eugène (Genia for short) Berman, who was then doing dark, romantic landscapes in something of an Italian seventeenth-century manner, and nocturnal quay-side scenes with sleeping beggars and mysterious pyramids of piled-up merchandise. Gertrude and Alice went to his studio and were delighted with the work. They at once bought a couple of pictures, and since they were leaving the next day for their summer home near Belley, they invited Genia to visit them there. Genia arrived and when he came down to breakfast a few mornings later he was brusquely told the time the next train left for Paris and dismissed. Gertrude explained later that he had behaved in an unpardonable manner, that he had become sexually excited at the sight of their maid and did not take the trouble to conceal it. Alice, in her published letters, gives a somewhat different account; that one night they rang for the maid who did not answer the bell, and when they went to her room to see why, they found Genia closeted with her.

This is a strange and unlikely story, like a misapprehension contrived to further the plot of a French farce, or more likely an excuse to justify a sudden ungovernable dislike. In Paris at that time, the details of everybody's sex life were public property. The source of a friend's income might remain obscure but not what he did in bed or whom he did it with. Genia was known to have passionate sentimental attachments (like his later unhappy union with the actress Ona Munsen). But he was judged by all, even by his devoted brother Léonid, to have no active sex life whatever. Anyway, Gertrude bought no more of his pictures.

My own painting she never paid the compliment of asking about, and she was quite right not to do so. I was still learning to paint and quite unready to be discovered. My peculiar literary gifts, which we employed in staging the two Stein-Thomson operas, *Four Saints* and *The Mother of Us All*, she took very seriously indeed, actually saying somewhere in print that I was the only one who knew how to put her plays on the stage but, unfortunately, I preferred to spend my time painting. I could have answered that putting her plays on the stage was scarcely a full-time job.

When I went back to France in 1953, after the war and after Gertrude's death, Alice and I became the best of friends. But in these earlier years my relations with Gertrude and Alice were not too easy, principally, I believe, because it was through Virgil that I came to know them. On my first visit to Paris four years before, I had been provided with a letter to Gertrude from her old friends, the philosopher Alfred North Whitehead and his beautiful wife. But I was too timid, and really not interested enough, to present it. This I have since regretted. Had I gone to see them then, I would probably have been accepted on my own merits. Coming as Virgil's friend, I was only the less interesting member of a pair. Consequently, I never developed any real intimacy with Gertrude. (As proof of this, my name does not occur in any of her poems.)

In fact, she rather intimidated me. Gertrude had a special way of dealing with couples. She would take over the artist or writer, leaving Alice to deal with the friend or wife. Alice would eventually get tired of the friend or wife, and if she got tired enough she would enlist Gertrude's help and try to make the pair break up. There is a typical example of this in *The Autobiography of Alice B. Toklas* where Alice begins taking French lessons from Fernande, at that time Picasso's mistress, so that Fernande would have money enough to leave him. At one point, I believe, Alice attempted to separate Virgil and me. One evening when Virgil was alone with them, his relations with me were vigorously attacked. Virgil stood up for me and the matter was not mentioned again.

Alice, in her quiet way, was very possessive. People that Gertrude became too fond of were liable suddenly to be dismissed, never to appear again. Gertrude would unexpectedly quarrel with the very people she had been the most intimate with, like her brother Leo, or Mabel Dodge, or Bravig Imbs, or Hemingway, or the poet Georges Hugnet, or Virgil himself (though Virgil and she resumed their friendship after the production of *Four Saints*). And I have always thought it was Alice who provoked the quarrels, though Gertrude herself was not averse to a change of scenery. "A Jew," she once said, "is a ghetto surrounded by Christians. What we need this year are some new

Christians." And since Gertrude's was the best-known English-French literary salon in Paris, there were always enough new Christians turning up.

As for the opera *Four Saints in Three Acts*, the whole business of its composition was somewhat peculiar. Virgil and Gertrude had settled on sixteenth-century Spanish saints for their subject, the saintly life being used, I suppose, as a metaphor for the devoted life of the artist we all considered ourselves to be leading. The text for the opera, when delivered, turned out to be just as obscure, and as full of repetitions and undecipherable private references as Gertrude's poetry always is. There were no indications of what was to be taken as stage directions and what was to be sung. Most of the speeches were unassigned. On two points, however, Gertrude was clear. The aria "Pigeons on the Grass, Alas," which occurs in the third act, was to be a vision of the Holy Ghost, and the long passage beginning "Dead, said, wed, led" was to be a religious procession such as is performed in Seville during Holy Week. Virgil, on his side, divided the role of Saint Teresa into two, there being too much of it for one singer alone. This also enabled her to sing duets with herself. He also introduced two characters, a Compère and a Commère, not saints at all but elegant laity, who were to act as end men in a minstrel show to introduce the saints and to comment on the action.

Virgil's way of writing the music was also a little peculiar. He would sing the text over to himself and when a passage came out always the same, he would write it down. At the end he found that he had set the whole text to music—stage directions, names of characters, as well as the numbers assigned to the scene and act divisions. So that when we came to think about staging the opera, all there was to work with was a dense mass of music which had absorbed everything else. My way to deal with this was to get Virgil to sit at the piano and sing the opera through. I would listen and try to imagine what was going on on the stage. It all came together very easily.

My scenario began with a sort of choral introduction which ended with the Commère and Compère introducing the saints by name. The first act that follows is a sort of Sunday school entertainment in which the two Saint Teresas act out on a small stage the principal events of their—or rather her—life. The second act is a garden party, which the Commère and Compère attend, seated together in an opera box at one side of the stage. The saints play various games like "London Bridge" and "Drop the Handkerchief." There is a ballet of angels, a love scene between the Commère and Compère, and a toast by the saints to the happy couple. Saint Ignatius arrives with a telescope through which he shows them a vision of the Holy City. Saint Teresa wants to keep the telescope. When it is explained that she cannot have it, she accepts the refusal gracefully and the act is over.

Act III takes place on a seashore where Saint Ignatius is training his disciples. The Holy Ghost appears to him and he sings about it and calls his distracted disciples to order with a sermon. There is a ballet of Spanish sailors and their girls. The saints form a propitiatory procession which slowly marches off the stage. The Commère and Compère come out in front of the curtain to discuss and introduce a fourth act. The curtain lifts to reveal the saints now in heaven and singing about their life on earth. This may sound rather silly, but when the opera was finally performed in Hartford four years later, my scenario turned out to be an ideal framework, and I am now convinced that the opera cannot be properly given without it. Except for Gertrude's two suggestions, the stage action was made up without her cooperation. In fact, by the time the scenario was set, Gertrude had quarreled with Virgil and they were no longer speaking.

The break between them came in the wake of a quarrel between Gertrude and the French poet Georges Hugnet. Georges was a Surrealist, even, I believe, an official member of the group. A tough, handsome, and rather truculent young man, he was a great friend of Virgil's, in fact Virgil had set a number of his poems to music.

Georges had recently completed a long series of poems about his childhood entitled "*Enfances*" which Gertrude—who at this time was seeing a great deal of him—found so admirable that she undertook to translate it into English. The two texts, Gertrude's translation and Georges's original, made up a remarkable pair, inasmuch as the obscurities of one acted to clarify the obscurities of the other. They decided to publish the two works under the title "*Enfances*, Poems by Georges Hugnet, Followed by an English Translation by Gertrude Stein," this being, of course, in French and not in the English I have given.

The title, however, did not long satisfy Gertrude. Her part of the work, she began to consider, was much too good to be dismissed as a mere translation. In fact, it was an important independent work, and the title had to be revised to read: "*Enfances, Poèmes de Georges Hugnet et Gertrude Stein.*" Even more, since Gertrude was a woman, it was only natural that her name should be given precedence and be cited first. Georges refused to accept the change and they fought bitterly over it. All the Quarter took sides, while Picasso, who loved a good literary quarrel, egged everybody on.

In the meantime Christmas was approaching and Gertrude and Alice invited Virgil and me to pass Christmas Eve—this was 1930— with them in their flat. We were four. We exchanged gifts, were given a ceremonial dinner, and passed a very pleasant evening. The subject of Hugnet came up, and Virgil, who did not at all approve of the behavior of either party, proposed a compromise, which he had already persuaded Hugnet to accept—something about adding after each name the date of the work's composition. Gertrude agreed to the compromise, apparently so did Alice, and we left with the impression of having spent with them a pleasant and friendly Christmas Eve.

Virgil then came down with his usual winter bronchitis and stayed at home in bed, his throat wrapped in flannel. One morning, a week or ten days after Christmas, he received in the mail a small stamped and addressed envelope containing a calling card which read: "Miss

Gertrude Stein" (this engraved) and underneath in Gertrude's spidery handwriting, "Declines further acquaintance with Mr. Virgil Thomson." That was all. Virgil was too hurt to answer or protest, and they did not see each other or speak again until the fall of 1934 when *Four Saints* was revived in Chicago and Alice and Gertrude came there to see it. The whole affair, aimless, silly, and wounding, I can explain only as another example of Alice's jealousy working on Gertrude's literary vanity, here acting to persuade her that Virgil had gone over to the enemy's camp.

Despite all this, the two *"Enfances"* nevertheless appeared together, on facing pages in Sherry Mangan's quarterly *Pagany*, Winter 1931, under the title Gertrude herself must have devised: "Enfances— Georges Hugnet" and "Poem Pritten on Pfances of George Hugnet— Gertrude Stein." Her translation was later published by itself, entitled, appropriately enough, *Before the Flowers of Friendship Faded Friendship Faded*.

—November 6, 1986

16

PRUDENCE CROWTHER
ON S. J. PERELMAN

SIDNEY JOSEPH PERELMAN was born in Brooklyn on February 1, 1904, to Russian Jewish immigrants. He was an only child. The family soon moved to Providence, Rhode Island, where his father, Joseph, opened a dry-goods store, earning a parlous living that did not improve after a switch to poultry farming ("to this day I cringe at the sight of a gizzard," Perelman wrote in a letter in 1966). He characterized his milieu as "lower middle bourgeois." His parents were not religious; Joseph was a socialist. In 1959, Sid told a panel of BBC interviewers:

> There was no particular persecution or pressure brought upon me because of my racial background. It just didn't exist. We were an extremely polyglot crowd.... The circumstances of my boyhood were, in fact, quite enjoyable in every way.... I never had any sense of being alienated from my background or culture whatever.

He claimed to have had the normal boy's ambitions but most wanted to become the rear driver on a hook and ladder fire truck. From an early age, he began drawing and cartooning. He received a solid public-school education and often worked after class.

In 1921 Perelman entered Brown University in Providence, where he met Nathanael ("Pep") West of New York City. West became his closest friend and, in 1929, his brother-in-law, when he married Laura West, who was eighteen. Perelman was made editor of the college humor magazine, *The Brown Jug*, his senior year. He left Brown without graduating, having failed the math requirement, and moved to Greenwich Village in 1924.

There he joined the staff of *Judge*, a weekly humor magazine, and the captions for his drawings began to grow into the singular style that characterized his life's work. Perelman also contributed to *College Humor*, until its demise in 1934. *That Old Gang o' Mine: The Early and Essential S. J. Perelman*, edited by Richard Marschall (Morrow, 1984), offers substantial and delightful evidence of his skill as an artist in the school of Ralph Barton and John Held, Jr., and as a well-advanced parodist and dementia praecoxswain, to turn Robert Benchley's phrase for the kinds of pieces they were both then writing.

Perelman went abroad for the first time in 1927 and again, on his honeymoon, in 1929, the year *Dawn Ginsbergh's Revenge*, a collection of his magazine pieces, was published by Horace Liveright. It was noticed by Groucho Marx, who soon latched onto Perelman as a writer. The movies *Monkey Business* (1931) and *Horse Feathers* (1932), both written in collaboration, show his handiwork. In December of 1930, he began his nearly half-century association with *The New Yorker*.

Although working with the Marx brothers provided him with inexhaustible storytelling capital—written and oral—over the years, Perelman often felt that the glamour of the connection upstaged the value of his work. In a 1976 letter to Deborah Rogers, his British agent at the time, he responded to a publisher's request to include extracts from his Marx Brothers scripts in his next book:

> I am fucking sick and tired of my endless identification with these clowns. If it is not yet apparent after 50 years of writing

for publication in the US, Britain, and elsewhere that my work is worth reading for its own sake; if illiterates and rock fans (synonymous) can only be led to purchase my work by dangling before them the fact that I once worked for the Marx brothers, then let us find some other publisher.

Over the next decade the Perelmans shuttled back and forth between coasts. In Hollywood they wrote as a couple for films; back East, for the stage. *All Good Americans* and *The Night Before Christmas* were both produced and made into films. By himself, Perelman wrote radio and theater sketches and continued to collect his magazine pieces: *Strictly from Hunger* appeared in 1937, *Look Who's Talking!* in 1940. With their two young children, Adam and Abby, the Perelmans lived in the Village and on their farm in Bucks County, Pennsylvania —purchased in 1932 with West, whom they later bought out. West intended to settle there as well, but in December 1940, during one of his own screenwriting stays in Hollywood, he and his wife of eight months, Eileen McKenney, were killed in a car accident.

Hollywood, with its "ethical sense of a pack of jackals" and producers who "had foreheads only by dint of electrolysis," was the place Perelman most loved to loathe. He did time there strictly for money, and as soon as he could afford to escape, he did. In 1943 he teamed up with Ogden Nash to write the musical *One Touch of Venus* (music by Kurt Weill), a Broadway smash that enabled him to end his servitude in the studio system. Not that he was set up for long: between private-school tuition, support of his mother (his father died in 1926), periodic psychiatric help, his determination to travel, and the costs of two households and an office, staying solvent was a frequent anxiety.

Hoping for another big score, Perelman wrote the musical *Sweet Bye and Bye* with his friend Al Hirschfeld in 1946 (songs by Vernon Duke). In the wake of its closing out of town, the editor of *Holiday* magazine proposed that Perelman and Hirschfeld go around the world. The accounts of that trip, with illustrations by Hirschfeld, were collected in *Westward Ha!*, brought out in 1948 by Simon and Schuster (Perelman's publisher from then until his death).

Perelman's passion for travel soon became inseparable from his search for copy. "The humorist," he said, "has to find himself in conflict with his environment.... He has to pretend that he's sublimely unhappy in most places, but that's a very small price for me to pay for the pleasure I derive from being in Africa or Asia." *The Swiss Family Perelman*, also illustrated by Hirschfeld, describes a second global trip in 1949, this time undertaken by the whole clan.

In 1955, the producer Mike Todd—"an ulcer no larger than a man's hand"—hired Perelman to write additional dialogue for his extravaganza *Around the World in 80 Days*. Much as Perelman professed to despise the job and the man, both together inspired him. At the point of maximum tension between his values and Todd's, he wrote some of his most ecstatic letters.

Perelman won an Oscar for the picture and parlayed the acclaim into a series of writing assignments for television. For the cultural series *Omnibus* he wrote "The Big Wheel," a tribute to burlesque starring Bert Lahr, and "Malice in Wonderland," three sketches about Hollywood. In 1962 he again wrote for Lahr, this time a star turn in *The Beauty Part*, a well-received play that had the ill luck to open—and close—during a printers' strike against the city's newspapers.

Toward the end of 1969, the Perelmans went to England for three months. In January they returned to Bucks County with the flu. Laura, in fact, was also suffering from a recurrence of breast cancer; she died in April of 1970 at the age of fifty-eight. Unable to work and claiming to find the States intolerable, Perelman fell back on his habitual recourse with a vengeance. He sold the farm in Bucks County, auctioned off nearly all of his and Laura's possessions, and announced his decision to move to England.

In an autobiographical reflection for *The New Yorker* that never ran, Perelman wrote:

> I clearly envisioned myself ripening there in the afternoon of life, a mellow old philosopher with an endearing twinkle, a familiar and beloved figure in the neighborhood. (How this transformation would be accomplished, I wasn't quite sure, but no matter.)

No sooner was he settled in than he again took off around the world, this time in imitation of Phileas Fogg's journey in the original Jules Verne story. On his return to London, he was lionized a little while longer before beginning to experience a more normal life. By the second year, it had palled. He was lonely; he was out of touch with his idiom. He found English life both "too couth" and too boorish. He told Alan Brien of *Punch*:

> I was talking in the street with a friend of mine, a real Cockney with a real Cockney accent. An upperclass Englishman I knew chanced by and I introduced them. I could see him looking at me and at my friend. He didn't say anything, of course. But I could see him altering his attitude toward me and wondering why I was mixing with people of that sort. I couldn't stand that. A barrier rang down.

By May of 1972, he was back in New York. He continued to travel and write. *Vinegar Puss* (his twentieth book) appeared in 1975; *Eastward Ha!*, an account of yet another global swing (his sixth), in 1977. The following year, when he was seventy-four, he proposed to the editor of the London *Sunday Times* the idea of recreating, in reverse, a famous 1907 road race.

In the fall of 1978, Perelman was driving his 1949 MG from Paris to Peking in company with an English friend, Eric Lister, and Sydney Beer, an MG specialist. He was looking for trouble for the last time, and finding more of it than he wanted. Although on the trip Beer bitterly accused him of being "a word man," Perelman gave up writing about the trip after finishing only thirty-eight pages—the first and last assignment he ever failed to complete. By September 30, however, the drive was not yet the debacle it would become. From Pakistan he writes: "Thus far the high point of the trip (in every sense) was Afghanistan—the people are the nicest, most colorful, and filthiest."

At the time I was also in a colorful and filthy place, or two of them: Manhattan and the production studio of *The New York Review of Books*, where I was setting type by day and by night working tentatively on my first piece of writing. After six years in New York, I was still burdened by naïveté and the feeling that my life was faintly absurd. Even so, I had a few preoccupations and thought that if I could express them, I would find some relief, if not a starting point. I was thirty.

One evening, an editor at the *Review* saw that I was working on something of my own and asked to see it. Since I wasn't sure yet what I was up to, I hoped her remarks would be brief. She said simply, "I think you should send this to Perelman."

As a teenager in Oklahoma City, my father, himself an exceedingly funny man, read Perelman's early work in *College Humor*, reprinted from *The Brown Jug*. By the time Dad became editor of the MIT *Voodoo*, Perelman had published *Dawn Ginsbergh's Revenge*. Dad's recollection of "How to Fall out of a Hammock," from that book, was nearly reverent. Lest he think he had any more influence over me than he already had, I'd never read it. Somehow I'd also never become aware of Perelman as a public figure. I was raised to think of him as living in the Pantheon, not in an apartment, much less fifteen blocks from where I lived.

Of course you could write to him in care of *The New Yorker*. But what could you say that wouldn't be a gross presumption? As he wrote E. B. White, the standard fan letter is so obnoxious it generally ends in a request for a small loan until Easter.

As a first exercise in sedulous aping, I paraphrased the youthful Heinrich Heine's first letter to Goethe, then seventy-two. I identified my source and tried to allow for the fact that I was not one of Germany's great lyric poets but instead probably one of the simpler people in town. I was pretty sure the letter would go straight into the wastebasket with the rest of that day's pile of unsolicited piety.

After reaching Peking, minus his car and companions but with a case of pneumonia, an exhausted Perelman flew home to New York in December and settled back into his modest apartment in the Gramercy Park Hotel.

Nobody suffers from future shock around Gramercy Park. *Michelin* calls it "one of the spots in New York which most recall the past," and indeed there are few signs of the present. The park is bounded by one of the city's earliest apartment buildings and by nineteenth-century townhouses, pristine classical revivals in several styles. Number 16 to the south is the Players Club (Perelman was a member), founded by the actor Edwin Booth in 1888. Next door is the National Arts Club, the handsome old home of a former governor: bas-relief heads of Shakespeare, Milton, Goethe, and Dante surround that of Ben Franklin on the wall outside. To the west are three-story red brick homes framed by wisteria and black cast-iron balconies. Perelman had a writer friend at number 4 and also occasionally visited number 19, Ben Sonnenberg's fine mansion to the southwest. Residents have keys to the kempt park, with its hearty trees and large black urns full of red geraniums. In the middle, an undefiled Edwin Booth rises from a throne chair as Hamlet, hand on heart.

From Room 1621 in the Gramercy Park Hotel, if Perelman stood at the window he could see just enough of the pretty parts to remind him of London. But the hotel is also on an axis that took him back to his earliest days in New York: two blocks north, at Twenty-third

Street and Lexington Avenue, is the Kenmore Hall Hotel, where between 1927 and 1932 Perelman used to visit his brother-in-law, Nathanael West, the assistant manager. West was already practicing the largess that he became better known for later at the Sutton, uptown. From the Kenmore, they could wander to the Village, nearer Perelman's digs, for a meal at Siegel's on Sixth Avenue—dinner was eighty-five cents. Perelman introduced West to the columnist known as Susan Chester there one night; West used the letters she showed him as the basis for *Miss Lonelyhearts*.

In 1979 the Gramercy Park Hotel was also reasonably cheap, and convenient to Perelman's essential haunts. Within a mile-and-a-half's walk were *The New Yorker*, the Mercantile Library, where he subscribed, the Coffee House—in its day an offbeat club frequented by editors and writers, like his beloved Robert Benchley—and the Century Club, to which he also belonged. Even handier were the Second Avenue Deli on Tenth Street and Hammer's Dairy Restaurant on Fourteenth. Right around the corner, at Walsh's Chop House on Twenty-third, he could dine on one of his favorite standbys—a ham steak with raisin sauce and sweet potatoes. Shops were a block away on Third Avenue. The cost of a Danish at the Gramercy Pastry Shop (since 1932) served as Perelman's consumer price index, and a jump seemed to alarm him more than a stock slide might. Three doors down was the Gramercy Park Flower Shop, where every Christmas he ordered a dozen yellow spider mums sent to "the two most angelic people in America," his old screenwriting friends Frances and Albert Hackett. If he was visiting Al Hirschfeld on Ninety-fifth Street, he could hop on the Third Avenue bus. As he wrote a friend in England, "Where I'm living there's an affable Chinese to whom I take the laundry; a discount store for drugs; and a bakery with seeds in the rye. What more do I need?"

The hotel itself gave no sign of its distinguished occupant, unless you thought to take Saul Steinberg's famous *New Yorker* cover, framed in the lobby, as a clue. Other than that, most of the color was provided by the rock 'n' roll clientele, putting up close to their gigs in the Village and nearby. If you'd asked them who wrote *The Road to Miltown*, they'd probably have guessed the Rolling Stones.

After catching up on his mail, Perelman answered my letter in January 1979. We wrote some more, and in the middle of March he invited me to meet for dinner. I was keen, of course, but also wary. As Perelman's friend Raymond Chandler wrote, "Never Meet a Writer if You Liked His Book." I girded myself for the possibility that fame had warped him, and spent the afternoon seeing the last of a silent film series as insurance against having nothing to say.

Perelman told me to meet him at Sal Anthony's, a two-story family restaurant on Irving Place, south of Gramercy Park. Outside the entrance, on the second floor, is a plaque that says O. Henry once lived there and wrote "The Gift of the Magi" in "two feverish hours." Perelman, who could spend a day on a paragraph, must have snorted at that.

Remembering a description of him from *Time* (and forgetting he'd written it himself as a parody of *Time*-ese), I expected a "tall, stooping figure," suave and self-important. Instead I saw, stylishly but unselfconsciously posed at the bar, a small man, quietly but beautifully dressed. He had freckled skin, cheeks mapped with spidery blood vessels, and light blue walleyes, large and expressive behind gold wire-rim glasses.

One eye found me, then the other followed; his stare was never quite dead-on. His hands were graceful, whether miming, smoothing his hair, or characteristically resting one finger across his mustache— a gesture both elegant and slightly protective. For a satirist he seemed fittingly, if barely, stigmatized: the index fingers curved gradually in opposite directions. His voice was pleasantly croaky, and his Rhode Island accent gained distinction as it stamped his precise and delightful speech.

Perelman was one of those people who make you feel as charming as they are. I talked about the Chaplin I'd just been watching; he *knew* Chaplin. I talked about Beerbohm; he'd once escorted Elizabeth Taylor to Oxford (she was consulting a doctor) and seen the undergraduates react just as violently as they had to Zuleika Dobson's first visit. He was dazzling company and yet completely modest—naturally so, and never as a point of style.

After dinner we walked back to the hotel, and Perelman excused himself for a minute—"I have to go to the sandbox." He never said anything in an ordinary fashion, but every spin was spontaneous. We had a nightcap in the bar, and I ordered an unusually stiff liqueur. Depression followed: the audience would shortly be over, and I'd probably live another forty years. He put me into a cab and said he hoped we'd become good friends.

I wrote Sid a follow-up note and included two articles from the *Times*, one concerning a snake heist, the other a university in Ohio that was giving college credit for delivering children by the Lamaze method. When I met him again for dinner he showed up with his own sheaf of clippings, plus a small present—a seam-ripper that doubles as the perfect tool for clipping items from a newspaper.

No longer Sid's guest, I insisted on paying for myself. He protested ("I mean to speak to you about this conceit"), but we split the tab thereafter. That may be why I never saw evidence of his putative stinginess, although once when he was giving me change and I said, "Are you sure you're not giving me too much?" he answered, "No, I have the soul of a bookkeeper." To me he seemed generous. There was a marked appropriateness about his gifts or gestures that gave them their value. Clare Hollingworth once told me about the time Sid took her to have her first pizza. I laughed, and she said, "Oh, but it was a *superior* pizza." No doubt it was.

His best gifts, of course, were his enthusiasms, and in spite of everything, one of them was still New York. Like a Kafka character, the New Yorker is "constantly on trial for something the nature of which he doesn't understand," he told Mary Shenker. The steady smell of garbage and the paucity of good slang were more recent complaints. But as he'd discovered in London, he needed New York for his work, and my own relative ignorance of the city may have served to resurrect some of his excitement about it. There was scarcely a block in the city, the Village especially, that didn't speak to him.

One night early on I was walking home late from a ballet class—"twirling," Sid called it—and swung by his hotel. I thought of phoning him from the lobby but hesitated, picturing him in the middle of a more or less permanent salon in his rooms, which I hadn't yet seen. After circling the block once I finally dialed and asked him what he was doing. "I'm poised here looking like I'm about to make an epigram, and all I've got in my head is butterscotch." I asked if he wanted to go have some dessert, and he sounded overjoyed to be sprung from his solitude. That was my first inkling that his life was not exactly the Olympian bower I'd imagined. He looked very sharp as usual, like an old artist, and wore a plaid shirt with a dark tie.

That night I borrowed a copy of *Dawn Ginsbergh's Revenge*, inscribed to his wife, Laura, "who is funnier than Jimmy Durante." He spoke of her infrequently but easily, with deference and affection. We talked about other books as well—a natural way for cautious people to reveal themselves and begin catechizing each other. Was I right in assuming he was a polymath along the lines of Edmund Wilson? He gave an embarrassed laugh (he never pretended to the erudition critics attributed to him) and, by way of answering, said the most learned people he'd known were Wilson, Ogden Nash, and Aldous Huxley. He showed me his signed copies of *The Waste Land* ("Inscribed for Sid Perelman by T. S. Eliot in homage") and *On Poetry and Poets* ("Some people think my books are funnier than yours") and talked about Chandler, whom he was rereading at the time. He was in the middle of V. S. Pritchett's *The Living Novel*, as well as Karl

Menninger's *Love and Death*. I also carted off Flann O'Brien's *At Swim-Two-Birds* and *Hand-Made Fables* by George Ade. Sid was particularly keen on "The Fable of the Waist-Band that was Taut up to the Moment it gave way" (it figures in a note to E. B. White). I got hooked on that, and sentences such as "Effie was just at the Age when a Girl has to be Deformed to prevent her from being a fairly Good Looker" and "Like all high-class Boarding Houses, it was infested by some Lovely People" (one Ring Lardner must have liked). The only passage Sid had marked, however, was from "The Civic Improver and the Customary Reward":

> The Plain People are worth dying for until you bunch them and give them the cold Once-Over, and then they impress the impartial Observer as being slightly Bovine, with a large Percentage of Vegetable Tissue.

He talked about his other favorites: Beerbohm's *Seven Men*, Zola's *Au Bonheur des dames*, which he loved for its mastery of department-store culture, and the Goncourt brothers' journals. This last brought him to a sore point about his own work, in particular the autobiography he'd long since contracted to do—he'd already cannibalized his life more than anybody realized. He said the trouble with old writers was that they repeated themselves, and in trying to mine the past for something new he just couldn't remember it right. The tediousness of having to dredge up period material—he was rereading the magazine *Snappy Stories* on microfilm in the public library—made him wish he'd kept even the skimpiest diary to jog his memory. The only advice he ever presumed to offer me about writing was that I keep a journal.

Sid read to feed his fancies, and even when he read more seriously he wasn't systematic. If he saw himself as part of a tradition, he derived no solace from identifying with his peers in an earlier age. (I once asked him if it was reassuring to read his praises, and he said wryly,

"Yes, every night.") He told me his two unachieved goals were to speak perfect French and play jazz piano.

In mid-April we had dinner at Sweet's on Fulton Street—another part of New York I'd never been to and a section Sid especially liked. In the cab downtown he said he'd had dinner the night before with Lillian Hellman and was finding her increasingly difficult to take. "Theirs was a very ambivalent relationship," a friend of his told me. "He detested her and she detested him." That night he said Lilly had once given him a play of hers to read and asked him to really lay it on the line. He demurred at first, but she insisted she could take it. When he went ahead, she didn't speak to him for a year and a half. All the same, in old age they vacationed together in Florida with other friends, and a card from her inside his copy of *The Hite Report* reads: "A testament to how young I think you are."

He mentioned that he'd agreed to have lunch with Dashiell Hammett's biographer, Diane Johnson, and was in a quandary what to tell her. After all, he had his own autobiography to think of, or as he put it: "Macy's doesn't tell Gimbel's." He alluded darkly to a tale involving Nathanael West (it found its way to her book anyway, through another source), but his own buttoned-up memoir of West in *The Last Laugh* doesn't mention it. West had saved Hammett by giving him free board at the Sutton Hotel while Hammett wrote *The Thin Man* and, as Sid told it, when West was on his uppers in Hollywood, the now-famous Hammett pointedly said that West could expect no financial help from him.

The story still galled Sid, as did another that concerned West. Sid claimed that within days of West's death in a car crash, Bennett Cerf called to ask for the return of the advance on West's next novel, a matter of about $150. When they next encountered each other, taking refuge under an awning during a rainstorm, Sid pounced on him. In Sid's version, Cerf was wearing a white suit that ended up covered in mud.

As fresh as his indignation over an old insult could be, Sid was too good a storyteller to be merely sore. His outrage was vigorous and entertaining. He told a story about a war-bond tour in the Forties that took him and several other writers as far as Texas. After the bond pitch, Stanley Marcus guided him personally through Neiman-Marcus in Dallas. After showing off a fine jewelry display, Marcus said with an air of noblesse oblige, "Surely there's something here your wife would like—earrings, a brooch . . . ?" Sid considered. "Well, yes, I think she'd like these earrings here." Marcus snapped his fingers at the saleswoman behind the counter, told her to wrap them up, and left. The woman said, "That'll be $1,200."

Sid had a highly polished repertoire of stories that he delivered as if they were brand-new, but even the new ones came out perfect the first time. When you realized how flawlessly he spoke and how slowly he wrote, you began to appreciate the standard he held himself to in his work.

At Sweet's I talked about the seder I'd just been to, in particular about the plague of frogs. Sid said, in earnest (I say that for readers who assume such a writer must be a relentless put-on artist, which he wasn't), that he'd read a book about the plague once and that in fact they were very tiny frogs. A short pause. "Blue points," he added. "Delicious."

Sid was a fanatic for dessert and ordered blueberry pie. The topping looked like spackling compound and a good bit of it somehow ended up plastered on his cuffs. Walking around the Village later, he said he wanted to find another restaurant so he could finish off the rest of his suit. Apropos the dry-cleaning problem, I mentioned having read that the curator Henry Geldzahler had once worn a porcelain bow tie to an art opening. Sid asked me if I'd be embarrassed if he wore a ceramic hat to the theater; I said fine, as long as it wasn't earthenware. He said thoughtfully, "In that case, maybe I'll wear my Spode vest." Then his hat blew into the street, and although he occasionally betrayed his age by shuffling slightly, he streaked after it as nimbly as a stunt man. He said it was the seventh time it had happened that day.

It seemed proper that Sid should live in a hotel, where he stood a greater chance of being abused in a stimulating way than if he'd lived entirely by himself. He wasn't a kvetch, as I knew him; his crotchets were comic, and while he was certainly capable of real rage, he could also feign an antic apoplexy. He complained that the morning maid (whom he calls Isosceles in a letter) was filching some special pencils he'd brought back from Japan and that she had stopped tucking in his bedclothes on the grounds that he was a "tousler." One morning he called, ostensibly beside himself, to say that after shaving he'd headed for the living room in his shorts and bumped into a couple standing there with suitcases. They insisted it was their room and were unimpressed by his claim to have lived there six years. When he phoned the desk, the clerk said the couple must have taken the wrong key. As Sid was pleased to point out, from the registration counter to the room keys is a reach of about six feet.

Sid said happiness was "a brown paper bag of possessions and a room in the Mills Hotel" (or Dixie, sometimes), and for a cosmopolite he'd come close to his ideal. His apartment consisted of two moderate-size rooms and a kitchenette, equipped with a hot plate and a counter oven, restaurant-style stainless steel for two, a sweet potato, and a rubber fried egg from Japan. In the living room, among a small but very personal collection of art works, was Saul Steinberg's *Egypt Still Life*, a collage whose focal motif is a wrapper of Chinese toilet paper with the happy brand name of Kapok. (Screenwriting, Sid wrote, was "an occupation akin to stuffing kapok in mattresses"; the air in New York was "like kapok twice-breathed.") Steinberg hadn't let him buy it but accepted in exchange Sid's offer of a copy of *Ulysses*, inscribed by Joyce. The set and costume designer Aline Bernstein, Thomas Wolfe's mistress, had given it to him.

Except for a Victorian swivel chair, the furniture was largely the hotel's, which made it all the more appropriate, somehow, that on his dresser were a number of Steinberg artifacts—a false matchbox, notebook, and fancifully labeled wine bottle, all gifts. Why so many tokens from the artist? Steinberg was indebted, he said, to anyone who saved him time, and when he arrived in America in 1942 and encountered Sid's work, his first experience of "the popular native avant-garde," it gave him an invaluable shortcut to the clichés of American culture.

At the time I met Sid, he was no longer so sure he had the inside track on those clichés. *The New Yorker* was hanging on to his pieces, and he said he'd recently got back a set of galleys edited by an unidentifiable hand. I asked him why he didn't try to find out the reason, and he said that, unlike Thurber, he'd never been able to be pushy about his work. "You know me, Patient Griselda. Can't you just see me in my pinafore?" He was anxious that his readers would think he'd stopped writing—they no longer sent him the oddball clippings that gave him ideas. I came over once just after he'd seen Robin Williams do a bit on a talk show, and he was both baffled and distressed. If people wanted to be bludgeoned to death by maniacs, where did that leave him?

In spite of such discouragement, Sid indulged himself very little in backward looks and not at all in self-pity—he had too much nerve and too much industry. He continued to examine his world as keenly as he knew how and, as far as I could tell, expected as much of himself as he ever had—that is, far more than most do. And reasonably or not, he still felt the financial necessity of working. If he occasionally thought he'd become an artifact—that literacy had outlived its day—his readers set him straight. Earlier in the day, he told me once, someone had called out to him as he was crossing the street in the middle of the block, "Be careful—we need you." This astonished and moved him.

When I was still thinking that Sid was probably used to a diet of high culture, I got tickets to the New York City Ballet. It was performing Vivaldi's *The Four Seasons*, which Sid had said was the only classical music he knew, as well as Stravinsky's *Agon*. In the cab to Lincoln Center I read him Lincoln Kirstein's synopsis of the Stravinsky: "Behind its active physical presence there was inherent a philosophy; *Agon* was by no means 'pure' ballet 'about' dancing only. It was an existentialist metaphor for tension and anxiety." Sid asked: "On the part of the audience?" He said the lights in the theater were the largest zircons he'd ever seen, and waited quietly for what he called "the resistance piece." When "Spring" came, he asked if the corps was supposed to be corn.

The mockery of superstition has been a hallmark of the satirist, and you could say that insofar as Sid dealt with cultural superstitions—that wealth confers character, say—he was true to his métier. At the same time, his fascination with the occult had a serious side, not always concealed by his also genuine desire to exploit the subject for comic purposes. (In his letters, for instance, he interprets one particular séance three ways for three separate correspondents.) That evening, Sid brought the subject up for the first time, so casually that I felt free to say something dismissive. At that he claimed he didn't put any credence in it either but simply liked to keep his hand "on the throttle of the future." He said he thought I'd like the language of the tarot even so, and when I went to London that summer, he gave me three addresses: his bookseller (Heywood Hill), his favorite candy dealer, and his "psychic surgeon." (I lost the note.)

Sid complained that our dining was getting too "Mimi-Sheraton-esque." I was content to give it up, since finding places quiet enough—that is, empty enough—for him to hear well was getting difficult. I proposed cooking at my place and asked my mother to send me a tablecloth. I don't know why I thought that would help, but when the evening rolled around, Aunty Con's double damask covered my unpainted trestle table clear to the floor. I seated Sid formally at one end, me at the other, and served a white fish with a white sauce that was hard to see on the plate. Some weeks later, I heard Sid express puzzlement that hostesses had stopped serving beef at parties and were now trying to fob off things like chicken as entrees. But that night, with a characteristic blend of shy grace and invention, he said only, "I feel like Marion Davies at San Simeon."

Not long after that he introduced me to the Second Avenue Deli, a genial place where the maitre d' treats you like family, barley counts as a second vegetable, and the waitresses call everyone "honey." I once overheard one of them declare that there were fifty Hebrew words that were cognate in Gaelic, a claim Sid nearly made credible in *Eastward Ha!* ("Pechand-Schwebyll of that Ilk," "Ichvaisnit Grange, the fief of Gornicht Kinhelfinn"). He admired the fact that you could actually buy a sandwich-and-a-half there, prorated.

My next and last attempt at mutual uplift was to get tickets for *Happy Days* at the Public Theater. I figured Beckett was close enough to Joyce, and we both liked the actress, Irene Worth. Sid said she had the décolletage of a young woman; he'd seen it once at a dinner party in London.

Unfortunately he didn't hear much of the play, and to salvage the price of the tickets we took a window seat at Lady Astor's across the street and ordered some cake. Sid forthrightly, but with no particular confidence, addressed the question of the gap in our ages, which he felt "was so great as to be ridiculous." I said I didn't see what the problem was, since he'd spent his whole life making the ridiculous into the sublime. It sounds too tidy now, but it seemed obvious, and he accepted it. As a friend of mine put it, "Yeah, too bad you couldn't have met when you were twenty-six and he was seventy—or when he was thirty, and your parents hadn't met yet." He seemed to be generally preoccupied about what his future would bring and appeared to put stock in Yevtushenko's prediction, made on Sid's last trip to the Soviet Union, that he'd live eight more years.

A friend of his had recently told him about a psychic, and he suggested that for the fun of it we should go separately, not letting on that we were acquainted, and compare prophesies to see if we were slated to figure in each other's lives. I think Sid liked to entertain the notion that some things were simply out of his hands, even while he was busy trying to influence them.

In May, then, I made an appointment with a character whose card identified him as a "humanistic astrologer" who read the tarot and practiced something called "TRANS formative counseling." A bachelor who worked out of his apartment, he gave me a cup of coffee and from a series of casual questions established that I was going to London that summer and was trying to write.

Finally we turned to the tarot, and he began laying out the themes of my life as he saw them. The "humanistic" part seemed to mean that whenever my expression indicated a reading was far-fetched he would change it—if necessary, to its opposite. As the session wore on, his desire to appear credible began to get the best of him, until he suggested, rather tentatively, that a trip to London might be in the offing, as well as some kind of creative work—writing, perhaps. More to the point, by the time we were done I was quite sure, from his detailed narrative, that Sid had inadvertently tipped him off: the King of Swords was all but identified as a seventy-five-year-old humorist with strabismus. He concluded by reading my palm and redeemed his integrity, after a fashion, by seeing in it a future completely unrelated to the one just foretold by the tarot, including a spell in a convent and the assurance that I would not have a hysterectomy. He was a harmless and well-meaning person and pretty clearly a psychotherapist manqué.

When Sid and I met to swap notes he was quite keyed up and showed a credulity that seemed odd in such a relentless student of scam; that it might have been a willful suspension only made it more intriguing. In any case, we had an occasion to talk about ourselves without getting too confessional, and with a good deal of amusement. (The astrologer had begun by asking Sid what his chief value was, to which he answered, "honesty.") My debunking account bothered him not at all.

As the summer approached, Sid pressed on doggedly but futilely with his Paris-Peking saga. Even so, he got around quite a bit and was not so isolated or bereft as his sometimes woebegone expression could suggest. Bette Midler sought him out to see if they could work together on cabaret patter (he felt they couldn't); he met London *Sunday Times* editor Harold Evans at the Century and turned down a proposal to revisit Hollywood, as a possible substitute for the China material. He scouted the charms of a new screen goddess, Laura Antonelli, and an old one, Louise Brooks in *Pandora's Box*.

William Shawn called to have lunch at the Algonquin ("you know, where the guests have those special swiveling heads"), and Perry Howze, an aspiring cartoonist he'd met after she too had written him a fan letter, took him to tea. He trained his usual sharp eye on the latest advertising bilge (one enclosure reads: "Pru—If you were a girl, wouldn't this be the man you'd most want to marry?") and kept stirring what he called his "vats" full of marinating ideas—he had several files full. He hiked up four flights of a walk-up to have dinner with my friend Roslyn, five flights to visit his friend Irene Kemmer, and six flights to come to my birthday party. (He brought a clipping from *The Observer* on "the pinching Lord of Fowey," who pleaded guilty to three cases of gross indecency—"Do you suppose there's such a thing as a 'net' indecency?")

In August we went to see "The Treasures of the Kremlin" at the Metropolitan, and after staring at the cases, Sid said he was going to have his boxer shorts sewn all over with tiny pearls. A trip to the Museum of Natural History was less stimulating—I think we saw a film about lava—but Sid got an idea for a book jacket, showing him typing inside either a mummy case or the black-bear diorama.

The September 10, 1979, issue of *The New Yorker* carried its last contribution by S. J. Perelman. "Portrait of the Artist as a Young

Cat's-Paw" describes his first trip to Europe in 1927 and how he got shanghaied into smuggling a conjugal bed from Paris back to the US. He's captured himself at age twenty-three, before the evolution of his worldly and world-weary persona:

> In the spring of 1927, I occupied a wee studio on West Ninth Street in the Village, where I drew cartoons that ultimately lowered the circulation of a weekly named *Judge* to the vanishing point.... It was on the sixth floor of a building equidistant from the Athens Chop House and a restaurant run by the Siegel brothers, and, what with my meagre sustenance and my constant toiling up those five flights, I became so thin that a Siegel brother inadvertently stuck me in a jardiniere, mistaking me for an umbrella.

I hadn't known this piece was in the works and came upon it by surprise in the subway one morning on the way to work. It was the only piece of his that appeared while I knew him, and I was amazed to think he'd been able to confect anything so perfect without letting on. I called him from work and said his phone must be ringing off the hook. Rather wistfully he said no and suggested we each take a door-to-door canvass to find out what people thought. I said, "Then what?" "We could hold hands."

Sid once advised the young Heywood Hale Broun, "No one ever laughed a girl into bed. What do you think they're always talking about Gary Gooper for?" I don't know if Sid ever took his own advice, but when I asked him once why his hands were so cold he said, "They've been insufficiently osculated." Something Gary Cooper would never have said.

Sid was a boon companion to women for many reasons. One was his attractive lack of swagger and proprietariness. As his friend Israel Shenker put it, Sid was "a collection of modesties, lightly worn and easily displayed," although when it came to flattering others, he never hung back. He favored the oblique ("Who does your burnishing?") and the hyperbolic remark. Outrageousness only made his compliments more delightful: since they were patently false, you could enjoy them without having to dimple. He regarded women as another species altogether—a view that may have accounted for his conscientiousness and lack of presumption. For him, certainly, it heightened their exoticism. One evening I wore a thrift-shop dress that had a peplum (an overskirt at the waistline), and Sid was enchanted to be reacquainted with the word, one of the few he was no longer able to retrieve. He could be immensely playful, and I suspect he found it easier to be so with women.

Sid also had an instinctive and sharp sense of the underdog. Once when we were riding a bus back from Pennsylvania, a woman he knew slightly came to say hello and perched on the armrest of my seat. She said things like, "Sid, you old card you," bragged about her how-to manual on tax evasion, and wound up by professing to find my work as a typesetter fascinating and enviable. After she'd returned to her seat, Sid rounded on me with a fuchsia face and said in a voice choked with indignation: "Did you see how she patronized you?"

As September came on, Sid heard the call of the foliage and began to get nostalgic about Bucks County, his home for forty-odd years. After Laura died in 1970, he said, his women friends told him not to "burn the wigwam" but to save something for when he recovered himself. He felt that he'd been impetuous in selling the farm—that grieving people ought to be locked up for a year to protect them from their mad behavior.

He suggested we take a bus out and pick up his old MG, which a mechanic in Pipersville was converting back to meet local inspection, and head southwest to see the Amish country. In the event, the mechanic was confounded by the English wiring, and we ultimately made the trip in a rented car. We saw Sid's old house and visited his painter friend Allen Saalburg; saw fabled farmland, horses and buggies, a cloister, a kosher chicken farm. The absence of glamour didn't seem to trouble Sid; he was content to ramble, and I saw no sign of the petulant persona from his work. The more bum the territory, the more inventive he became—his romanticism was sui generis.

In October, Morley Safer of *60 Minutes* brought a crew to Sid's apartment to do a segment focusing on his travels. ("Unlike Las Vegas, which I very much like, Hollywood has very little charm. I think that anybody who wants to wrap up a four-year course of sociology has only to walk from Vine Street to La Brea to get a swift kind of pastiche of the worst that has been thought and said in our century.") Sid claimed the filming improved his status at the hotel immensely, although the program never ran.

On the first Saturday in October, Sid and I took the train up to Rhinebeck to see Clermont, a stately home on the Hudson open to the public. It was a spectacular day; Sid suspected the lawn had been professionally dappled. We toured the house and on the way out studied an *objet* decorated with a frieze of Apollo in a chariot drawn by butterflies. I said the motif might be another good one for a book jacket, Sid drawn by wasps—"yes," he added, "or drawn and quartered by Anatole Broyard." It was warm enough to eat lunch on the grass, overlooking the river, and as we heard a whistle in the distance, Sid said: "We need never leave here. We can steal vegetables from the passing trains."

The travel section of the October 14 Sunday *New York Times* ran an article on cruise liners with an addendum on freighters, their itineraries, and the cost of passage. Sid had recently been talking about the wonders of Hong Kong and said the ideal way to get there was by tramp steamer—twelve passengers maximum and no doctor on board. On his second global trip, in 1949, he wrote Leila Hadley: "I prefer the previous way I girdled this ocean, viz., a cargo ship which gave you some sense of accomplishment." American President

Lines had several vessels that sailed east every two weeks from Oakland, California. Sid and I hadn't girdled much of anything, apart from each other, but so far the companionship looked promising. Undaunted by his last punishing venture, he clipped the schedule and began scheming how he could pay for the trip by writing.

The morning of October 17, a Wednesday, I was wandering down Madison Avenue and spotted in the window of a fancy hardware store a rather good-looking carryall—something I figured I ought now to have. I bought it and walked to work, wondering what winter in New York would be like knowing someone like Sid. An idle thought, but I remember it because that afternoon, as we were closing pages of the *Review*, the woman I worked with heard on the radio that S. J. Perelman was dead.

In collecting his letters, I was searching for a man I did not know well but was certain I wanted to know better. I've not been disappointed; I hope others will not be. His letters do not describe a happy life: "I alternate between violence and despair when I consider what faces anybody who wants to really write as well as he can." How much more astonishing, then, the work it produced. "You can be as deeply moved by laughter as you can by misery," Sid wrote Abby. Whether the collection bears him out, I'd like to dedicate my share of it to the memory of my father, with whom it really began.

—July 16, 1987

17

MICHAEL IGNATIEFF
ON BRUCE CHATWIN

HIS OWN CHARACTER was one of his greatest inventions: traveler, adventurer, storyteller, mimic, the most English of eccentrics abroad, and at the same time the most restlessly cosmopolitan English writer of his generation. This multifaceted persona became an essential part of the appeal of his writing. In his books you were addressed not merely by a distinctive voice, but by the fabulous character he had fashioned for himself.

His life could be described as a sequence of escapes—from the English class system and his public school education; from Sotheby's, where he made himself a career as an art dealer when in his twenties only to throw it all away when he felt he was becoming a "smarmy" and inconsequential success. After a period studying anthropology and archaeology, he escaped into journalism and then into a life on the road, which produced the book—*In Patagonia*—that heralded his arrival as a writer of extraordinary promise.

He was a master, in his life and in his work, of the art of eluding expectations. When he felt pigeonholed as a travel writer in the English tradition of Patrick Leigh-Fermor and Wilfred Thesiger, he wrote *The Viceroy of Ouidah*, a surreal fable of slavery set in Dahomey, and then when his public began to think of him as a writer of the exotic, he produced *On the Black Hill*, about two Welsh hill farmers who had never left the confines of the Welsh valleys. And when he felt enclosed again by the idea that he was an English realist, he wrote *Songlines*, a metaphysical novel about nomads and wandering, set in the Australian outback, which—like all of his work—was unclassifiable. Was this anthropology, fiction, an essay, disguised autobiography? It was all of these. His best work redrew the borderline between fiction and nonfiction.

Songlines brought him success but did not tempt him into repeating himself. No sooner had he finished it than he began exploring radically different terrain. The result was *Utz*, a strange miniature, in the tradition of Borges, on a porcelain collector in Prague, a pertinacious eccentric who pursued his obsessions in healthy obliviousness to the Iron Curtain across the heart of European culture. As a parable about the human fascination with the beautiful, *Utz* was also Chatwin's oblique commentary on the art of writing. When the book was nominated for the Booker Prize, he said *Utz* was about art and then added, "Art is never enough. Art always lets you down."

Illness began to engulf him in the autumn of 1986 as he struggled to complete *Songlines*. There was then a miraculous period of remission in 1987, when he composed *Utz*; and then illness returned again in 1988. Throughout the final years, he was cared for with devotion by his wife Elizabeth.

To the astonishment of those who visited him this past winter, reduced and emaciated, he managed to complete the editing of a collection of his short writing and journalism called *What Am I Doing Here?* (to be published later this year). He rediscovered and rewrote these old pieces with pleasure, as if they reminded him of old selves left behind on his travels.

By the autumn of 1988, he was too weak to work, too weak to hold a pen. But the bed was still covered with books. He would still toss odd and unfashionable treasures at you and say, Had you read that? In a weak but excited whisper, he would sketch out scenes from a projected novel. On good days, the best scenes, set in the all-black apartment of a bizarre Russian painter, came alive as vividly as his written books. If you ventured to hope he would soon be able to dictate, he would snap—blue eyes flashing—that he was not going to dictate anything. He was bloody well going to write it, on his yellow pads. His hope was contagious.

The novel died with him, and half a lifetime of the work that was in him will not see the light of day. What he did have time to write had a piercing clarity and economy. His books are models of transparency, lightness, and elusiveness in literature; he never mined the same vein of inspiration twice. As a writer, he was a magician of the word; as a man, he lived with a verve that left his friends breathless. He traveled light, and there was nothing—except friendship—he wasn't prepared to leave behind.

On the final page of *Songlines*, composed when he was beginning to die, he wrote: "The mystics believe the ideal man shall walk himself to a 'right death.' He who has arrived 'goes back.' . . . The concept is quite similar to Heraclitus' mysterious dictum, 'Mortals and immortals alive in their death, dead in each other's life.'"

I shall always think of him on a day in the last autumn of his life, lying on the grass outside his house, wrapped in blankets, weak, gray-haired and emaciated, but still incorrigibly stylish in a pair of high-altitude ski sunglasses. He said he had bought them for his next trip to the Himalayas. He lay there and talked in a faint whisper, full of cackles and laughter like some grand and unrepentant monarch in exile, or like one of the fantastic and touching figures of his own fiction, staring up at the bright blue sky, while the white clouds scudded across his black glasses.

—March 2, 1989

18

JOSEPH BRODSKY
ON ISAIAH BERLIN

I FIRST SAW him seventeen years ago, when he was sixty-three and I thirty-two. I had just left the country where I'd spent those thirty-two years and it was my third day in London, where I knew nobody.

I was staying in St. John's Wood, in the house of Stephen Spender, whose wife had come to the airport three days before to fetch W. H. Auden, who had flown in from Vienna to participate in the annual Poetry International Festival in Queen Elizabeth Hall. I was on the same flight, for the same reason. As I had no place to stay in London, the Spenders offered to put me up.

On the third day in that house in the city where I knew nobody the phone rang and Natasha Spender cried, "Joseph, it's for you." Naturally, I was puzzled. My puzzlement hadn't subsided when I heard in the receiver my mother tongue, spoken with the most extraordinary clarity and velocity, unparalleled in my experience. The speed of sound, one felt, was courting the speed of light. That was Isaiah Berlin, suggesting tea at his club, the Atheneum.

I accepted, although of all my foggy notions about English life, that of a club was the foggiest (the last reference I had seen to one was in Pushkin's *Eugene Onegin*). Mrs. Spender gave me a lift to Pall Mall and before she deposited me in front of an imposing Regency edifice with a gilded Athena and Wedgewoodlike cornice, I, being unsure of my English, asked her whether she wouldn't mind accompanying me inside. She said that she wouldn't, except that women were not allowed. I found this puzzling, again, opened the door, and announced myself to the doorman.

"I'd like to see Sir Isaiah Berlin," I said, and attributed the look of controlled disbelief in his eyes to my accent rather than to my Russian clothes. Two minutes later, however, climbing the majestic staircases and glancing at the huge oil portraits of Gladstones, Spencers, Actons, Darwins, et alia, that patterned the club's walls like wallpaper, I knew that the matter with me was neither my accent nor my turtleneck but my age. At thirty-two I was as much out of sync here as if I were a woman.

Presently I was standing in the huge, mahogany-cum-leather shell of the club's library. Through high windows the afternoon sun was pouring its rays onto the parquet as though testing its resolve to refract light. In various corners two or three rather ancient members were sunk deep in their tall armchairs, in various stages of newspaper-induced reverie. From across the room, a man in a baggy three-piece suit was waving to me. Against the sunlight, the silhouette looked Chaplinesque, or penguinish.

I walked toward him and we shook hands. Apart from the Russian language, the only other thing we had in common was that we both knew that language's best poet, Anna Akhmatova, who dedicated to Sir Isaiah a magnificent cycle of poems, *Sweetbriar's Bloom*. The cycle was occasioned by a visit Isaiah Berlin, then secretary of the British embassy in Moscow, paid to Akhmatova in 1946. Aside from the poems, that encounter provoked Stalin's wrath, the dark shadow of which completely enveloped Akhmatova's life for the next decade and a half.

Since in one of the poems from that cycle—spanning in its own turn a decade—the poet assumed the persona of Dido, addressing her visitor as Aeneas, I wasn't altogether surprised by the opening remark of that bespectacled man: "What has she done to me? Aeneas! Aeneas! What sort of Aeneas am I really?" Indeed, he didn't look like one, and the mixture of embarrassment and pride in his voice was genuine.

Years later on the other hand, in his own memoirs about visiting Pasternak and Akhmatova in 1946, when "the world's strength was all spent/and only graves were fresh," Sir Isaiah himself compares his Russian hosts to victims of a shipwreck on a desert island, inquiring about the civilization which they've been cut off from for decades. For one thing, the essence of this simile echoes somewhat the circumstances of Aeneas's appearance before the queen of Carthage; for another, if not participants themselves, then the context of their meeting was epic enough to endure subsequent disclaimers.

But that was years later. Now I was staring at a face I saw for the first time. The paperback edition of *The Hedgehog and the Fox* that Akhmatova had once given to me to pass on to Nadezhda Mandelstam lacked a picture of its author; as for a copy of *Four Essays on Liberty* it came to me from a book shark with its cover torn off—out of caution, given the book's subject. It was a wonderful face, a cross, I thought, between a wood grouse and a spaniel, with large brown eyes ready at once for flight and for hunting.

I felt comfortable with this face being old because the finality of its features alone excluded all pretension. Also, in this foreign realm where I had suddenly found myself, it was the first face that looked familiar. A traveler always clings to a recognizable object, be it a telephone or a statue. In the parts I was from that kind of face would belong to a physician, a schoolteacher, a musician, a watchmaker, a scholar—to someone from whom you vaguely expect help. It was also the face of a potential victim, and so I suddenly felt comfortable.

Besides, we spoke Russian—to the great bewilderment of the uniformed personnel. The conversation naturally ran to Akhmatova until I asked Sir Isaiah how he had found me in London. The answer made me recall the front page of that mutilated edition of *Four Essays on Liberty*, and I felt ashamed. I should have remembered that that book, which for three years served me as an antidote to all sorts of demagoguery in which my native realm was virtually awash, was dedicated to the man under whose roof I now stayed.

It turned out that Stephen Spender was Sir Isaiah's friend from their days at Oxford. It turned out that so, though a bit later, was Wystan Auden, whose "Letter to Lord Byron" had once been, like those *Four Essays*, my daily pocket companion. In a flash I realized that I owed a great deal of my sanity to men of a single generation, to the Oxford class, as it were, of circa 1930; that I was, in fact, also an unwitting product of their friendship; that they wandered through each other's books the way they did through their rooms at Corpus Christi or University College; that those rooms had, in the end, shrunk to the paperbacks in my possession.

On top of that, they were sheltering me now. Of course, I wanted to know everything about each one of them, and immediately. The two most interesting things in this world, as E. M. Cioran has remarked somewhere, are gossip and metaphysics. One could add, they have a similar structure: one can easily be taken for the other. That's what the remainder of the afternoon turned into, owing to the nature of the lives of those I was asking about, and owing to my host's tenacious memory.

The latter of course made me think again about Akhmatova, who also had this astonishing ability to retain everything: dates, details of topography, names and personal data of individuals, their family circumstances, their cousins, nephews, nieces, second and third marriages, where their husbands or wives were from, their party affiliations, when and by whom their books were published, and, had they come to a sorry end, the identities of those who had denounced them. She, too, could spin this vast, weblike, palpable fabric on a minute's notice, and even the timbre of her low monotone was similar to the voice I was listening to now in the Atheneum's library.

No, the man before me was not Aeneas, because Aeneas, I think, remembered nothing. Nor was Akhmatova a Dido to be destroyed by one tragedy, to die in flames. Had she permitted herself to do so, who could describe their tongues? On the other hand, there is indeed something Virgilian about the ability to retain lives other than your own, about the intensity of attention to others' fates, and it is not necessarily the property of a poet.

But, then again, I couldn't apply to Sir Isaiah the label "philosopher," because that mutilated copy of *Four Essays on Liberty* was more the product of a gut reaction against an atrocious century than a philosophical tract. For the same reason, I couldn't call him a historian of ideas. To me, his words always were a cry from the bowels of the monster, a call not so much for help as of help—a normal response of the mind singed and scarred by the present, and wishing it upon nobody as the future.

Besides, in the realm I was from, "philosophy" was by and large a foul word and entailed the notion of a system. What was good about *Four Essays on Liberty* was that it advanced none, since "liberty" and "system" are antonyms. As to the smart-alecky retort that the absence of a system in itself is a system, I was pretty confident that I could live with this syllogism, not to mention in this sort of system.

And I remember that as I was making my way through that book without a cover I'd often pause, exclaiming to myself: How Russian this is! And by that I meant not only the author's arguments, but also the way that they were presented: his piling up of subordinate clauses, his digressions and questions, the cadences of his prose which resembled the sardonic eloquence of the best of nineteenth-century Russian fiction.

Of course I knew that the man entertaining me now in the Atheneum was born in Riga—I think Akhmatova told me so. She also thought that he was a personal friend of Churchill's, whose favorite wartime reading had been Berlin's dispatches from Washington. She was also absolutely sure that it was Berlin who arranged for her to receive an honorary degree from Oxford and the Etna Taormina Prize for Poetry in Italy in 1963. (Having seen something of Oxford dons years later, I think that making these arrangements was a good deal rockier than she could have imagined.) "His great hero is Herzen," she would add with a shrug and turn her face to the window.

Yet for all that, what I was reading wasn't "Russian." Nor was it Western rationalism marrying Eastern soulfulness, or Russian syntax burdening English clarity with its inflections. It appeared to me to be the fullest articulation of a unique human psyche, aware of the limitations imposed upon it by either language, and cognizant of those limitations' perils. Where I had cried, "Russian!" I should have said "human." The same goes for the passages where one might have sighed, "How English!"

The fusion of two cultures? Reconciliation of their conflicting values? If so, it would only reflect the human psyche's appetite for and ability to fuse and reconcile a lot more. Perhaps what could have been perceived here as faintly Eastern was the notion that reason doesn't deserve to have such a high premium put on it, the sense that reason is but an articulated emotion. That's why the defense of rational ideas turns out sometimes to be a highly emotional affair.

I remarked that the place looked positively English, very Victorian, to be precise. "Indeed so," replied my host with a smile. "This is an island within an island. This is what's left of England, an idea of it, if you will." And, as though not sure of my fully grasping the nuance, he added, "a Herzen idea of London. All it lacks is fog." And that was itself a glance at oneself from the outside, from afar, from a vantage point which was the psychological equivalent of the mid-Atlantic. It sounded like Auden's "Look, stranger, on this island now. . . ."

No, neither a philosopher nor a historian of ideas, not literary critic or social utopian, but an autonomous mind in the grip of an outward gravity, whose pull extends its perspective on this life insofar as this mind cares to send back signals. The word, perhaps, would be "*penseur*," were it not for the muscular and crouching associations so much at odds with this civilized, alert figure comfortably reclining in the bottle-green leather armchair at the Atheneum—the West and the East of it mentally at the same time.

That is where an Indian scout normally is, that's where one would be looking for him. At least in the beleaguered fort I was from one learns not to look in one direction only. The sad irony of all this is of course that, so far as I know, not a line of Berlin's writings has been translated into the language of the country which needs that intellect the most, and which could profit from those writings enormously. If anything, that country could learn from him a lot more about its intellectual history—and by the same token about its present choices —than it seems capable of thus far. His syntax, to say the least, wouldn't be an obstacle. Nor should they be perturbed by Herzen's shadow, for while Herzen indeed was appalled by and sought to change the mental climate of Russia, Berlin seems to take on the entire world's weather.

Short of being able to alter it, he still helps one to endure it. One cloudless—if only a cloud in one's mind—is improvement enough, like removing from a brow its "tactile fever." An improvement far greater is the idea that it is the ability to choose that defines a being as human; that, hence, choice is the species's recognized necessity— which flies into the moronic face of the reduction of the human adventure to the exclusively moral dimensions of right and wrong.

Of course, one says all this with the benefit of hindsight, sharpened by what one could have read of Berlin since. I think, however, that seventeen years ago, with only *The Hedgehog and the Fox* and *Four Essays on Liberty* on my mind, I could not have reacted to their author differently. Before our tea at the Atheneum was over I knew that others' lives are this man's forte, for what other reason could there be for a sixty-three-year-old knight of England to talk to a thirty-two-year-old Russian poet? What could I possibly tell him that he didn't already know, one way or the other?

Still, I think I was sitting in front of him on that sunny July afternoon not only because his work is the life of the mind, the life of ideas. Ideas of course reside in people, but they can also be gleaned from clouds, water, trees; indeed, from a fallen apple. And at best I could qualify as an apple fallen from Akhmatova's tree. I believe he wanted to see me not for what I knew but for what I didn't—a role in which, I suppose, he quite frequently finds himself vis-à-vis most of the world.

To put it somewhat less stridently, if not less autobiographically, with Berlin the world gets one more choice. This choice consists not so much of following his precepts as of adopting his mental patterns. In the final analysis, Berlin's notion of pluralism is not a blueprint but rather a reflection of the omniscience of his own unique mind, which indeed appears to be both older and more generous than what it observes. This omniscience in other words is very man-like and therefore can and should be emulated, not just applauded or envied.

Later the same evening, as we sat for supper in Stephen Spender's basement, Wystan said, "Well, how did it go today with Isaiah?" And Stephen immediately asked, "Yes, is his Russian really good?" I began, in my tortured English, a long story about the nobility of old Petersburg pronunciation, about its similarity to Stephen's own Oxonian, and how Isaiah's vocabulary was free of unpalatable accretions of the Soviet period and how his idiom was so much his own, when Natasha Spender interrupted me and said, "Yes, but does he speak Russian as fast as he speaks English?" I looked at the faces of those three people who had known Isaiah Berlin for much longer than I had lived and wondered whether I should carry on with my exegesis. Then I thought better of it.

"Faster," I said.

—August 17, 1989

19

CAROLINE BLACKWOOD
ON FRANCIS BACON

I FIRST BECAME aware of Francis Bacon shortly after World War II. I was then eighteen, and I was invited to a formal London ball given by Lady Rothermere, who was later to become Mrs. Ian Fleming. Princess Margaret was among the guests and could immediately be seen on the parquet floor wearing a crinoline and being worshiped by her adoring set who were known at the time as "the Smarties." She was revered and considered glamorous because she was the one "Royal" who was accessible. Princess Margaret smoked, and she drank, and she flirted. She went to nightclubs and she loved show business and popular music.

As a guest Princess Margaret used to send out confusing signals. At times she seemed to ask to be treated as an ordinary racy young girl. But her conception of "ordinariness" sometimes made her behave in a manner that embarrassed rather than reassured those who entertained her. In order to put them at their ease so that they could forget that they had a royal figure at their table, she would pick up strings of tomato-pasted spaghetti from her plate and make loud sucking noises as she ate them with her hands. However, because she had emerged from the insulated capsule of her regal upbringing with ideas of "normality" that were askew, Princess Margaret inspired fear among her contemporaries. She encouraged familiarity and then, without warning, drew herself up to her full, small height and administered chilling snubs in which she reminded the socially inept that they had offended the daughter of the King of England.

Toward the end of the ball given by Lady Rothermere, after much champagne had been consumed, Princess Margaret seemed to be seized by a heady desire to show off. She grabbed the microphone from the startled singer of the band and she instructed them to play songs by Cole Porter. All the guests who had been waltzing under the vast chandeliers instantly stopped dancing. They stood like Buckingham Palace sentries called to attention in order to watch the royal performance.

Princess Margaret knew the Cole Porter lyrics by heart but she sang all his songs hopelessly off-key. She was given unfair encouragement by the reaction of her audience. All the ladies heavy-laden with jewelry, all the gentlemen penguin-like in their white ties and perfect black tails clapped for her. They shouted and they roared, and they asked for more.

Princess Margaret became a little manic at receiving such approval of her musical abilities, and she started wriggling around in her crinoline and tiara as she tried to mimic the sexual movements of the professional entertainer. Her dress with its petticoats bolstered by the wooden hoops that ballooned her skirts was unsuitable for the slinky act but all the rapturous applause seemed to make her forget this. Just when she had embarked on a rendering of "Let's Do It," a very menacing and unexpected sound came from the back of the crowded ballroom. It grew louder and louder until it eclipsed Princess Margaret's singing. It was the sound of jeering and hissing, of prolonged and thunderous booing.

Princess Margaret faltered in mid-lyric. Mortification turned her face scarlet and then it went ashen. Because she looked close to tears, her smallness of stature suddenly made her look rather pitiful. She abandoned the microphone and a phalanx of flustered ladies-in-waiting rushed her out of the ballroom. The band stopped playing because they felt it was unseemly to continue in the face of this unprecedented situation. There was a buzzing of furious whispers as Lady Rothermere's guests started to take in what they had witnessed.

"Who did that?" I asked the nearest white-tied and black-tailed man who happened to be standing next to me. His face was already red but rage made it look apoplectic. "It was that dreadful man, Francis Bacon," he said. "He calls himself a painter but he does the most frightful paintings. I just don't understand how a creature like him was allowed to get in here. It's really quite disgraceful."

Later when I was married to Lucian Freud and I got to know Francis he once referred to this incident, which caused a scandal.

"Her singing was really too awful," he said. "Someone had to stop her. I don't think people should perform if they can't do it properly."

Francis had an anarchic fearlessness which was unique. I can think of no one else who would have dared to boo a member of the Royal family in a private house. Among all the guests assembled in Lady Rothermere's ballroom, more than a few were secretly suffering from Princess Margaret's singing, but they suffered in silence, gagged by their snobbery. Francis could not be gagged. If he found a performance shoddy no conventional trepidation prevented him from expressing his reactions. Sometimes his opinions could be biased and perverse and unfair, but he never cared if they created outrage.

He could be fearlessly outspoken and crushing if provoked. I remember him being pestered in a bar by a very bad and irritating artist who was trying to make him come to his studio to look at his work. The artist said that he had the feeling that Francis only refused to come and look at his paintings because they threatened him. Francis replied that he didn't feel in the least threatened by the man's paintings.

"I don't want to come to your studio because I've seen your tie."

This same quality of fearlessness manifested itself in his work. The critics who found his painting obscene and ugly did not intimidate him. With big and masterful brush strokes he continued to stamp his canvases with the bleak but beautiful images that expressed his darkly Irish, pessimistic, and extremely personal vision.

There was also a fearlessness in his attitude to money, a wildness in his reckless generosity. When I first got to know him in Soho he was forty and he had not yet found any gallery prepared to give him a show because his work was considered too off-putting. Francis was broke at that time but somehow, mysteriously, he still managed to pay for rounds of drinks and he kept the champagne flowing. Later when he became world-famous and very rich there was no basic change in his behavior. He continued to keep the champagne flowing, the only difference was that he filled his friends' glasses with champagne of a very much higher quality.

His generosity like his fearlessness was infectious. Extremely stingy and mean-fisted people who hated to pay for others would suddenly and amazingly offer to pay for a round of drinks while they were in his company. He could always shame the miserly.

In the Fifties, I remember Francis joining Lucian and me for dinner in his favorite fish restaurant, Wheelers, in Soho. The owner was perceptive and he allowed him to eat and drink there in return for his paintings, which were still spurned by the art world. Francis arrived late because he'd just been to the doctor. He came rolling in with the confident walk of a pirate making adjustments to the slope of the wind-tilted deck. As usual his round cheeks made him look cherubic, but his eyes were far more intelligent than those of the average cherub.

He said that his doctor had just told him that his heart was in tatters. Not a ventricle was functioning. His doctor had rarely seen such a hopeless and diseased organ. Francis had been warned that if he had one more drink or even allowed himself to become excited, his useless heart would fail and he would die.

Having told us the bad news he waved to the waiter and ordered a bottle of champagne, and once we had finished it he went to order a succession of new bottles. He was ebullient throughout the evening but Lucian and I went home feeling very depressed. He seemed doomed. We were convinced he was going to die, aged forty. We took the doctor's diagnosis seriously. No one was ever going to stop him from drinking. No one would ever prevent him from becoming excited. We even wondered that night if we would ever see him again. But he lived to be eighty-two. His attitude toward doctors and death was disdainful. They didn't frighten him. In his way, he jeered at them just as he jeered at the bad singing of Princess Margaret.

A younger British painter, Michael Wishart, once said to me that he thought that Francis had two major ambitions. He wanted to be one of the world's best painters and he wanted to be one of the world's leading alcoholics. Whereas most people discovered that these two ambitions were contradictory and self-defeating he felt that Francis had pulled them both off.

There was an "Irishness" in Bacon's temperament, although he vehemently denied it, having experienced his childhood in Ireland as traumatically painful. He found it impossible to return to Ireland although he loved its countryside. He developed a neurotic attack of asthma on the plane whenever he tried to get there. He could fly to any country in the world without physical mishap, but any flight to his homeland always proved disastrous.

"My father was a horse trainer," I remember him saying to me with a shudder. "A *failed* horse trainer," and he stressed the word "failed" with such disgust and anger that he made his father's occupation sound utterly repulsive. When he was a little boy his parents had put him astride a pony and they had forced him to go fox hunting. He loathed the brutality of the "Sport of Kings" and developed a violent allergy to horses. He turned blue once he found himself on the hunting field and he started to choke with chronic asthma. His parents were very soon made to realize that he was never going to be the son they had wanted.

"Surely there's nothing worse," Francis once said to me, "than the dusty saddle lying in the hall."

Coming from Ireland myself, I sometimes tried to make him tell me more about his unlikely and horsey Irish upbringing. I wanted him to go on, I longed to hear more about his loathing of the awful dusty saddles that symbolically litter the Irish hall. But the subject made him freeze. He became agitated whenever I broached it. He started to tug at the collar of his shirt as if he were trying to loosen some kind of noose which he found asphyxiating; for a moment he resembled the agonized figures in his paintings whose faces turn a truly dangerous shade of indigo purple as they go into the last stages of strangulation. I always stopped my questioning because it seemed cruel and tactless to upset him. I was told by a homosexual friend of Francis's that he'd once admitted that his father, the dreaded and failed horse trainer, had arranged that his small son spend his childhood being systematically and viciously horsewhipped by his Irish grooms.

But with all his horror of Ireland he had the intellectual Irishman's traditional dislike of Catholicism. The Popes that he painted were all screaming and distorted. Some of them were sitting on the lavatory. Although he stubbornly denied that he had been influenced by his Irish upbringing, the desolation of his vision was very similar to that of Beckett.

There was nothing tragic or untimely about his end, although his gallantry, his fearlessness, and his exuberance made one feel he could last drinking champagne forever. Fascinated by the inevitability of human physical decay, Francis, himself, never believed that he would last forever for one moment.

—September 24, 1992

20

ELIZABETH HARDWICK
ON MARY MCCARTHY

INTELLECTUAL MEMOIRS: New York 1936–38.[1] I look at the title
of these vivid pages and calculate that Mary McCarthy was only
twenty-four years old when the events of this period began. The pages
are a continuation of the first volume, to which she gave the title *How
I Grew*. Sometimes with a sigh she would refer to the years ahead
in her autobiography as "I seem to be embarked on how I grew and
grew and grew." I am not certain how many volumes she planned,
but I had the idea she meant to go right down the line, inspecting the
troops you might say, noting the slouches and the good soldiers, and,
of course, inspecting herself living in her time.

Here she is at the age of twenty-four, visiting the memory of it, but
she was in her seventies when the actual writing was accomplished.
The arithmetic at both ends is astonishing. First, her electrifying ("to
excite intensely or suddenly as if by electric shock") descent upon
New York City just after her graduation from Vassar College. And
then after more than twenty works of fiction, essays, cultural and
political commentary, the defiant perseverance at the end when she
was struck by an unfair series of illnesses, one after another. She bore

---

1. An unfinished memoir by Mary McCarthy, published in 1992 by Harcourt Brace Jovan-
ovich; this essay appeared as the introduction.

these afflictions with a gallantry that was almost a disbelief, her disbelief, bore them with a high measure of hopefulness, that sometime
companion in adversity that came not only from the treasure of consciousness, but also in her case from an acute love of *being there* to
witness the bizarre motions of history and the also, often, bizarre
intellectual responses to them.

Intellectual responses are known as opinions and Mary had them
and had them. Still she was so little of an ideologue as to be sometimes unsettling in her refusal of tribal reaction—left or right, male or
female, that sort of thing. She was doggedly personal and often this
meant being so aslant that there was, in this determined rationalist,
an endearing crankiness, very American and homespun somehow.
This was true especially in domestic matters, which held a high place
in her life. There she is grinding the coffee beans of a morning in a
wonderful wooden and iron contraption that seemed to me designed
for muscle building—a workout it was. In her acceptance speech
upon receiving the MacDowell Colony Medal for Literature she said
that she did not *believe* in labor-saving devices. And thus she kept on
year after year, up to her last days, clacking away on her old green
Hermes nonelectric typewriter, with a feeling that this effort and the
others were akin to the genuine in the arts—to the handmade.

I did not meet Mary until a decade or so after the years she writes
about in this part of her autobiographical calendar. But I did come to
know her well and to know most of the "characters," if that is the
right word for the friends, lovers, husbands, and colleagues who
made up her cast after divorce from her first husband and the diver-
sion of the second, John, last name Porter, whom she did not marry.
I also lived through much of the cultural and political background
of the time, although I can understand the question asked, shyly, by
a younger woman writing a biography of Mary: "Just what is a Trotskyite?" Trotskyite and Stalinist—part of one's descriptive vocabulary, like blue-eyed. Trotsky, exiled by Stalin and assassinated in

Mexico in 1940, attracted leftists, many of them with Socialist leanings, in opposition to the Stalin of the Moscow Trials, beginning in 1936, which ended in the execution of most of the original Bolsheviks and the terror that followed.

The preoccupation with the Soviet Union which lasted, with violent mutations of emphasis, until just about yesterday was a cultural and philosophical battleground in the years of Mary McCarthy's "debut" and in the founding, or refounding, of the magazine *Partisan Review*. In that circle, the Soviet Union, the Civil War in Spain, Hitler, and Mussolini were what you might call real life, but not in the magazine's pages more real, more apposite, than T. S. Eliot, Henry James, Kafka, and Dostoevsky.

Her memoir is partly "ideas" and very much an account of those institutional rites that used to be recorded in the family Bible: marriage, children, divorce, and so on. Mary had only one child, her son Reuel Wilson, but she had quite a lot of the other rites: four marriages, interspersed with love affairs of some seriousness and others of none. Far from taking the autobiographer's right to be selective about waking up in this bed or that, she tempts one to say that she remembers more than scrupulosity demands. Demands of the rest of us at least as we look back on the insupportable surrenders and dim our recollection with the aid of the merciful censor.

On the other hand, what often seems to be at stake in Mary's writing and in her way of looking at things is a somewhat obsessional concern for the integrity of sheer fact in matters both trivial and striking. "The world of fact, of figures even, of statistics...the empirical element in life...the fetishism of fact...," phrases taken from her essay "The Fact in Fiction," 1960. The facts of the matter are the truth, as in a court case that tries to circumvent vague feelings and intuitions. If one would sometimes take the liberty of suggesting caution to her, advising prudence or mere practicality, she would look puzzled and answer: But it's the truth. I do not think she would have agreed it was only her truth—instead she often said she looked upon her writing as a mirror.

And thus she will write about her life under the command to put it all down. Even the name of the real Man in the Brooks Brothers Shirt in the fiction of the same name, but scarcely thought by anyone to be a fiction. So at last, and for the first time, she says, he becomes a fact named George Black, who lived in a suburb of Pittsburgh and belonged to the Duquesne Club. As in the story he appeared again and wanted to rescue her from New York bohemian life, but inevitably he was an embarrassment. As such recapitulations are likely to be: Dickens with horror meeting the model for Dora in later life. Little Dora of *David Copperfield*, "What a form she had, what a face she had, what a graceful, variable, enchanting manner!" Of course, the man in the Brooks Brothers shirt did not occasion such affirmative adjectives, but was examined throughout with a skeptical and subversive eye. About the young woman, the author herself more or less, more rather than less, she would write among many other thoughts: "It was not difficult, after all, to be the prettiest girl at a party for the share-croppers."

The early stories in *The Company She Keeps* could, for once, rightly be called a sensation: they were indeed a sensation for candor, for the brilliant, lightning flashes of wit, for the bravado, the confidence, and the splendor of the prose style. They are often about the clash of theory and practice, taste and ideology. Rich as they are in period details, they transcend the issues, the brand names, the intellectual fads. In "The Portrait of the Intellectual as a Yale Man," we have the conflict between abstract ideas and self-advancement, between probity and the wish to embrace the new and fashionable. About a young couple, she writes: "Every social assertion Nancy and Jim made carried its own negation with it, like an Hegelian thesis. Thus it was always being said by Nancy that someone was a Communist but a terribly nice man, while Jim was remarking that someone else worked for Young and Rubicam but was astonishingly liberal."

In the memoir, we learn that we can thank Edmund Wilson for turning the young Mary away from writing reviews to undertaking fiction and thereby producing these dazzling stories. We also learn that she thanks him for little else. A good deal of these pages left at her death tell about her affair with Philip Rahv and *analyze* the break, in fact a desertion, from him and her marriage to Wilson. I must say that much of this drama was new to me. I was not in New York at the time. I met Mary for the first time in the middle 1940s when I was invited to Philip Rahv's apartment. She was with a young man who was to be her next husband after the "escape" from Wilson, that is she was with Bowden Broadwater. Philip was married to Nathalie Swan, Mary's good friend from Vassar.... A lot of water had flowed by.

The picture of Mary and Philip Rahv living in a borrowed apartment on East End Avenue, a fashionable street over by the wrong river, since Philip was very much a downtown figure, rambling round the streets of Greenwich Village with a proprietary glance here and there for the tousled heads of Sidney Hook or Meyer Schapiro and a few others whom he called "Luftmenschen." The memory, no matter the inevitable strains of difference between them, has an idyllic accent, and she appears to have discovered in the writing, decades later, that she loved Rahv—a discovery I will call amusing for want of a better word. There was to be an expulsion from the garden when Edmund Wilson meets Mary, pursues her, and finally, a not very long "finally," gets her to marry him.

The account of her moral struggles is a most curious and interesting one, an entangled conflict between inclination and obligation; the inclination to stay with Rahv and the obligation to herself, her principles, incurred when she got drunk and slept with Wilson and therefore had to marry him. The most engaging part of this struggle is not its credibility or inner consistency but the fact that Mary believed it to be the truth. There was a scent of the seminarian in Mary's moral life which for me was part of her originality and also one of the baffling charms of her presence. Very little was offhand; habits, prejudices, moments, even fleeting ones, had to be accounted for, looked at, and written in the ledger. I sometimes thought she felt the command to prepare and serve a first course at dinner ought to be put in the Bill of Rights.

I remember telling her about some offensive behavior to me on the part of people who were not her friends, but mere acquaintances, if that. When she saw them on the street up in Maine she would faithfully "cut them"—a phrase she sometimes used—while I, when her back was turned, would be waving from the car. Yet it must be said that Mary was usually concerned to make up with those she had offended in fiction, where they were amusingly trapped in their peculiarities, recognizable, in their little ways, not to mention their large ways. Among these were Philip and Nathalie Rahv whom she had wounded, painfully for them, in a novella, *The Oasis*. They too made up, after a time, after a time.

Details, details. Consider the concreteness of the apartments, the clothes, the inquisitive, entranced observing that had something in it of the Goncourt Brothers putting it all down in the Paris of the second half of the nineteenth century. They will write: "On today's bill of fare in the restaurants we have authentic buffalo, antelope, and kangaroo." There it is, if not quite as arresting as Flaubert making love in a brothel with his hat on. Mary remembers from the long-flown years that they on a certain occasion drank "Singapore Slingers." And the minutiae of her first apartment in New York: "We had bought ourselves a 'modernistic' Russell Wright cocktail shaker made of aluminum with a wood top, a chromium hors d'oeuvres tray with glass dishes (using industrial materials was the idea), and six old-fashioned spoons with a simulated cherry on one end and the bottom of the spoon flat for crushing sugar and Angostura." The cocktail age, how menacing and beguiling to the sweet tooth, a sort of liquid mugger.

Unlike the Goncourts' rather mad nocturnal stenography to fill their incomparable pages, I don't think Mary kept a diary. At least I never heard mention of one or felt the chill on rash spontaneity that such an activity from this shrewdly observing friend would cast upon an evening. From these pages and from the previous volume, it appears that she must have kept clippings, letters certainly, playbills, school albums, and made use of minor research to get it right—to be sure the young man in Seattle played on the football team. In these years of her life, she treasured who was in such and such a play seen in an exact theater. On the whole, though, I believe the scene setting, the action, the dialogue came from memory. These memories, pleasing and interesting to me at every turn, are a bit of history of the times. Going to *Pins and Needles*, the Federal Theater's tribute to the Ladies Garment Workers Union, a plain little musical with fewer of the contemporary theater's special effects than a performance of the church choir.

The pages of this memoir represent the beginning of Mary McCarthy's literary life. She was a prodigy from the first. I remember coming across an early review when I was doing some work in the New York Public Library. It was dazzling, a wonderfully accomplished composition, written soon after she left college. As she began, so she continued, and in the years ahead I don't think she changed very much. There was a large circle of friends in France, England, and Italy, as well as here at home, but Mary was too eccentric in her tastes to be called snobbish and I did not find her an especially worldly person. She was not fashionable so much as discriminating; but beyond it all there was the sentimental and romantic streak in her nature that cast a sort of girlish glow over private and public arrangements.

Year in and year out, she made fantastical demands on her time and her budget for birthdays, Christmas; presents, banquets, bouquets, surprises, a whole salmon for the Fourth of July, traditional offering. I remember Natasha Nabokov, the mother of Ivan Nabokov, a publisher in Paris, telling me of a Thanksgiving in Paris where

Mary found an approximation of the American turkey and brought forth "two dressings, one chestnut and one oyster." Keeping the faith it was. I often thought the holiday calendar was a command like the liturgical calendar with its dates and observances. Perhaps it was being an orphan, both of her parents having died in the flu epidemic of 1918, that led her to put such unusual stress on the reproduction of "family" gatherings.

Here she speaks of her "patrician" background, a word I never heard her use about herself. It was true that she came from the upper-middle class, lawyers and so on, but all of it had been lived so far away in Minnesota and the state of Washington that one never thought of her as Middlewestern or Western, but instead as American as one can be without any particularity of region or class. In any case, she created, even in small, unpromising apartments, a sort of miniature *haut bourgeois* scenery, without being imitative. And she would arrive in New York with Mark Cross leather luggage, a burdensome weight even when empty, pairs of white leather gloves, a rolled umbrella, all of it reminding of ladies of a previous generation, and no thought of convenience. Of course, she didn't believe in convenience.

Wide friendships and hospitality, yes, but there were, in my view, only two persons, outside the family circle, for whom she felt a kind of reverence. The two were Hannah Arendt and Nicola Chiaromonte, both Europeans. Chiaromonte, a beautiful man with dark curls and brown, I think, eyes, was a curiosity in the *Partisan* circle because of his great modesty and the moderation of his voice in discussion, a gentle word for what was usually a cacophony of argument. An evening at the Rahvs was to enter a ring of bullies, each one bullying the other. In that way it was different from the boarding school accounts of the type, since no one was in ascendance. Instead there was an equality of vehemence that exhausted itself and the wicked bottles of Four Roses whiskey around midnight—until the next time.

Chiaromonte, with his peaceable, anarchist inclinations, was outclassed here.

I suppose he could be called a refugee, this Italian cultural and social critic and antifascist. Here he published essays, but did not create a literary presence equal to his important career when he returned to Italy in the late 1940s. After his death, Mary wrote a long, interesting essay in order to introduce an American edition of his writings on the theater.[2] I remember an anecdote she told me about Chiaromonte and it alone is sufficient to show why she so greatly admired him. The story went as follows: stopped at a border, trying to escape the Nazi drive across Europe, Nicola was asked for his passport and he replied: Do you want the real one or the false one?

Hannah Arendt, of course, was or became an international figure with *The Origins of Totalitarianism*, *Eichmann in Jerusalem*, and other works. I can remember Mary at Hannah's apartment on Riverside Drive, a setting that was candidly practical, a neat place, tending toward a mute shade of beige in its appointments. For an occasional gathering there would be drinks and coffee and, German style it seemed to us, cakes and chocolates and nuts bought in abundance at the bakeries on Broadway. Mary was, quite literally, enchanted by Hannah's mind, her scholarship, her industry, and the complexities of her views. As for Hannah, I think perhaps she saw Mary as a golden American friend, perhaps the best the country could produce, with a bit of our western states in her, a bit of the Roman Catholic, a Latin student, a sort of New World, blue-stocking *salonnière* like Rachel Varnhagen, about whom Hannah had, in her early years, written a stunning, unexpected book. The friendship of these two women was very moving to observe in its purity of respect and affection. After Hannah's death, Mary's extraordinary efforts to see her friend's unfinished work on questions of traditional philosophy brought to

---

2. "Nicola Chiaromonte and the Theatre," *The New York Review*, February 20, 1975.

publication, the added labor of estate executor, could only be called sacrificial.

I gave the address at the MacDowell Colony when Mary received the Medal and there I said that if she was, in her writing, sometimes a scourge, a Savonarola, she was a very cheerful one, lighthearted and even optimistic. I could not find in her work, trace of despair or alienation; instead she had a dreamy expectation that persons and nations should do their best. Perhaps it would be unlikely that a nature of such exceptional energy could act out alienation, with its temptation to sloth. Indeed it seemed to me that Mary did not understand even the practical usefulness of an occasional resort to the devious. Her indiscretions were always open and forthright and in many ways one could say she was "like an open book." Of course, everything interesting depends upon which book is open.

Among the many charms and interests of her unfinished memoir are the accounts of the volatility of her relations with the men in her life. She will say that she doesn't know why she left her first husband, backed out on John Porter, and deserted Philip Rahv. That is, she doesn't know *exactly*, but can only speculate. What, perhaps, might be asked nowadays, is why the gifted and beautiful young woman was so greatly attracted to marriage in the first place, why she married at twenty-one. She seemed swiftly to overlook the considerable difficulties of unmarried couples "living together" at the time: the subterfuge about staying overnight, facing the elevator man, hiding the impugning clothes when certain people appeared, keeping the mate off the phone lest there be a call from home—unimaginable strategies in the present-day cities. There were many things Mary didn't believe in, but she certainly believed in marriage, or rather in being married. She had no talent at all for the single life, or even for waiting after a divorce, a break. However, once married, she made a strikingly independent wife, an abbess within the cloister, so to speak.

In a foreword to the paperback edition of *Memories of a Catholic Girlhood*, she speaks of the treasures gained from her education in Catholic convent and boarding schools, even finding a benefit in the bias of Catholic history as taught.

> To care for the quarrels of the past, to identify oneself with a cause that became, politically speaking, a losing cause with the birth of the modern world, is to experience a kind of straining against reality, a rebellious nonconformity that, again, is rare in America, where children are instructed in the virtues of the system they live under, as though history had achieved a happy ending in American civics.

Nonconformity may be a tiresome eccentricity or arise from genuine skepticism about the arrangements of society. Think of the headache of rejecting charge cards, the universal plastic that created a commercial world in which trying to use a personal check could bring oneself under suspicion. Going along with fidelity to old-fangledness, Mary and her husband declined the cards and had to carry about large sums of money, rolls of bills that reminded me of nothing so much as men in fedoras in gangster movies. Still they did it and I think with some amusement in a trendy restaurant or Madison Avenue shop.

So, we meet her here, in 1936, marching in a Communist May Day parade, marching along with John Porter, a new man who looked like Fred MacMurray. The conjunction of romance and the events of the day is characteristic of Mary at all points in her life. At the end of her memoir two years have passed and she has covered a lot of ground; divorce, a new marriage, unhappy, that lasted seven years, "though it never recovered." Never recovered from Wilson's mistakes and shortcomings as she saw them.

I would have liked Mary to live on and on, irreplaceable spirit and friend that she was; even though I must express some relief that her memoirs did not proceed to me and my life to be looked at with her smiling precision and daunting determination on accuracy. She had her say, but I never knew anyone who gave so much pleasure to those around her. Her wit, great learning, her gardening, her blueberry pancakes, beautiful houses. None of that would be of more than passing interest if it were not that she worked as a master of the art of writing every day of her life. How it was done, I do not know.

—March 26, 1992

21

TATYANA TOLSTAYA
ON JOSEPH BRODSKY

WHEN THE LAST things are taken out of a house, a strange, resonant echo settles in, your voice bounces off the walls and returns to you. There's the din of loneliness, a draft of emptiness, a loss of orientation and a nauseating sense of freedom: everything's allowed and nothing matters, there's no response other than the weakly rhymed tap of your own footsteps. This is how Russian literature feels now: just four years short of millennium's end, it has lost the greatest poet of the second half of the twentieth century, and can expect no other. Joseph Brodsky has left us, and our house is empty. He left Russia itself over two decades ago, became an American citizen, loved America, wrote essays and poems in English. But Russia is a tenacious country: try as you may to break free, she will hold you to the last.

In Russia, when a person dies, the custom is to drape the mirrors in the house with black muslin—an old custom, whose meaning has been forgotten or distorted. As a child I heard that this was done so that the deceased, who is said to wander his house for nine days saying his farewells to friends and family, won't be frightened when he can't find his reflection in the mirror. During his unjustly short but endlessly rich life Joseph was reflected in so many people, destinies, books, and cities that during these sad days, when he walks unseen among us, one wants to drape mourning veils over all the mirrors he loved: the great rivers washing the shores of Manhattan, the Bosporus, the canals of Amsterdam, the waters of Venice, which he sang, the arterial net of Petersburg (a hundred islands—how many rivers?), the city of his birth, beloved and cruel, the prototype of all future cities.

There, still a boy, he was judged for being a poet, and by definition a loafer. It seems that he was the only writer in Russia to whom they applied that recently invented, barbaric law—which punished for the lack of desire to make money. Of course, that was not the point—with their animal instinct they already sensed full well just who stood before them. They dismissed all the documents recording the kopecks Joseph received for translating poetry.

"Who appointed you a poet?" they screamed at him.

"I thought.... I thought it was God."

All right then. Prison, exile.

> *Neither country nor churchyard will I choose*
> *I'll come to Vasilevsky Island to die,*

he promised in a youthful poem.

> *In the dark I won't find your deep blue façade*
> *I'll fall on the asphalt between the crossed lines.*

I think that the reason he didn't want to return to Russia even for a day was so that this incautious prophecy would not come to be. A student of—among others—Akhmatova and Tsvetaeva, he knew their poetic superstitiousness, knew the conversation they had during their one and only meeting. "How could you write that... Don't you know that a poet's words always come true?" one of them reproached. "And how could you write that...?" the other was amazed. And what they foretold did indeed come to pass.

I met him in 1988 during a short trip to the United States, and when I got back to Moscow I was immediately invited to an evening devoted to Brodsky. An old friend read his poetry, then there was a performance of some music that was dedicated to him. It was almost impossible to get close to the concert hall, passersby were grabbed and begged to sell "just one extra ticket." The hall was guarded by mounted police—you might have thought that a rock concert was in the offing. To my utter horror I suddenly realized that they were counting on me: I was the first person they knew who had seen the poet after so many years of exile. What could I say? What can you say about a man with whom you've spent a mere two hours? I resisted, but they pushed me on stage. I felt like a complete idiot. Yes, I saw Brodsky. Yes, alive. He's sick. He smokes. We drank coffee. There was no sugar in the house. (The audience grew agitated: Are the Americans neglecting our poet? Why didn't he have any sugar?) Well, what else? Well, Baryshnikov dropped by, brought some firewood, they lit a fire. (More agitation in the hall: Is our poet freezing to death over there?) What floor does he live on? What does he eat? What is he writing? Does he write by hand or use a typewriter? What books does he have? Does he know that we love him? Will he come? Will he come? Will he come?

"Joseph, will you come to Russia?"

"Probably. I don't know. Maybe. Not this year. I should go. I won't go. No one needs me there."

"Don't be coy! They won't leave you alone. They'll carry you through the streets—airplane and all. There'll be such a crowd they'll break through customs at Sheremetevo airport and carry you to Moscow in their arms. Or to Petersburg. On a white horse, if you like."

"That's precisely why I don't want to. And I don't need anyone there."

"It's not true! What about all those little old ladies of the

intelligentsia, your readers, all the librarians, museum staff, pension-
ers, communal apartment dwellers who are afraid to go out into the
communal kitchen with their chipped teakettle? The ones who stand
in the back rows at philharmonic concerts, next to the columns,
where the tickets are cheaper? Don't you want to let them get a look
at you from afar, your real readers? Why are you punishing them?"

It was an unfair blow. Tactless and unfair. He either joked his way
out of it: "I'd rather go see my favorite Dutch." "I love Italians, I'll go
to Italy." "The Poles are wonderful. They've invited me." Or would
grow angry: "They wouldn't let me go to my father's funeral! My
mother died without me—I asked—and they refused!"

Did he want to go home? I think that at the beginning, at least, he
wanted to very much, but he couldn't. He was afraid of the past, of
memories, reminders, unearthed graves, was afraid of his weakness,
afraid of destroying what he had done with his past in his poetry,
afraid of looking back at the past—like Orpheus looked back at
Eurydice—and losing it forever. He couldn't fail to understand that
his true reader was there, he knew that he was a Russian poet,
although he convinced himself—and himself alone—that he was an
English-language poet. He has a poem about a hawk ("A Hawk's Cry
in Autumn") in the hills of Massachusetts who flies so high that the
rush of rising air won't let him descend back to earth, and the hawk
perishes there, at those heights, where there are neither birds nor people, nor any air to breathe.

So could he have returned? Why did I and others bother him with
all these questions about returning? We wanted him to feel, to know
how much he was loved—we ourselves loved him so much! And I
still don't know whether he wanted all this convincing or whether it
troubled his troubled heart. "Joseph, you are invited to speak at the
college. February or September?" "February, of course. September—
I should live so long." And, tearing yet another filter off yet another
cigarette, he'd tell another grisly joke. "The husband says to his wife:

'The doctor told me that this is the end. I won't live till morning. Let's drink champagne and make love one last time.' His wife replies: 'That's all very well and fine for you—you don't have to get up in the morning!'"

Did we have to treat him like a "sick person"—talk about the weather and walk on tiptoe? When he came to speak at Skidmore, he arrived exhausted from the three-hour drive, white as a sheet—in a kind of condition that makes you want to call 911. But he drank a glass of wine, smoked half a pack of cigarettes, made brilliant conversation, read his poems, and then more poems, poems, poems—smoked and recited by heart both his own and others' poems, smoked some more, and read some more. By that time, his audience had grown pale from his un-American smoke, and he was in top form—his cheeks grew rosy, his eyes sparkled, and he read on and on. And when by all counts he should have gone to bed with a nitroglycerin tablet under his tongue, he wanted to talk and went off to the hospitable hosts, the publishers of *Salmagundi*, Bob and Peggy Boyers. And he talked, and drank and smoked and laughed, and at midnight when his hosts had paled and my husband and I drove him back to the guest house, his energy surged as ours waned. "What charming people, but I think we exhausted them. *So now* we can really talk!" "Really," i.e., the Russian way. And we sat up till three in the morning in the empty living room of the guest house, talking about everything—because Joseph was interested in everything. We rummaged in the drawers in search of a corkscrew for another bottle of red wine, filling the quiet American lodging with clouds of forbidden smoke; we combed the kitchen in search of leftover food from the reception ("We should have hidden the lo mein.... And there was some delicious chicken left...we should have stolen it.") When we finally said goodbye my husband and I were barely alive and Joseph was still going strong.

He had an extraordinary tenderness for all his Petersburg friends, generously extolling their virtues, some of which they did not possess.

When it came to human loyalty, you couldn't trust his assessments—
everyone was a genius, a Mozart, one of the best poets of the twentieth
century. Quite in keeping with the Russian tradition, for him a human
bond was higher than justice, and love higher than truth. Young writers and poets from Russia inundated him with their manuscripts—
whenever I would leave Moscow for the US my poetic acquaintances
would bring their collections and stick them in my suitcase: "It isn't
very heavy. The main thing is, show it to Brodsky. Just ask him to read
it. I don't need anything else—just let him read it!" And he read and
remembered, and told people that the poems were good and gave
interviews praising the fortunate, and they kept sending their publications. And their heads turned, some said things like: "Really, there are
two genuine poets in Russia: Brodsky and myself." He created the
false impression of a kind of old patriarch—but if only a certain young
writer whom I won't name could have heard how Brodsky groaned
and moaned after obediently reading a story whose plot was built
around delight in moral sordidness. "Well, all right, I realize that after
this one can continue writing. But how can he go on living?"

He didn't go to Russia. But Russia came to him. Everyone came to
convince themselves that he really and truly existed, that he was alive
and writing—this strange Russian poet who did not want to set foot on
Russian soil. He was published in Russian in newspapers, magazines,
single volumes, multiple volumes, he was quoted, referred to, studied,
and published as he wished and as he didn't, he was picked apart, used,
and turned into a myth. Once a poll was held on a Moscow street:
"What are your hopes for the future in connection with the parliamen-
tary elections?" A carpenter answered: "I could care less about the par-
liament and politics. I just want to live a private life, like Brodsky."

He wanted to live, and not to die—neither on Vasilevsky Island,
nor on the island of Manhattan. He was happy, he had a family he
loved, poetry, friends, readers, students. He wanted to run away from
his doctors to Mount Holyoke, where he taught—then, he thought,

they couldn't catch him. He wanted to elude his own prophecy: "I will fall on the asphalt between the crossed lines." He fell on the floor of his study of another island, under the crossed Russian-American lines of an émigré's double fate.

And two girls—sisters from un-lived years
running out on the island, wave to the boy.

And indeed he left two girls behind—his wife and daughter.

"Do you know, Joseph, if you don't want to come back with a lot of fanfare, no white horses and excited crowds, why don't you just go to Petersburg incognito?" "Incognito?" Suddenly he wasn't angry and didn't joke, but listened very attentively. "Yes, you know, paste on a mustache or something. Just don't tell anyone—not a soul. You'll go, get on a trolley, ride down Nevsky Prospect, walk along the streets—free and unrecognized. There's a crowd, everyone's always pushing and jostling. You'll buy some ice cream. Who'll recognize you? If you feel like it you'll call your friends from a phone booth—you can say you're calling from America, or if you like you can just knock on a friend's door: 'Here I am. Just dropped by. I missed you.'"

Here I was, talking, joking, and suddenly I noticed that he wasn't laughing—there was a sort of childlike expression of helplessness on his face, a strange sort of dreaminess. His eyes seemed to be looking through objects, through the edges of things—on to the other side of time. He sat quietly, and I felt awkward, as if I were barging in where I wasn't invited. To dispel the feeling, I said in a pathetically hearty voice: "It's a wonderful idea, isn't it?"

He looked through me and murmured: "Wonderful... Wonderful..."

—February 29, 1996;
translated from the Russian by Jamey Gambrell

22

ENRIQUE KRAUZE
ON OCTAVIO PAZ

IN 1968, OCTAVIO PAZ founded a culture of intellectual dissidence in Mexico. The Mexican political system had no concentration camps. It proposed no ideology of a Supreme State. But it did exercise an almost absolute power based on precedents drawn from Spanish and pre-Hispanic culture. It was a government opposed to free discussion and criticism. Intellectuals had traditionally been integrated into the structure of the state. Their function was to collaborate in the "building of the nation," as educators, advisers, ideologues, ambassadors. When there were exceptions—intellectuals who tried to form opposition parties or offer independent criticism—the machinery of the Partido Revolucionario Institucional would crush their efforts.

On October 2, 1968, the government of Gustavo Díaz Ordaz massacred hundreds of students in the ancient Plaza of Tlatelolco. Their crime had been to raise the flag of political liberty. On the following day, Octavio Paz resigned as Mexican ambassador to India. It was his finest hour, an unheard-of gesture in Mexico. And it would not only change his life but the intellectual life of Mexico and, to a great degree, of Latin America.

Shortly afterward, Paz would begin to publish his first bitter criticisms of the PRI: "In Mexico there is no greater dictatorship than that of the PRI and no greater danger of anarchy than that provoked by the unnatural prolongation of the PRI's political monopoly." Since 1943, Paz had lived largely abroad, as a Mexican diplomat, primarily in France and later in India. It was natural that now, on his return, the youth of Mexico—with their feelings of intense and recent grievance —should expect him to become a leader of revolutionary opposition to the petrified regime of the PRI. But Paz opted for a different gesture of dissidence, not only with respect to the PRI but toward the dominant political culture of the left. He ruptured the ideological unity in the intellectual life of the country and founded the magazine *Plural* (1972–1976), which, following the much earlier tradition of *Partisan Review*, criticized—from a democratic and liberal standpoint—not only the military dictatorships of South America but also Castro's dictatorship in Cuba and various guerrilla movements that had begun to proliferate throughout most of Latin America.

In 1976, the government engineered an internal coup against the newspaper *Excelsior*, which published *Plural*. The magazine closed, but Paz almost immediately founded *Vuelta*, an independent monthly magazine of literature and criticism. It would be distributed throughout the Spanish-speaking world, initiating an intellectual debate that sometimes seemed to verge on civil war. It was then that I first met him. And for the next twenty years, along with a small group of kindred writers, I was privileged to work with him in carrying on that debate.

Vuelta was his fortress but also his literary workshop. From his library, in his apartment on the historic avenue of the Paseo de la Reforma where he lived for almost all those twenty years, he spoke with me daily by telephone. He would propose or discuss articles, reviews, translations, stories, poems. Alfonso Reyes, the prolific man of letters who had preceded Octavio Paz as the presiding eminence of Mexican literature, had once complained that "Latin America is a late arrival at the feast of world culture." Since his early youth, Paz had decided to join that feast, and *Vuelta* would set out places for the earliest companions of his intellectual life: Ortega y Gasset, Sartre, Camus, Breton, Neruda, Buñuel. Right up until his death, on April 19, at age eighty-four, he saw himself as an ally and interpreter of the Surrealists, and he was, in fact, the most distinguished survivor of that movement. But *Vuelta* would also create a banquet of its own, with the presence of Borges, Kundera, Brodsky, Milosz, Kolakowski, the Americans Irving Howe and Daniel Bell, and hundreds of others.

Paz gave no classes nor did he ever pontificate. Conversation with him was a constant exploration. Although he did have the "irritable nature" that Horace ascribed to poets and was invariably serious about all issues, he could also show an almost childlike enthusiasm in the breadth and degree of his intellectual curiosity. Large themes fascinated him and he wrote about them at length: reflections on poetic creation and language; his vision of the course of Western poetry from the enthusiasms of Romanticism to the ironic vision of the modern avant-garde, in which he compared not only works in different languages but placed them against the background of other, non-Western poetics; his thoughts on modern culture, politics, and society, always emphasizing the need for a careful, critical outlook on the world. And he was excited by new scientific discoveries or intellectual inquiries: the latest theory on the Big Bang, debates about the nature of the mind or the decipherment of the Mayan script. As he wrote in these pages:

> The immense and prolonged historical solitude of Mesoamerica is the reason for its grandeur and its weakness. Grand because it was one of the few truly original civilizations in history: it owed nothing to the others. Weak because its isolation made it vulnerable to that essential experience, the same in social life as in biology: the encounter with the Other.

Then unexpectedly—and the idea of "unexpectedly" signaled by a sudden change of gesture or of manner marks my memories of him—his conversation would swerve toward unpredictable subjects: French erotic literature of the eighteenth century, the political maxims of an ancient Chinese scholar, medieval theories on love or melancholy....

I remember that I once felt tempted to become his Boswell and take notes on everything he said and did. Fortunately I resisted the temptation, and our friendship flowed more easily for it. He was a man who lived in a constant state of exaltation. He looked like a lion with a full mane and that was how he behaved. Other great Latin American writers built up, as he did, their personal body of work, but either they inhabited Olympus, like Borges, practiced a cult of personality like a political *caudillo* (García Márquez), or thought of Marxist or populist "revolution" as the only possible road for Latin America (as did practically all the writers of the Latin American Renaissance except Ernesto Sábato, the later Vargas Llosa, and Heberto Padilla). None of them founded or directed a literary and political magazine. Paz continually did so, almost without interruption, since the 1930s.

Paz converted Mexico into a sacred text that cried out to be deciphered, to be revealed. He was a miner and an alchemist of Mexican identity. Through his explorations, in *The Labyrinth of Solitude*, among the images and rites of his culture, its desires and popular myths; through the poetic freedom of the prose poems of *Eagle or Sun* (the direct predecessor of Latin American Magic Realism); through his books on the writers and artists of Mexico and especially his brilliant meditation on Sor Juana Inés de la Cruz; in his essays of historical interpretation or political criticism; and through a number of long poems ("Pasado en claro," "Nocturno de San Ildefonso," "Vuelta"), Paz attempted, in his own words, "to tear the veil and see":

> I felt myself alone and I felt that Mexico was a lonely country, isolated, far from the central flow of history.... Thinking about the strangeness of being Mexican, I discovered an old truth:

everyone carries a stranger hidden within himself.... I wanted to dive within myself, to dig up this stranger, to speak with him.

For Paz, a poet of love, "woman is the gate of reconciliation with the world." His mother, his aunt (the first to encourage him as a writer), the women he loved as a young man, and especially Marie José, his wife since 1964, with whom he found a very special happiness—they lessened his sense of emptiness, his feelings of need; they were the inspiration of his passion for poetry, and they saved him from the labyrinth.

> *Your gaze scatters seed.*
> *It planted a tree.*
> *I speak*
> *because you stir the leaves.*

His father, on the other hand, was not a gate for him but a mute wall. There perhaps, I remember thinking, lay the key to unearthing the stranger, a way for me to understand the fighter that Octavio Paz was: within the Mexico of the Revolution that forever changed the life of his family, in the old house on the outskirts of Mexico City where his grandfather, Ireneo Paz, and his father, Octavio Paz Solorzano, argued about the future of a country dramatically linked to the course of their own lives. And in that house, the poet as a child was the silent witness to their differences.

His grandfather had been a nineteenth-century liberal rebel, a participant in numerous uprisings, a soldier in the war against the French intervention that tried to create, out of the raw material of the European nobles Maximilian and Carlota, an emperor and empress of Mexico. Later Ireneo Paz became a novelist and was for many years the editor of a famous newspaper, *La Patria*. And he wrote about power and about freedom. He had satirized Benito Juárez in poetry and been a companion of Porfirio Díaz, but at the age of seventy-five he turned against the old dictator, welcomed the democratic revolution led by Madero in 1910, endured imprisonment, and would finally retire to die in his bed, a very old man, in 1924, close by his huge library of history and literature, and surrounded by images of Danton, Mirabeau, Victor Hugo, and Lamartine. Uneasy with the "anarchy of the chieftains and petty chieftains," he saw them as threats to his Mexico. In the watching eyes of his ten-year-old grandson, he was a wise and powerful patriarch.

Ireneo Paz's son, Octavio Paz Solorzano, was a different being, a sort of "mutineer," the kind of man to whom phrases later written by his son could well be applied, "the macho, the *caudillo*, the terrifying man, the 'hell-of-a-guy,' the man who left his wife and children" under the spell of the Revolution, "the magic word, that will change everything and grant us intense pleasure and a quick death." In 1914, the year his only son was born, Octavio Paz Solorzano joined the peasant army of Emiliano Zapata. He would rise to be Zapata's personal emissary in the United States. And his obsessions would be equality and social justice, his life a string of misfortunes: defeat, frustration, alcoholism, exile in San Antonio and Los Angeles, and a passionate revolutionary vocation that would eventually, in 1936, end with a premature and violent death:

> *Between vomiting and thirst,*
> *lashed to the colt of alcohol,*
> *my father passed back and forth in flames.*
> *Among the sleeping cars and the rails*
> *of a fly-blown, dusty railroad station,*
> *one evening, we picked up the pieces of him.*

It was natural enough that the young man, the poet Octavio Paz, should identify with both his grandfather and his father, and yearn to be "a revolutionary, a hero, dying by the bullet, a liberator." On his own, he had to seek out not only the innocent liberal rebellion of his grandfather, who merely wanted a democratic political life for Mexico, and not only the rousing Zapatista cry of Revolution by his father, who sought to recover a lost unity between humanity and the earth. He had to do more, he had to serve the Revolution, "the great Goddess, the eternal Beloved, the great Whore of poets and novelists."

Paz remained obsessed by the idea of the Revolution, but he discovered and reworked it in only one part of experience, the incessant subversion and free experimentation of his poetry. He came to feel that Surrealism, with its emphasis on releasing emotions through access to the unconscious (and its interest in non-European cultures), was an ideal poetic and intellectual medium for confronting the multilayered reality of Mexico. With less luck but with nobility and enthusiasm, he sought the Revolution also in action: he worked as a country schoolmaster in the henequen country of Yucatan, with its tragic social history of racial conflict and economic slavery; he wrote for revolutionary Mexican newspapers; he went to Spain during the Civil War because he saw—on the side of the Republic—the unforgettable visage of hope, of possible fraternity, the "creative spontaneity and direct and daily participation of the people." But perhaps, above all, he went looking for the Revolution in the world of thought, among the great "possessed" writers of Russia, in the canonic texts of Marxism, the heretical texts of Trotsky, and, later, the polemics of Camus and Sartre.

Like many other European and Latin American intellectuals, Paz fell in love with the Revolution, but his disenchantment, though gradual, would be irreversible. It began with the Hitler–Stalin pact, and continued to grow. During the Sixties, he still saw hope in some revolutionary movements but rapidly became skeptical about Cuba. With the definitive revelations by Solzhenitsyn of the Soviet Gulag, his love affair with the Revolution ended for good: "Now we know that the splendor, which seemed to us the coming of dawn, was a blood-soaked, burning pyre."

In a sense, it can be said that this too was the source of his combativeness—his awareness that the Revolution had turned against itself. During the full cultural hegemony of the Latin American left, intolerant of the slightest criticism directed toward Cuba or the slightest doubt about the "globally positive" balance of "genuine socialism" in Eastern Europe, Paz declared his dissenting opinion. And, in Mexico, the scholastic and inquisitorial instincts of its Catholic culture reappeared in a new form to combat his "heterodoxy." He was accused of being a reactionary, insulted in the halls of the universities, in newspapers and academic reviews. In 1984, his effigy was burned before the American embassy. (A cruel paradox, since no one in Latin America had looked more closely at the United States and criticized the provincial, puritanical, and materialistic aspects of its culture and the shortsightedness of American diplomacy.)

"We Mexicans must reconcile ourselves with our past," Paz insisted. In *The Labyrinth of Solitude*, he had reconciled himself with his father and with the Zapatista revolt, seeing in that Revolution "a communion of Mexico with itself," with its Indian and Spanish roots. But during the last decades of his life, another character sat down at his table—his grandfather, Ireneo Paz. Confronted with the corrupt, inefficient, paternalistic, and authoritarian Mexican state, it seemed right to recover liberal and democratic values. From the time he resigned his ambassadorship in 1968, Paz no longer had faith in the Revolution but he still wore the badge of individual rebellion his grandfather had worn. In 1985, he published "The PRI, Its Final Hour," and in 1986 denounced the PRI's electoral fraud in the state of Chihuahua, which would initiate a long and as yet incomplete Mexican transition toward democracy.

When the Berlin Wall fell in 1989 and—no less a miracle—Latin America began to move toward democracy, Paz felt that history had justified his convictions. In 1990, *Vuelta* organized a conference called "The Experience of Freedom" during which, without any trace of triumphalism, an international group of intellectuals analyzed the glow and the shadows of that watershed of history. During the same year Paz was awarded the Nobel Prize for Literature. After that, in the Spanish-speaking world, he held a place that had only been matched earlier by Ortega y Gasset. Paz had emerged from the labyrinth and had—to a considerable degree—brought Mexico out of its tangential position and into the full light of Western culture.

Toward the end, even his face began to look more and more like that of his grandfather. He said he wanted a quick and serene death, like Don Ireneo, but that final blessing was not granted to him. He had been born during the historic conflagration of 1914, and the final stage of his life would be marked by a tragic fire, which, in 1996, destroyed much of his apartment and library. Shortly afterward, he was diagnosed as having spinal cancer. And toward the end, just like his grandfather, he became concerned about the shadow of anarchy that seemed to be spreading over Mexico.

During a public ceremony of farewell, he turned once again to the image of Don Ireneo, the protective, wise patriarch. He repeated his favorite metaphor of Mexico as "a country of the sun" but then immediately reminded the audience about the darkness of our history, our "luminous and cruel" duality that already reigned within the cosmogony of the Aztec gods and had been an obsession for him since childhood. He wished that some Socrates might appear who could free his people of the darker side, of all the destructive passions. Unusual for him, he was actually preaching "like my grandfather," he said, "who loved to preach after a meal." And suddenly he looked up toward the cloudy sky, as if he wanted to touch it with his hand. "Up there," he said, "there are clouds and sun. Clouds and sun are related words. Let us be worthy of the clouds of the Valley of Mexico. Let us be worthy of the sun of the Valley of Mexico." For an instant the sky cleared, leaving only the sun, and then Octavio Paz said, "The Valley of Mexico, that phrase lit up my childhood, my maturity, and my old age."

During the following weeks, both his father and grandfather dropped out of his consciousness. He was left with only the memory of his mother and the presence of his wife. And one day, unexpectedly, she heard him whisper to her, "You are my Valley of Mexico."

—May 28, 1998;
translated from the Spanish by Hank Heifetz

23

RICHARD SEAVER
ON JÉRÔME LINDON

HE WAS TALL, thin, with a hairline that had so receded that only two white, barely discernible tufts remained above his prominent ears. His dark, flashing eyes fixed on you as if you were the only person in the universe, and his nervous energy, even in the forty-ninth year of our friendship, was so ill-contained that he constantly shifted in his chair behind a disconcertingly clean desk. He was, without question, the most prestigious French publisher of the second half of the twentieth century and, arguably, the most important publisher in the Western world. And yet, since 1948, when he assumed the direction of the fledgling publishing house Les Éditions de Minuit (Midnight Press), Jérôme Lindon brought out no more than fifteen to twenty books a year. In half a century the people on his payroll never exceeded the magic number of ten.

What made Lindon so special? His total integrity. He never published a manuscript he had not read and approved of personally. No committees. No readers' reports. Until recently, when his daughter Irène began forming her own list of authors within the house, he read every manuscript submitted to Minuit. "I read, and I decide," he once told me. Most often he would respond the very next day, either to accept the work or summon the author to discuss what he thought needed to be done to make it publishable. In an era of increasingly impersonal publishing, of gluttonous conglomeratization, Lindon remained the consummate personal publisher. To me he was an inspiration throughout my own publishing life.

Les Éditions de Minuit was born in 1941, during the darkest days of the Nazi occupation. A clandestine house founded by two members of the French Resistance, Pierre de Lescure and Jean Bruller, Minuit published a score of underground titles between then and the end of the war, the most famous of which is the now-classic *Le Silence de la mer* (*The Silence of the Sea*) by Vercors, which was Jean Bruller's pseudonym.

Lindon, too young in 1939 to be conscripted, moved with his family—his father, Raymond Lindon, was an eminent lawyer and jurist—to the south of France, the so-called free zone. The end of the war found him in Constance, Germany, as part of General Lattre's First Army.

In 1946, Lindon, who was then barely twenty, joined Les Éditions de Minuit as an unpaid intern, bearing nonetheless the imposing title of "assistant production manager," bestowed no doubt because he had a year's experience working in a printshop. The publishing house was losing money, and young Lindon convinced his family to invest, to help keep it afloat. A year later, with the company still badly in the red, the Lindon family's further investment gave it the majority share, and Bruller/Vercors promptly left, taking his backlist with him to a rival publishing house, Albin Michel.

"So there I was," Lindon said to me years later, "a mere kid, completely ignorant of how businesses were or should be run, knowing little or nothing about publishing, the proud owner of a prestigious name, Les Éditions de Minuit, with terrifying debts to be met and a publishing house to rebuild or, rather, to be built from scratch." For the next decade, despite an increasingly impressive roster of authors —Georges Bataille, Pierre Klossowski, Maurice Blanchot—Minuit continued to lose money, its losses covered by loans or investments from both Lindon's and his wife's families. A breakthrough came as early as 1950, when a manuscript by an unknown Irishman writing in French landed on his desk: *Molloy*, by Samuel Beckett, which had already been turned down by several major French publishers. Reminiscing, Lindon once described to me the mounting excitement he had felt as he feverishly turned the pages of the novel. That night, he took it home with him on the Métro and remained so engrossed that he missed his stop.

"Suddenly," he said, "nothing else seemed important. Beckett for me was like a meteor streaking across the sky. I simply could not understand how anyone could not have recognized the man's brilliance. From that day on, if before I had had any doubts about my chosen profession, my fate was sealed."

Molloy appeared the following year, to excellent reviews and modest sales. Two other Beckett novels—volumes two and three of the trilogy he had finished—*Malone Dies* and *The Unnamable*—were waiting and followed in quick succession. Minuit's publication of Beckett also quickly gave Lindon the reputation of a publisher of taste and courage, and a number of younger writers began sending him their manuscripts. Alain Robbe-Grillet's *Les Gommes* (*Erasers*) appeared in 1953, about the same time as Beckett's first play, *Waiting for Godot*, which opened at the tiny Babylon Theater on the Left Bank —the equivalent of an off-off-Broadway house—to generally puzzled reviews and, for Lindon, again modest sales. Beckett himself, who was twenty years older than Lindon, was the first to worry about and commiserate with his newfound friend and publisher. "He's such a nice young man, Lindon," he said to me one afternoon at the Dôme in Montparnasse, where we were working together translating one of his short stories, "La Fin" ("The End"), into English. "And to think that because of me he may well go bankrupt!" (Ironically, it was Beckett who would "save" Minuit, for Lindon owned world rights to most of Beckett's work, which he would later sell around the world to dozens of countries.)

Despite all those lean years when, in Lindon's own words, he went on the assumption that he "was living in a state of constant financial crisis," he never yielded to the temptation to compromise; his intellectual rigor never wavered. The financial turning point for Lindon and Minuit came in 1957, when he published four key titles: Nathalie Sarraute's *Tropisms*, Beckett's *Endgame*, future Nobel laureate Claude Simon's *Le Vent* (*The Wind*), and Michel Butor's *La Modification* (*A Change of Heart*), the last of which won the Renaudot Prize and sold a phenomenal (for Minuit) 90,000 copies. That year Minuit became profitable, and it has remained so ever since.

Lindon is generally credited with being the force behind the so-called *nouveau roman*, a loose label that included, in addition to Robbe-Grillet, Butor, and Simon, the novelists Robert Pinget, Claude Ollier, and Marguerite Duras. In fact, that generic term was coined not by Lindon but by the literary critic for *Le Monde* at the time, Émile Henriot, who was grasping for a label to define, or describe, this new novelistic approach.

I first met Lindon in 1952, a year after he published *Molloy*, and our link was Beckett. That year, in the Paris-based literary review *Merlin*, an equally impecunious quarterly headed by a towering, charismatic Scotsman, Alex Trocchi, I had written an article on Beckett, recommending him, with all the authority of my twenty-plus years, "to anyone interested in twentieth-century literature." Having heard a rumor that Beckett had written, before *Molloy*—a work that had overwhelmed me as much as it had Lindon—an earlier novel in English entitled *Watt*, I took a copy of *Merlin* #2, containing my piece on Beckett, together with a letter to the author, and asked Lindon if he would kindly forward the package to him.

Lindon received me in his austere office on the third floor of a four-story building on the rue Bernard-Palissy, just behind St.-Germain-des-Prés and around the corner from where I was living on the rue du Sabot. Minuit, the most austere and rigorous of publishers, was housed in a former bordello, the front door of which still bore a grille through which the erstwhile customers used to announce their names and bona fides before being admitted. Now, below the Éditions de Minuit sign, sat another, ENTREZ SANS SONNER—come in without ringing—proving to any do-gooder doubters that the business of the place had indeed changed.

I shall never forget our first meeting: dressed impeccably in a dark suit and equally dark tie, Lindon sat behind the same imposing desk where he remained enthroned for the next half-century. Casually dressed, to say the least, I felt not humiliated but certainly humble before this imposing presence, while he listened politely, but slightly impatiently, to my request. Never divining his own strong feelings, I went on at great length about the indelible impression that Beckett had made on me, as if I had to convince him of the man's importance. Little did I know that my impassioned peroration endeared me to Lindon for life. He promised to forward the material and, as we parted, graced me with a broad smile.

Three months later, having heard nothing from Beckett, I went to see Lindon a second time, essentially, I suspect, to make sure he had indeed kept his word. He assured me he had, but added: "Mr. Beckett is a very private person. And in fact he's been away from Paris for the past couple of months. I'm sure you'll hear from him one way or another."

A few weeks later, on a night that was dark and stormy, Beckett, unlike Godot, did indeed appear at my rue du Sabot digs, bearing the original typescript of *Watt*, which in due course the hardy *Merlin* group published. This led eventually to my third encounter with Lindon. *Merlin*, having expanded its horizon into the even more financially precarious realm of books, wanted to publish *Molloy* in English, while Lindon wanted to translate *Watt* into French. This time we were meeting not as acolyte to high priest but (almost) as equal to equal. Negotiating. For the occasion, I put on a tie (borrowed), a freshly laundered shirt, and my only jacket (a present from my father when I had set out for France four years before, and scarcely worn).

Despite all my sartorial efforts, I still had the feeling, as I entered Lindon's office, that I was at a distinct negotiating disadvantage. He was much older than I (or so I thought), he ran a real publishing house, in contrast to *Merlin*'s shoestring operation. I asked him what kind of an advance he expected for *Molloy*. He barely paused and said, "How about 50,000 francs?" That was more than what *Merlin* had in the bank—I know, since by then I had become a director—not to mention printers' debts of triple that amount. "And *Watt*," I said, "how much would you be willing to pay for the rights to that?" He looked at me with a straight face. "How about 50,000 francs?" he said. I searched for a smile, the trace of a smile, but found none. But there was an undeniable twinkle in his eye, one that I would observe a thousand times over the next half-century.

On the spot, we struck a deal: the only caveat I raised—no, humbly requested—was that Lindon not cash *Merlin*'s check for four days. "Why is that?" he asked, raising an eyebrow. "We're expecting an infusion of capital next week," I lied. I handed him our check for 50,000 francs, he handed me his for the same amount, which I rushed to deposit, for only when his cleared, I knew, would ours be honored. I thought I had pulled a fast one, but years later, Lindon teased: "That *Merlin* check," he said, "I want you to know I waited five days before depositing it." What I did not know at the time was that Minuit, almost as much as *Merlin*, was on the financial precipice. Thus Jérôme's Alphonse–Gaston gesture was far more generous than I had suspected.

Those early meetings cemented our relationship for life—a relationship both personal and professional. In my first job in publishing at George Braziller's, who was just branching out from his book club base to mainstream publishing, I read in 1957 a recent Minuit *succès de scandale*, Henri Alleg's *The Question*, a book that denounced the torture being inflicted on the Algerians by the French Army during the Algerian war. I told Braziller it would not sell—who in America was interested in a French colonial war?—but added that he should publish it anyway. To my surprise, he did. And to the surprise of us both, the book was soon on the *New York Times* best-seller list. But in France, Jérôme Lindon, far closer to the fire, was quickly embattled: harassed at work and at home, he saw his books seized, and he was indicted, under various sections and subsections of French law, no fewer than eighteen times.

He whose first and foremost love was literature, and above all the discovery of new talent, was nevertheless political in the purest sense of the term. Following hard on his publication of *The Question*, Lindon, despite the legal war being waged against him, was nevertheless instrumental in disseminating the "Manifesto of the 121"—121 French writers and artists against the war in Algeria. (At Grove Press where I then worked, we published, as an act of solidarity, the manifesto in *Evergreen Review*, though I'm sure 90 percent of our readers had no idea what we were protesting.) This retiring, self-effacing, seemingly disengaged man, who proclaimed himself nonpolitical, was unflinching in the face of repression. I once accused him—if that is the permissible term—of being far more engaged than he ever admitted. "No," he said, shaking his head, "it's simply that if one is lucky enough to live in a free country, to enjoy the extraordinary privilege of total freedom of expression, you have to speak out when that freedom is threatened." "In totalitarian countries," he added, "the first ones to be attacked are always the publishers, of both newspapers and books."

Over the next forty-nine years I never went to Paris without seeing Jérôme. Inevitably, we met in his office—that same immaculate space I had timorously visited in 1952, the only difference being that in the intervening years the shelves behind him and to his right slowly filled with the impressive results of his foresight and dedication. From there we would go to the Sybarite, a restaurant around the corner on the rue du Sabot, two doors down from where I had lived. It was a typical low-key, rustic Left Bank place, run by the owners, a husband and wife. Jérôme, who had his table, always ordered the same: *steak frites*, with a salad following, and Badoit water, then coffee. No wine. Ever. "But please," he would always insist, "you should have some." We would talk books, to a lesser degree politics, and in the later years, after Beckett had died, always about Beckett. That first lunch after Beckett's death, we—Lindon, my wife Jeannette, and I—tried to avoid the subject, but to no avail, and as we reminisced, jovially and joyously, tears began streaming down all our faces, to the consternation of the waiter and diners around us, I am sure, but to little or no embarrassment on any of our parts.

Our last lunch was this past October: same fare, same immediate connection as though no time had passed since that first meeting, almost half a century earlier. I remember remarking how little Jérôme had changed over the years. At his office, he did not climb the narrow circular staircase up which we inched gingerly: he bounded, doubtless wondering what was keeping us. At the restaurant, he talked enthusiastically about his latest discovery, whose first work he was about to publish; he worried about an author whose fourth novel he was expecting (would it be good? would it be up to his previous three?); he railed against the attempts to overturn *la loi Lang*—the law, named after the former minister of culture Jacques Lang, for which he had fought so long and hard, to prevent the discounting of books, which he saw as the death knell of the independent bookstores, on which he knew the fate of new voices depended.

As we left each other at the doorstep of Minuit, we fixed a date for the following month, to pursue a common project we had agreed to work on. When Jeannette wrote in November to confirm our date, we learned that Jérôme was out of the office, for an indeterminate period. He had had an operation, from which he was recovering, we were assured. When in early February my wife talked to Jérôme's daughter Irène, who was running the company in his absence, the date of his return still remained vague. Arriving in Paris on April 10 of this year, we were received immediately by Irène, who told us that her father was *au plus mal*—in terrible shape. What she did not tell us—because she could not, without betraying his strict instructions—was that he had died two days before. No notice was to be given of his death, he had mandated, until after his burial, which took place on Thursday the 12th.

True to himself to the end, this great publisher, this mentor to so many, remained in death what he had always been in life: discreet, forever staying out of the limelight, honest and courageous. Despite all his efforts to pass from this world discreetly, he could not prevent the outpouring of homages that filled the newspapers in the following days. He who had supported two generations of writers was eulogized by hundreds, from the president of France, Jacques Chirac, to the prime minister, Lionel Jospin, to writers, publishers, and friends from all corners of Europe. He was buried in the strictest privacy, in the Montparnasse cemetery, not far from his great friend Samuel Beckett.

Bonjour, Sam. Bonjour, Jérôme....

—June 21, 2001

24

SEAMUS HEANEY
ON THOMAS FLANAGAN

"URBANITY FLUNG LIKE a careless cloak across a murderous sword":
Tom Flanagan's relish for what he is describing in his characterization
of the young James Joyce's style is unmistakable and understandable.
His own style had a definite urbanity and panache, and while it would
be wrong to ascribe murderousness to the blade he wielded, there was
nevertheless a Toledo steel spring and edge to it. He was more like a
fencer with a foil than a combatant with a weapon, but you were
always aware that he could make a rent if he had to. Nobody was
more capable of glee and happy, intuitive enjoyment in the company
of friends, but his long familiarity with companies where the knives
were out meant that he knew how to take care of himself. "I was
proffered gossip, malice, and oblique, knife-edged anecdote," he says
at one point, speaking of the Dublin where he came to be so at home,
but something tells you that in the circumstances the visitor didn't
exactly quail.

It was appropriate, therefore, that the last thing he published in his
lifetime should have been in *The Irish Times*, a review of a history of
St. Patrick's Day where he was identified by the paper's literary editor
as "a novelist and scholar... currently working on a book about
Irish-American writers." And given his own deeply felt and deeply
pondered Irish-American identity (I can just hear a faint rattle of the

foil as I use that hackneyed phrase), it was equally appropriate that when he died in Berkeley five days after the review appeared in Dublin, he had submitted to *The New York Review of Books* a piece on William Kennedy.

The Kennedy essay was the last in a series on Irish-Americans that he was hoping to publish as a separate book. As he continued to write with his usual mordant appreciation about the works and pomps and personalities of Scott Fitzgerald, Eugene O'Neill, John Ford, and others, there was a sense of a life's work being completed. His 1959 study *The Irish Novelists, 1800–1850* not only rescued the work of Maria Edgeworth, Lady Morgan, John Banim, Gerard Griffin, and William Carleton from critical neglect, it turned the novelists themselves into vividly imagined figures and created a country of the mind as well as a field of study. Fifty years ago, after all, what are now called "Irish Studies" did not have any institutional existence in American (or Irish) universities, but once the Flanagan book appeared, it showed what was needed and how it should be done.

In the age of the New Critic, Tom was a history and biography man. There was, moreover, a touch of the artist about him. At the same time as he was doing his academic research, he was writing crime mysteries and gaining Ellery Queen awards. Here, indeed, was somebody whose narrative gifts and feel for the social and cultural conditions of nineteenth-century Ireland made him the artistic heir to the writers in question, a role which he would fulfill ever more copiously and confidently in the ensuing years with the publication of *The Year of the French* (1979), *The Tenants of Time* (1988), and *The End of the Hunt* (1994). These novels, covering the history of Ireland from the 1798 rebellion to the War of Independence and Civil War, have earned Flanagan a place in Irish literature alongside the writer friends he knew and loved: Frank O'Connor, Benedict Kiely, and others.

Yet the novelist who could imagine with total sympathy the mental and physical toils of an eighteenth-century Gaelic-speaking poet on the bog roads of Mayo began life with no great devotion to the old sod. Even though, as he tells us, "the words 'Ireland' and 'Irish'... had for me a special resonance, striking, somewhere within me, a faint clear bell," the pale shade of green which his father had retained from earlier immigrant Flanagans was paling "to the point of translucency" in his well-assimilated son. Graduating from "a most excellent college which had developed as a part of the New England Protestant tradition," he had gone on to study with Lionel Trilling at Columbia, and ended up teaching courses in the humanities program. And it was then that bells of Ireland, whose sound had once broken the hearts of the legendary children of Lir, began to ring in his ears with a new, commanding resonance.

Tom Flanagan amazed literary Dublin in the early Sixties by his encyclopedic knowledge of the history and topography of the country: the story goes that on his first taxi ride from the airport he was so immersed in Joyce that he could name the streets and buildings they passed en route to his hotel. He became something of a legend, so that when I eventually met him in Berkeley, where I taught for the year 1970–1971, I was ready to be in awe but found myself treated with great affection and would eventually feel like his literary foster child.

To begin with, the Flanagans took great care of us as a family when we landed. Jean was our chauffeur as we looked for an apartment and their house was a home away from home all that year. But as well as feeling total welcome on the domestic front, I was under the spell of Tom's strong Hibernocentric mind and imagination. It's no exaggeration to say that he reoriented my thinking. When I landed in California I was somebody who knew a certain amount of Irish literature and history, but my head was still basically wired up to Eng. Lit. terminals. I was still a creature of my undergraduate degree at Queen's University, Belfast. When I left, thanks mostly to Tom's brilliantly sardonic conversation, I was in the process of establishing new coordinates and had a far more conscious, far more charged-up sense of

Yeats and Joyce, for example, and of their whole Irish consequence. I was starting to see my situation as a "Northern poet" more in relation to the wound and the work of Ireland as a whole, and for that I shall be ever in his debt.

In the end, however, Tom was reckoning with the American side of his heritage. He had spent the last St. Patrick's weekend in New York where he met his agent, linked up with old friends from earlier days in Manhattan, with poets and diplomats in town from Dublin, and watched the parade from the balcony of the American Irish Historical Society's premises on Fifth Avenue. It was a lap of honor, and was probably understood as such by all concerned, since he had grown frailer in the previous year, after Jean's death, and in the words of Hopkins, "a heavenlier heart began."

Not that he ever lost any of his earthly powers. He was still the brilliant raconteur with a sense of humor as pungent as his sense of history. The great ironical intelligence never failed; he remained to the end as exhilaratingly capable of scorn as of merriment. He winced rather than winked at stupidity and generally kept us up to scratch by never himself falling below intellectual par. Whether you met him in the snug of Doheny & Nesbitt's civil public house among the conversational cutters and thrusters or in his home in the tonic company of Jean and his daughters, you came away the better for it.

In Ireland, we looked forward to his annual visits. For the best part of forty years, he and the family came to Dublin, and during those migrant weeks he took to the country and the country took to him. He was like a bard on his circuits. In fact, when *The Irish Times* called him a scholar, they could well have been using the word in the older Hiberno-English sense, meaning somebody not only learned but ringed around with a certain *draoícht*, or magical aura, at once a man of the people and a solitary spirit, a little separate but much beloved.

Since that first meeting in 1970 I felt, like the typical Irish son, closest at our times of greatest silence and remoteness: walking the fields of County Leitrim where the 1798 insurgents had been cut down in the Battle of Ballinamuck, climbing down a cliff path on the Antrim coast where Roger Casement would have wished to be buried, gazing out along the stony pier at Portland Bill on the south coast of England where the Fenian prisoners had done hard labor a century before. "And there was nothing between us there," as I once wrote of my own father, "That might not still be happily ever after."

—January 25, 2002

25

LARRY MCMURTRY
ON KEN KESEY

THE MINUTE KEN KESEY walked into the Stegner Fellowship Class in Fiction, at Stanford in September of 1960, he made it plain that he meant to be the stud-duck—in today's parlance, the alpha male. Wallace Stegner was away that year. Malcolm Cowley took the fellowship class for the fall semester; Frank O'Connor taught us in the spring. There were about a dozen of us assembled when Ken made his entrance, and he was hardly the only competitive person in the room. Like stoats in a henhouse, we were poised to rend and tear. Except for the lovely Joanna Ostrow, protected by her elegant Afghan—a dog, not a Mujahideen—we were all young males. Ken plopped himself down at the right hand of Mr. Cowley and got set to read what turned out to be the first chapters of *One Flew Over the Cuckoo's Nest*. This was stud-duckery indeed, for at least two members of the class, Christopher Koch of Tasmania and Peter Beagle, youthful pride of Brooklyn, had already published books and might be thought to have a better claim to read. My own first novel was in press; Jim (James Baker) Hall and Gurney Norman from Kentucky, Dave Godfrey from Canada, and Robin Macdonald from Scotland—who was soon to marry the lovely Joanna—all had arrived with books or parts of books that would in time be published. Mr. Cowley, still an editorial force at Viking—he had helped reel in *On the Road*—was keeping a paternal eye on Peter Beagle, also a Viking author (as Kesey soon would be). We were primed, and we were anything but slackers: when I lost count in the Nineties the class had produced about sixty books.

So who was this lumberjack, a figure so Paul Bunyanesque that I would not have been surprised to see Babe, the Blue Ox, plod in behind him? When he took out his pages, casually assuming the first position, there was a momentary bristle of egos, powerful enough to cause Malcolm Cowley, seasoned literary warrior that he was, to turn off his hearing aid. I believe he kept it turned off the whole semester, a tactic that allowed him to indulge in comfortable fantasies about how nice and how well educated we were. (I think this because in an interview given years later about our by then famous class he said that I had read all of French literature and had written a thesis on the naughty poetry of John Wilmot, Earl of Rochester: in fact I was still struggling through *Madame Bovary* and have never written a word about Rochester.)

Ken cleared his throat, we bristled, and then relaxed and decided to be bemused, rather than annoyed. Why? Because Ken Kesey was a very winning man, and he won us. In Robertson Davies's *Fifth Business*, Mrs. Dempster, the minister's wife, is caught in the bushes with a tramp; when her husband asked why she did it she said, "...He was very civil, 'Masa. And he wanted it so badly." As with Mrs. Dempster and the tramp, so with Ken's determination to be the center of attention: he wanted it so badly; so we let him get away with it, and, with one tragic exception, he kept getting away with a good deal of it for the next forty-one years, until the day came when he couldn't, when it stopped.

On the ground at Stanford in 1960, we blithely let Ken get away with murder, but then refused, perversely, to let Peter Beagle, who read second, get away with French, the language in which he had written large hunks of his second novel. We attacked this book so savagely that Peter, from then on, retired behind a copy of *The New York*

Times, where he peacefully snoozed out the year. We soon repented of our brutality and attempted to make it up with Peter by finding him girls, a coals to Newcastle sort of thing, since he had already secured, on his own, more girls than the rest of us put together could locate. Every time I crossed the Camino Real, in Palo Alto or Menlo Park, there would be Peter, zipping along on his motor scooter, traveling from lady to lady. Thanks to his habit of feminizing the universe—which couldn't have hurt him with the ladies—it was a while before we figured out that the Jenny he talked about constantly was his motor scooter, not another girlfriend.

Most of the fellowship class lived on the Peninsula, but Chris Koch and I preferred San Francisco; we drove down to Stanford twice a week in my jalopy. Chris was already deep into his obsession with South Asian politics, the fruit of which was *The Year of Living Danger-ously*. After a class or two, Ken, the stud-duck, invited us to his duck pond, the famous Stanford Bohemia, Perry Lane, preferred residence of advanced spirits since the time of Thorstein Veblen. To me Perry Lane looked not unlike cheap graduate student housing anywhere; similar hotbeds of low-rent revolt could have been found in Iowa City, Ann Arbor, or New Haven. But Perry Lane meant much to those who lived there, so much that when it was bulldozed in 1963 to make way for pricier structures Faye Kesey, Ken's quiet, shy wife, was so frenzied by the destruction of her habitat that she chopped up a piano with an axe. Despite this moment of wildness Faye was the unwob-bling pivot and the unmeltable glue that kept a very complex domes-tic situation from spinning into fragments. She and Ken, country kids, married young; at the time of his death in November 2001 they had been married forty-five years. I don't know a wife I respect more.

What was evident from my few visits to Perry Lane was that Ken already had a court; and he kept a court. Courtiers might leave, be chased off, die; but there would be replacements. The Merry Prank-sters, once they evolved, functioned as a floating court. There were always a few good friends who were not of the court: Wendell Berry, Robert Stone, myself. To enjoy the strength of Ken's friendship it was necessary to separate him, for a time, from the court, because if the court was sitting he would play to it, meddle with it, charm it, vex it.

The Stegner class soon mellowed, as we became friends. By the time Frank O'Connor took over there was no need to turn off hearing aids. If a dull or vapid piece got read in class we didn't savage it, as we had Peter Beagle's hopeful French. If there was savaging to be done, Mr. O'Connor did it. I was denounced for having read Smollett, a Scotch author evidently intolerable to Irishmen. Ken continued to read chapters of *Cuckoo's Nest* as he wrote them. I liked it; it was clear that he had a powerful story going. I think most of the class felt the same way, though we weren't quite 100 percent seduced. When the hero, Randle P. McMurphy, appears, Ken, the stud-duck, has McMurphy introduce himself to the loonies on the ward with a challenge. McMurphy speaking:

> "This busy man Mr. Harding, is he the bull goose loony?" He looks at Billy with one eye and Billy nods his head up and down real fast; Billy's tickled with all the attention he's getting.
>
> "Then you tell Bull Goose Loony Harding that R. P. McMurphy is waiting to see him and that this hospital ain't big enough for the two of us. I'm accustomed to being top man. I been a bull goose catskinner for every gyppo logging operation in the Northwest and bull goose gambler all the way from Korea, was even bull goose pea weeder on that pea farm at Pendleton—so I figure if I'm bound to be a loony, then I'm bound to be a stompdown dadgum good one. Tell this Harding that he either meets me man to man or he's a yaller skunk and better be outta town by sunset."

In class, with him performing it, this works; on the page, without the author's voice, it flattens a little. Ken's reaching for an old vernacular, the frontier yarn, which sometimes works and sometimes doesn't. By giving a bravura reading I suspect Ken was trying to slide us past a big question, which is how probable is it that Randle P. McMurphy would be on that loony ward. Ken attempts to finesse this by having McMurphy's eventually victorious enemy, Nurse Ratched, explain that he probably thinks the ward offers an easier life than the prison farm. Coming at a time when more and more of America's young, in their struggle to defy authority, were cracking up, *Cuckoo's Nest* was a fresh-sounding antiauthoritarian fable, a big advance over the *Snake Pit* model of mental-ward fiction. Little wonder that it was popular.

Somewhere at Stanford there were poets, under the stern tutelage of Yvor Winters, but I never met one. The Age of Criticism was in its twilight; Winters was one of its last resplendent figures. He must have kept the poets in sweatshops, training them to be fanatical metricists. I doubt that he wanted them rubbing shoulders with a bunch of wormy fiction writers.

Soon enough the year ended, and the Stegner class scattered to the four winds. Thirty years passed before I saw Chris Koch again, but we kept in touch. *Cuckoo's Nest* was soon published, to much acclaim; I had only occasionally news of the Keseys. There seemed to be a cultural revolution cranking up, but few tremors of it had reached Rice, where I was teaching.

The tremors struck Houston on a fine spring morning in 1964, when Ken called and said they were on a bus and were coming to see me; little did I know that the breeze of the future was about to blow through my quiet street. A very few minutes later there it came, the bus whose motto was FURTHER, and whose occupants probably indulged in a bit of drugs, sex, and rock-and-roll, as well as almost continuous movie-making and a great deal of rubber-necking as they sped across America. There were Pranksters sitting on top, waving at my startled neighbors with day-glo hands. Ken was playing a flute.

Living legend Neal Cassady—who had inspired both *On the Road* and Allen Ginsberg's beautiful poem "The Green Automobile"—was at the wheel. My son James, aged two, was sitting in the yard in his diapers when the bus stopped and a naked lady ran out and grabbed him. It was Stark Naked (later shortened to Stark), who, being temporarily of a disordered mind, mistook him for her little girl. James, in diapers, had no objection to naked people, and the neighbors, most of them staid Republicans, took this event in stride: it was the Pranksters who were shocked.

To that point virtually every moment of the trip had been filmed, but there was Stark, wearing not a stitch, and the Pranksters were not camera-ready. I soon coaxed Stark inside, where she rapidly took seven showers. Neal Cassady came in, said not a word, went to sleep, and didn't stir until the next day, when it was time to leave.

The Pranksters, at this stage only on the road a few days, were extremely appealing. They were young, they were beautiful, they were fresh, and they were friendly. My neighbors at once adopted them; soon cookies were being baked and doughnuts fetched. I was glad to see the Keseys but also nervous. Who knew what Stark would do when she finished taking showers? The Kens, Kesey and Babbs, parked a mysterious jar in my kitchen cabinet—I didn't investigate but I suspect we'd all be just getting out of jail now if that jar had fallen into official hands.

I never got a solid count of Pranksters on that visit, but there were enough of them to cover most of the floor space in my small house. In the night, despite my vigilance, Stark slipped away, having no idea what city or state she was in. The police found her and at once popped her into what Carl, the Billy Bob Thornton character in *Slingblade*, calls the "nervous hospital."

In the morning the Pranksters—who would soon be advising America to tear up their schedules and embrace spontaneity and disorder—remembered that they had a schedule: Ken's book party for

Sometimes a Great Notion was happening in New York in only a few days. They lingered long enough for Ken to teach James his first word —"ball"—before hurrying off, Cassady again at the wheel. (In the last decade or so, touring the Northwest with his band, James has seen more of our old friends the Keseys than I have.)

This smooth departure left me, my lawyer, and Stark's lovelorn boyfriend to extract Stark from the nervous hospital. It didn't help that all our first names were Larry, but, in time, we got her out. The boyfriend was screamed at and driven off. My lawyer advised me to get her on the next plane to San Francisco, which happened to be the red-eye. In the airport, with several hours to wait, I asked her if she was hungry and she said she might eat a grilled cheese sandwich. She ate $78 worth, a big meal for an airport restaurant in 1964. As she munched she slowly regained a measure of her sanity, enough of it that when her boyfriend straggled up, the picture of woe, she meekly took his hand and got on the plane.

Three years passed. I was in the process of giving James a fifth birthday party when the bus whose motto was FURTHER pulled up at my door again. I had given James a small log fort for his birthday; it was set up in the back yard. Soon birthday party guests and Prankster children, of which there seemed to be a good number, merged in a wild melee. The confusion was so great that when I took the party guests home I forgot a little boy; he was found, hours later, sitting quietly in the darkened fort.

In the morning I came down to find another little boy sitting on my kitchen counter, digging Cheerios out of a box and eating them by the fistful. For a moment I feared I had forgotten yet another party guest, but this little boy was young Jed Kesey, who offered me a Cheerio. The image of the little boy eating Cheerios out of his fist has stayed with me to this day. Jed Kesey was killed in a car wreck while on a winter trip with his wrestling team in 1984; that's the tragic exception, of which more later.

In 1967 the Pranksters were still beautiful, but they were far from fresh. They looked mushed, crushed, smushed, as bedraggled as World War I aviators who had just managed to get their Sopwith Camels safely on the ground. The neighbors were deeply concerned; even more cookies were baked, even more doughnuts fetched. On this visit the neighbors were particularly taken with a small man named Hermit, who was said to live on honey and roadkill. His honey was certainly excellent, but the roadkill in that neighborhood must have seemed paltry, I'm afraid.

At this juncture the ideal of companionship seemed to be cracking under the strain of travel—and of Ken's celebrity. Ken Babbs, a very able man, was, I believe, getting a little tired of always being second in command. Mutiny threatened. Out of steam physically, the Pranksters had begun to pin their hopes on the spirit. I remember having a hot argument with the Prankster *nomenklatura* about a weighty piece of metaphysical (in the bad sense) slush called *The Urantia Book*, the manuscript of which was said to have been deposited in a Chicago bank vault by an alien. I wasn't buying the alien, or the book either.

The next time I saw the Keseys they were living in La Honda, high in the fogs above Stanford. Both Hunter S. Thompson in *Hell's Angels* and Tom Wolfe in *The Electric Kool-Aid Acid Test* have given full accounts of the Keseys in La Honda, so I'll be brief. I went there with Jane Burton, a Texan with impeccable Perry Lane credentials. Jane said we should take food, so we took a carful, which was immediately inhaled. Faye hurried out to warn me to keep a close eye on my car—people had begun to cannibalize any vehicle that moved in hopes of getting one of the several rusting hulks scattered around running again. Ken was in a work shack, editing the many thousands of feet of bus film. Mountain Girl (later, as Mrs. Jerry Garcia, the matriarch of the Grateful Dead) was much in evidence; though it might be more accurate to say that much of Mountain Girl was in evidence. She was scantily clad.

Then Ken became a fugitive; the Pranksters went to Mazatlán, from whence Ken sent me a journal which seems to have passed through several hands before reaching me. I believe Tom Wolfe saw it, and was soon working on his brilliant reconstruction of the whole strange Grail Quest on which the Pranksters and others were leading the Flower Children—a quest not without victims. At La Honda the happy dream of Pranksterism had turned to nightmare, and, still to come, were the Acid Tests—big dances or parties at which the Kool-Aid was sometimes laced with LSD and other provocative substances —in my staid opinion a thoroughly bad idea.

I saw little of the Keseys from the mid-Sixties to the late Seventies, though there was one nice visit in Houston, no bus, just Ken and Faye; a few years later Ken and I did an evening together at Northlake College, outside of Dallas, after which I took him to my home in Archer City for a visit. On April 10, 1979, Wichita Falls had been hit by a devastating tornado, which killed nearly fifty people and destroyed thousands of homes, my brother's included. I took Ken over to the site; by then the debris had been scraped away, leaving thousands of bare foundations, with the naked plumbing sticking up. Even more startling were the naked trees, from which all vestiges of bark had been sucked. Ken said little at the time but the sight of the naked plumbing and the naked trees resulted, fifteen years later, in a kind of happening called "Twister," on the theme of ecological doom, that the Kens and perhaps others had cooked up.

On the way up from Dallas Ken told me a story, which became, for me, emblematic of his new working methods. He had been visiting Hugh Romney, known as Wavy Gravy, at the Pig Farm in Los Angeles when, while taking a walk, he came face to face with an immense and angry boar. Ken reasoned that the boar recognized him as a meat-eater and was prepared to eliminate him at once. Ken quickly resolved to convert to vegetarianism; the boar intuited and accepted this somewhat opportunistic conversion and let him pass in peace.

When I was three some evil cousins threw me into our pig pen, where, stuck in the muck, I was for several minutes the cynosure of a number of unfriendly porcine eyes. I'll believe a lot about pigs, but not that they can intuit incipient vegetarianism. I said nothing. Finally Ken giggled. I don't think he expected me to believe that story; I don't think he even wanted me to. He was just beginning to craft it, orally, and the more resistant the listener was, the more it suited his immediate purpose.

His ultimate purpose was harder to guess at. There began to be shamanistic elements in his stories, elements whose meaning might not be revealed for several years. When Ken talked, I listened. He might say ten nonsensical things in a row and then come out with a perception of genius. I'm sure he told and retold the story of his confrontation with Wavy Gravy's pig; he probably somewhere convinced an audience that Wavy Gravy had once owned a very civilized pig who was a good judge of character. In fact the pig was *no* judge of character; Ken duped him. I don't know how long his vow of vegetarianism was to stay in effect, but on this visit he tucked, without apparent guilt, into a couple of hefty steaks.

Ken had by this time moved his family to the farm near Pleasant Hill, Oregon, where they still live. There were soon to be more consequences of the broken vow, as the group entered what in Prankster mythos is called the time of Hamburger's Revenge. Hamburger was the family bull, I guess; I prefer to think Hamburger may have been a steer because bulls are not really meant for the table; steers are tender, bulls are tough. But, tough or tender, Hamburger got eaten, after which there was disorder in the heavens, with Lear-like confusions and alarums.

I'll try to give the common-sense version: Faye had had enough. Ken was a very famous man in an Age of Groupies. He reminded me at times of LBJ. Faye thus had a lot to contend with—Lady Bird Johnson, in a different context, had the same thing to contend with. Faye's forbearance was great—but it wasn't total; neither was Lady Bird's.

Ken, ever boyish himself, refused to register the fact that women aged. In his mind's eye I believe he saw all women as being about the same age: young, as Faye had been when they married. But more than twenty years had passed; it was the groupies, not Faye, who were evergreen. Ken didn't see jealousy of any sort as a problem. How could it be a problem? So Faye finally detonated, and a just thunder was heard far across the land. Courtiers and groupies fled. The marriage went on.

There was, also, a major scare. Ken was in his hometown of Springfield, Oregon, on his way to see his brother, when he crossed a long-defunct railroad track. But the track had been reactivated and a train hit them. Ken, his daughter, Shannon, his son, Jed, and his dog, Pretzels, were in the car. Dog and daughter were not much hurt, but Jed appeared to be dead. Ken, through a combination of will, prayer, and mouth-to-mouth resuscitation, coaxed Jed back from the Shadows. I don't know the exact dates but I think his father's refusal to give him up gained Jed about fifteen years. Then, in 1984, the Shadows pulled him in.

In the Eighties I saw the Keseys only sporadically, once or twice in Oregon, in New York, Washington, here and there. When Ken traveled with Faye he was calm and kindly; when he traveled without her he was the wild boy from the hills. He worked up a little folk story his grandmother had told him: "Little Trickster the Squirrel Meets Big Double the Bear." He began to perform this story with orchestras, and on the radio, and at shindigs of all sorts. He got interested in Alaska and, in 1992, published his third novel, *Sailor's Song*—a good novel, too.

The three novels, published over a thirty-year span, seem to me to be roughly of a piece, in quality. But the best writing, for my money, is in the second book, *Sometimes a Great Notion*. This:

> Along the western slopes of the Oregon Coastal Range...come look: the hysterical crashing of tributaries as they merge into the Wakonda Auga River...

The first little washes flashing like thick rushing winds through sheep sorrel and clover, ghost fern and nettle, shearing, cutting...forming branches. Then, through bearberry and salmonberry, blueberry and blackberry, the branches crashing into creeks, into streams. Finally, in the foothills, through tamarack and sugar pine, shittim bark and silver spruce—and the green and blue mosaic of Douglas fir—the actual river falls five hundred feet...and look: opens out upon the fields.

Metallic at first, seen from the highway down through the trees, like an aluminum rainbow, like a slice of alloy moon. Closer, becoming organic, a vast smile of water with broken and rotting pilings jagged along gums, foam clinging to the lips....

I quoted that at length to get to the metaphor, always the heart of Ken Kesey's purest gift in prose or conversation. *Sometimes a Great Notion*, the story of the Stamper family, is as much a realistic novel of manners as *The Forsyte Saga*, and, for that very reason, always seemed to irritate Ken, although it is the book in which he does the most with his gift and his heritage. Those of us who insisted through his showman years on thinking of him as a writer were not wrong.

Certainly, though, he got more interested in performance. What Ken would have been happiest doing, it seems to me, would have been to run a traveling medicine show. I can see him trucking on, with a mule and a monkey, a wagon gaily painted, a juggler, a magician, perhaps a dancing girl, and himself as master of ceremonies, driving around America, adding a little vividness, a splash of color, to the lives of people in remote communities. The Pranksters at their best and bounciest were, in effect, a rolling medicine show.

I saw Ken for the last time in 1995. Sara Ossana, the daughter of my screenwriting partner, Diana Ossana, was in the Northwest wing looking at colleges. Diana and I tagged along, as well as Sara's then boyfriend Matt. Finished in Portland, we dropped down to see the

Keseys for a day. Ken immediately captured the kids. He took them into his editing room and let them watch a film of *Twister*, the ecological doom-story that he claimed was the result of seeing all that naked plumbing and those skinned trees in Wichita Falls. Sara and Matt were at first bemused. Why were these old guys dressed up like characters in *The Wizard of Oz*? Why were they singing "They Called the Wind Maria," only with different words? But then Ken took them into a big shed and let them sit in the bus—that bus whose motto is FURTHER. He stayed with them a long time, telling them his adventures. The bus was hardly a thing of their generation. They didn't know exactly why they were sitting in it, but, as he talked, it became, in the teen words of the time, an awesome experience, sitting with this winning man in his wild Picasso bus that had somehow, before their time, been a bright thread in the fabric of American life.

For most of the time we were there, Ken kept on rapping with the kids. Faye showed us Jed's grave, which was not far behind the house. A llama was moping about, lending this lovely Oregon pastoral a bleak Andean look. I missed the dead boy, and I felt misgivings. Families must put their dead where they want them to be; but there is, still, an argument to be made for cemeteries and Rilke has made it immortally if complexly in the great poem "Requiem for a Friend," which he wrote in response to the death of his friend the artist Paula Modershon-Becker, after childbirth in 1907. Excerpts can't do this poem justice but a stanza or two can at least suggest some of the questions it raises about the distancing that must go on between the living and the dead:

> *I have my dead, and I have let them go,*
> *and was amazed to see them so contented,*
> *so soon at home in being dead, so cheerful,*
> *so unlike their reputation. Only you*
> *return; brush past me, loiter, try to knock*
> *against something, so that the sound reveals*

> *your presence. Oh don't take from me what I*
> *am slowly learning....*

And:

> *For this is wrong, if anything is wrong:*
> *not to enlarge the freedom of a love*
> *with all the inner freedom one can summon.*
> *We need, in love, to practice only this:*
> *letting each other go. For holding on*
> *comes easily; we do not need to learn it.*

And, finally:

> *For somewhere there is an ancient enmity*
> *between our daily life and the great work.*
> *Help me, in saying it, to understand it.*
> *Do not return. If you can bear to, stay*
> *dead with the dead. The dead have their own tasks....* [1]

These are my memories of things that mostly happened long ago. I have not done a necrology but I think most of the Stegner Fellowship class of 1960 is creaking on, in Australia and Scotland, in Canada and Kentucky, in California and Texas. Sad it is—sad—that our lumberjack is gone; but so it is. In Oregon now father has been laid by son, the two of them gone FURTHER indeed, into that mystery that neither *The Urantia Book* nor any other can explain.

—December 5, 2002

---

1. The quotes are from Stephen Mitchell's beautiful translation, to be found in *Ahead of All Parting: The Selected Poetry and Prose of Rainer Maria Rilke* (Modern Library, 1995).

26

BRAD LEITHAUSER
ON ANTHONY HECHT

I CAUGHT MY final glimpses of Anthony Hecht in Tennessee last July. This was at the Sewanee Writers Conference, where he was a guest of honor. I was one of a panel of five writers and editors come to pay tribute. Each panel member was to present a brief talk about Hecht's work. It was a task turned all the more imposing by having the object of our remarks, the eighty-one-year-old poet himself, seated in the audience. The look he trained upon us was—to my eyes—neither encouraging nor censorious but simply, deeply thoughtful. Though Hecht had as healthy an appetite for acclaim as most writers, he was typically far less tolerant than most of "damned nonsense"—a favorite phrase of his. The shared sentiment on the panel was that observations had better be defensible and all facts correct.

Today, when poets tend to feel less appreciated and less well read than novelists or journalists, one will frequently hear somebody praised because he or she "really loves poetry." This was damned nonsense in Hecht's view—why should anybody be commended for this? Poetry was the apex of the art, the sum and summit; it was the true stuff. You found in Hecht neither that apologetic diffidence nor that insular smugness, with its fierce pride in small numbers, so common among poets.

At Sewanee, I gave him a number of those close covert inspections reserved for cherished friends whose health has been shaky. He'd suffered various medical trials and scares over recent years and had almost died not long before of heart problems. The poet I saw at Sewanee looked solider than I'd imagined. But as it turned out, those July days in Tennessee were a sort of sunlit valediction, for it was shortly after his return home to Washington, D. C., that he received the diagnosis of advanced lymphoma that was his death sentence. He died on October 20.

I left Sewanee with two impressions. The first was purely literary: having entered his eighties, Hecht was still at the top of his powers. On the evening after our panel, he gave a reading—the last public reading of his life—and introduced work completed only in recent months: rich and delicate poems, all the old music freshly intact.[1]

The second impression may surprise those acquainted with Hecht only on the page: I was struck by the charm and frequency of his laughter. Hecht's poetry is well known for its bleak subjects, for a grimness that often veers into gruesomeness. He created some of the most harrowing images I've met in poems: the half-decapitated soldier in "Venetian Vespers," the live burials of "'More Light! More Light!'" and "The Short End," the flaying in "Behold the Lilies of the Field," the crowded gas chamber of "Rites and Ceremonies." "The Deodand," which closes with an image of a bedizened, perfumed, dismembered prisoner of war, holds the distinction of being the most excruciatingly violent poem I know. But at Sewanee I was heartened to hear again and again—sometimes from an adjoining table, sometimes from an adjoining room—the characteristically low, resounding laugh of that man whose poems occasionally descended from their elevated heights for an erudite, atrocious pun: "civilization and its discothèques," "truth and booty," "*mens sana* in men's sauna." He was somebody who relished good company and good conversation.

---

[1] For my fuller discussion of Hecht's poetry, see my "Poet for a Dark Age," *The New York Review*, February 13, 1986.

That laugh of his was a true belly laugh: it emerged from the core of the man.

In the spring semester of 1973, Hecht came to Harvard as a visiting professor and I enrolled in his poetry-writing class. I understood quickly that I had stumbled into the classroom of a master—a man who was erudite, funny, intuitive, and, in the critical business of tendering advice to undergraduates, self-effacing. What took longer to clarify was that I had found something of a lifelong friend and guide. I was nineteen.

The relationship of literary mentor and apprentice creates its own set of idiosyncratic complexities. A number of these were sensitively explored in Alec Wilkinson's recent *My Mentor: A Young Man's Friendship with William Maxwell.* (As it happens, Hecht was a huge admirer of Maxwell's, who slowly produced novels while busy editing fiction at *The New Yorker.* Contemporary fiction was of limited appeal to Hecht—his fiction-writing peers excited him far less than his fellow poets but he loved unreservedly Maxwell's understated midwestern novels.) Even the greatest of teachers might know nothing of their students, who may be enlivened and transformed across a cavernous lecture hall. The mentor's relationship is something else again, an imbalanced but reciprocal give-and-take.

An initial search of my filing cabinet has turned up some eighty-six letters and postcards from Hecht, who, shortly after that spring semester of 1973, became Tony to me. Once he left Harvard, we wrote to each other. Outside my family, Tony became my first reader. He found time to write to me, and to comment on my poems, while in England, Italy, Austria. I mailed off whatever I was working on—and waited nervously for his usually prompt replies. The nervousness wasn't needless or misplaced, for he could be a stern judge. Some twenty-seven years after receiving a particularly exacting letter, I still shudder when I remember that the last line of one of my stanzas was "metrically outrageous," and that one of my neologisms suggested "pet dragons who are trained to light people's cigarettes." To look through those letters after his death is to be overwhelmed by the man's kindness. He was a born encourager of the most useful sort: he had suggestions to propose. He thought hard about how this or that struggling poem might be wrested into presentability.

In time, I began teaching writing classes myself—and marveled all the more at the care and effort Tony was willing to expend on someone else's work. Anybody who has ever taught a writing class knows how feelings of duty, professional pride, guilt, an urge to cultivate goodwill, and perhaps a raw desire to hold on to a job may combine to induce lengthy and enthusiastic commentary on apprentice work. And anyone who has ever taught a writing class would instantly recognize in Tony's letters an intellectual and imaginative effort extending beyond all such calls to duty, pride, guilt, and the rest. I've met a number of younger poets similarly touched by how unstinting Tony Hecht was when they were beginning their careers.

In many ways, he and I held on to the roles we began with. Decades after I'd stepped out of his classroom, we regularly recreated that classroom. As time went on, I saw far less of him than I would have wished—we lived thousands of miles apart for a number of years—but when we did get together we would often hold informal two-person seminars. He'd ask me to suggest poems I wanted to discuss. I remember separate afternoons devoted to Shakespeare, Donne, Hopkins, Yeats, Ransom, Auden.... He had a rare gift for untangling complexities, especially with Auden, whose poetry eventually inspired his longest book, a critical study called *The Hidden Law: The Poetry of W. H. Auden.* But some of our happiest moments were the result of a carefully arrived at, shared incomprehension. We both loved Ransom's "Vision by Sweetwater," but what exactly was the poem about? Built into such a relationship was a careful psychological distance. Given the central role he played in my life and in my wife's life (he and his wife were godparents to our older daughter), you might have expected more intimate confidences. But much of what I know about the darker aspects of Hecht's past—his unhappy first marriage, his hospitalization for depression, his traumatic experiences during the Second World War, culminating in extensive involvement with survivors of Flossenburg, the Nazi death camp—was derived from mutual friends or from published interviews.[2] He talked rarely of such things, and I didn't press him. It seemed his poems, calculated and tormented, said what needed to be said.

He always seemed a little taken aback when—as occasionally happened—I would challenge him on a small matter: the interpretation of a line of poetry, a prosodic distinction, the source of a quotation. For a moment, he would look startled and vaguely affronted; then, for another moment, thoughtful, as he mulled over the proposed emendation; and then pleased, for he enjoyed spirited debate. The very last time I saw him we argued the pros and cons of Frost's dictum "No tears in the writer, no tears in the reader." (I was in support, Hecht in opposition.)

Prosody was a lifelong interest of Tony's and many of our discussions turned on minute issues of meter and rhyme. He took quiet but deep satisfaction in knowing that he'd written a matchless sestina, "The Book of Yolek." One of the most strict and elaborate of all poetic forms, whose pattern of six end-words marches inflexibly and repetitively from start to finish, sestinas are all but impossible to write. Hecht's is the most moving sestina I've ever read—more so even than Elizabeth Bishop's or W.H. Auden's. If I could keep only one Hecht poem, it might be this one.

"The Book of Yolek"—which honors a little boy, "who wasn't a day over five years old," swallowed up by the Nazi death camps—

---

2. For some especially gripping accounts, see *Anthony Hecht in Conversation with Philip Hoy* (Between the Lines, 1999). I would highlight one sentence from Hecht's wartime reminiscences: "There is much about this I have never spoken about, and never will."

encapsulates a number of Hecht hallmarks: formal ease; a juxtaposing of the pleasurable and the painful, the luxurious and the necessitous; a sense of a carefully graduated, growing menace; and, at the close, an unblinking look into the infernal. The opening stanza about Yolek's life before his family is arrested is a pastoral idyll:

> *The dowsed coals fume and hiss after your meal*
> *Of grilled brook trout, and you saunter off for a walk*
> *Down the fern trail, it doesn't matter where to,*
> *Just so you're weeks and worlds away from home,*
> *And among midsummer hills have set up camp*
> *In the deep bronze glories of declining day.*

In the ideal sestina—and this comes pretty close to ideal—every one of the six end-words will make a meaningful journey by the poem's close. The poem is like a short theatrical play, in which half a dozen passengers in a closed train compartment begin to speak and interact; the laws of dramatic economy would seem to insist that each must have his or her revelatory moment. In "The Book of Yolek," each of the end-words deepens, darkens. The delicious campfire meal of stanza one becomes a "meal of bread and soup" at the Home for Jewish Children; the sauntering walk down the fern trail turns into a walk in close formation; the "to" of "doesn't matter where to" changes into a numeral tattoo; the camper's fondly recalled home yields to a prisoner's "long home," and the holiday camp to a concentration camp; finally, the "bronze glories of declining day" inevitably lead us to Judgment Day.

It wasn't until the dusk of Tennyson's career—the late nineteenth century—that emerging audio technology allowed poets to record their poems, and not until the twentieth century that this became a common practice. Many imperishable voices have perished.

It's comforting to think that there are tapes and disks of Hecht's readings, for it would have been a great loss if this particular voice—quite an idiosyncratic voice—had vanished. His was a middle-of-the-Atlantic accent, though located far closer to the English than the American shore. Given his background—he was born in New York City, and spent much of his adult life in Rochester—his voice was clearly a willed and self-designed creation: a deliberative and pointedly cultured, a plummy and yet cleanly enunciated deployment of well-rounded tones.

The last time I heard that voice was not long before he died. Tony had been undergoing chemotherapy treatments, with ravaging results. Given the painful range of physical ailments afflicting him over the years, he was a remarkably stoical man. This was the only occasion I ever heard him complain at any length about medical problems—and the form of his complaint was touchingly revealing. He explained that the difficulties of the chemotherapy were twofold. There was, first, a great deal of physical discomfort, much of it lingering. Second, and more important, there was a resultant loss of energy and concentration. For the first time in his adult life, he lamented, he found himself unable to read anything of length or complexity. In addition, the treatments had slowed and disjointed his thinking—and meanwhile I, on the other end of the phone, was noting how beautifully articulate he contrived to be even while complaining about his inarticulateness.

Shortly after his death, while I was sorting through his letters, the word *noble* sprang to mind, with a ring of rightness to it. It's not a word I'd think to apply to many of the people I've been closest to—not a word, probably, most of them would wish to see applied. But with all its old-fashioned connotations, its echoes of the gentlemanly and the mannerly, the high-minded and the honor-bound, *noble* seemed perfectly to evoke my departed friend, whose greatest nobility lies in the seven volumes of poetry he so meticulously assembled.

That work was both painful and painstaking. And yet within it Tony often managed, usually by unexpected psychological pathways, to locate and to extol some rare natural wonder, some light-enkindled joy. If a well-made poem is a regimented attempt, against all odds, to safeguard against time some important facet of oneself, I'm struck, surveying those seven volumes, at how much of himself, both the darkness and the light, Anthony Hecht succeeded in preserving. At how much, even now, remains.

—December 2, 2004

27

OLIVER SACKS
ON FRANCIS CRICK

I

I READ THE famous "double helix" letter by James Watson and Francis Crick in *Nature* when it was published in 1953—I was an undergraduate at Oxford then, reading physiology and biochemistry. I would like to say that I immediately saw its tremendous significance, but this was not the case for me or, indeed, for most people at the time.

It was only in 1962, when Francis Crick came to talk at Mount Zion Hospital in San Francisco, where I was interning, that I started to realize the vast implications of the double helix. Crick's talk at Mount Zion was not on the configuration of DNA but on the work he had been doing with the molecular biologist Sidney Brenner to determine how the sequence of DNA bases could specify the amino acid sequence in proteins. They had just shown, after four years of intense work, that the translation involved a three-nucleotide code. This was itself a discovery no less momentous than the discovery of the double helix.

But Crick's mind was always moving forward, and clearly he had already moved on to other things. There were, he intimated in his talk, two "other things," great enterprises whose exploration lay in the future: understanding the origin and nature of life, and understanding the relation of brain and mind—in particular, the biological basis of consciousness. Did he have any inkling, any conscious thought, when he spoke to us in 1962, that these would be the very subjects he himself would address in the years to come, once he had "dealt with" molecular biology, or at least taken it to the stage where it could be delegated to others?

It was not until May of 1986 that I met Francis Crick, at a conference in San Diego. There was a big crowd, full of neuroscientists, but when it was time to sit down for dinner, Crick singled me out, seized me by the shoulders, sat me down next to him, and said, "Tell me stories!" I have no memory of what we ate, or anything else about the dinner, only that I told him stories about many of my patients, and that each one set off bursts of hypotheses, theories, suggestions for investigation in his mind. Writing to Crick a few days later, I said that the experience was "a little like sitting next to an intellectual nuclear reactor.... I never had a feeling of such *incandescence.*"

He was especially eager to hear stories of visual perception, and was fascinated when I told him of a patient who had consulted me a few weeks before, an artist who had experienced a sudden and total loss of color perception following a car accident (his loss of color vision was accompanied by an inability to visualize or to dream in color). Crick was also fascinated when I told him how a number of my migraine patients had experienced, in the few minutes of a migraine aura, a flickering of static, "frozen" images in place of their normal, continuous visual perception. He asked me whether such "cinematic vision" (as I called it) was ever a permanent condition, or one that could be elicited in a predictable way so that it could be investigated. I said I did not know.

During 1986, encouraged by the questions Crick had fired at me, I spent a good deal of time with my colorblind patient, Mr. I., and in January of 1987, I wrote to Crick. "I have now written up a longish report on my patient.... Only in the actual writing did I come to see how color might indeed be a (cerebro-mental) construct." I had now started to wonder, I added, whether all perceptual qualities, including the perception of motion, were similarly constructed by the brain. I had spent most of my professional life wedded to notions of "naive realism," regarding visual perceptions, for example, as mere transcriptions of retinal images—this was very much the epistemological atmosphere at the time. But now, as I worked with Mr. I., this was giving way to a very different vision of the brain-mind, a vision of it as essentially constructive or creative. (I also included a copy of my book *A Leg to Stand On*, because it contained accounts of personal experiences of both motion and depth blindness.)

I got a letter back a few days later—Crick was the promptest of correspondents—in which he sought more detail about the difference between my migraine patients and a remarkable motion-blind patient described by the German neuropsychologist Josef Zihl. My migraine patients experienced "stills" in rapid succession, whereas in Zihl's patient (who had acquired motion blindness following a stroke), the stills apparently lasted much longer, perhaps several seconds each. In particular, Crick wanted to know whether, in my patients, successive stills occurred within the interval between successive eye movements, or only between such intervals. "I would very much like to discuss these topics with you," he wrote, "including your remarks about color as a cerebro-mental construct."

In my reply to Crick's letter, I enlarged on the deep differences between my migraine patients and Zihl's motion-blind woman. I mentioned too that I was working on Mr. I.'s case with several colleagues. My ophthalmologist friend Bob Wasserman had examined Mr. I. several times and discussed his case with me at length, and we had also been joined by a young neuroscientist, Ralph M. Siegel, who had just come to New York from the Salk Institute, where, as it happened, he had been close to Crick. Siegel collaborated with us, designing and conducting a variety of psychophysical experiments with our patient. I mentioned, too, that the neurophysiologist Semir Zeki had visited us from London, and had tested our patient with his color "Mondrians," using light of different wavelengths, and with these, had confirmed that Mr. I. showed excellent wavelength discrimination. His retinal cones were still reacting to light of different wavelengths, and his primary visual cortex (an area which has been named V1) was registering this information, but it was clear that this wavelength discrimination was not in itself sufficient for the experience of color. The actual perception of color had to be constructed, and constructed by an additional process in another part of the visual cortex. Zeki felt, on the basis of animal experiments, that color was constructed in the tiny areas of the visual cortex called V4, and wondered whether Mr. I. had damage to these areas resulting from his stroke.

At the end of October 1987, I was able to send Crick the paper that Bob Wasserman and I had written, "The Case of the Colorblind Painter,"[1] and having sent this article off to him, I was assailed by intense anxieties—what would he say?—but also by great eagerness to hear his reactions. Both of these feelings waxed in the weeks that followed, for Crick was out of town, his secretary told us, until mid-December.

Early in January, then, I got a response from Crick—an absolutely stunning letter, five pages of single-spaced typing, minutely argued, and bursting with ideas and suggestions. Some of them, he said, were "wild speculation," but it was the sort of wildness that had intuited the double-helix structure of DNA thirty-five years before. "Do please excuse the length of this letter," he added. "We might talk about it over the phone, after you've had time to digest it all." Bob and I, Ralph too, were mesmerized by the letter. It seemed to get deeper and more suggestive every time we read it, and we got the sense that

---

1. *The New York Review*, November 19, 1987.

it would need a decade or more of work, by a dedicated team of psychophysicists, neuroscientists, brain imagers, and others, to follow up on the torrent of suggestions Crick had made.

I wrote back to Crick, saying that we would need weeks or months to digest all he had said, but would be getting to work in the meantime, doing tests of motion vision, stereo vision, and contrast vision in Mr. I., as well as more sophisticated color vision testing, and that we hoped to get high-quality MRI and PET scans to look at the activity in his visual cortex.

In his five-page letter, Crick had written, "Thank you so much for sending me your fascinating article on the color-blind artist.... Even though, as you stress in your letter, it is not strictly a scientific article, it has aroused much interest among my colleagues and my scientific and philosophical friends here. We have had a couple of group sessions on it and in addition I have had several further conversations with individuals." He added too that he had sent a copy of the article and his letter to David Hubel, who, with Torsten Wiesel, had done pioneering work on the cortical mechanisms of visual perception.

Writing to me again in January of 1988, he said, "So glad to hear from you and to learn that you plan more work on Mr. I. All the things you mention are important, especially the scans.... There is no consensus yet among my friends about what the damage might be in such cases of cerebral achromatopsia. I have (very tentatively) suggested the V1 blobs plus some subsequent degeneration at higher levels, but this really depends on seeing little in the scans (if most of V4 is knocked out you should see something). David Hubel tells me that he favors damage to V4, though this opinion is preliminary. David van Essen tells me that he suspects some area further upstream."

He mentioned two of Antonio Damasio's cases: in one of these, the patient had lost color imagery, but still dreamed in color. (She later regained her color vision.) "I think the moral of all this," he concluded, "is that only careful and extensive psychophysics on [such] a patient *plus* accurate localization of the damage will help us. (So far, we cannot see how to study visual imagery and dreams in a monkey.)"

I was very excited to think that Crick was opening our paper, our "case," for discussion in this way. It gave me a deeper sense of science as a communal enterprise, of scientists as a fraternal, international community, sharing and thinking on each other's work—and of Crick himself as a sort of hub, or center, in touch with everyone in this neuroscientific world.

Eighteen months passed without further contact between us, for I was largely occupied now with other, nonvisual, conditions. But in August of 1989, I wrote to Crick again, saying that I was still working with our colorblind patient. I also enclosed a copy of my just-published book, *Seeing Voices*, on sign language and the culture and history of congenitally deaf people. I was especially fascinated by the way in which novel perceptual and linguistic powers could develop in congenitally deaf people, and the brain changes which both resulted from and allowed a very different perceptual experience in them, and in my book I had cited some of Crick's thoughts in this context—he had just published a paper called "The Recent Excitement About Neural Networks." (I also cited Gerald M. Edelman in the same context, and wondered what the relationship of these two extraordinary figures might be, since Edelman had recently relocated his Neurosciences Institute to La Jolla, practically next door to the Salk Institute, where Crick was working.)

Crick wrote back a few days later, and said that he had read my original articles about the deaf and American Sign Language in *The New York Review*. He had become intrigued by the subject, and looked forward to reading the book ("including the many fascinating footnotes"). "Over the years," he added, "Ursula [Bellugi, his colleague at the Salk] has been patiently educating me about ASL." He urged me, too, to continue my investigation of Mr. I., and enclosed the manuscript of a new article of his: "At the moment I am trying to come to grips with visual awareness, but so far it remains as baffling as ever."

The "short article" he enclosed, "Towards a Neurobiological Theory of Consciousness," was one of the first synoptic articles to come out of his collaboration with Christof Koch at Caltech. I felt very privileged to see this manuscript, in particular their carefully laid out argument that an ideal way of entering this seemingly inaccessible subject would be through exploring the mechanisms and disorders of visual perception.

Crick and Koch's paper covered a vast range in a few pages, was aimed at neuroscientists, and was sometimes dense and highly technical. But I knew that Crick could also write in a very accessible and witty and personable way—this was especially evident in his two earlier books, *Life Itself* (1981) and *Of Molecules and Men* (1966). So I now entertained hopes that he might give a more popular and accessible form to his neurobiological theory of consciousness, enriched with clinical and everyday examples. He intimated, in one of his letters, that he would attempt such a book, and in September 1993, his publishers sent me a proof of *The Astonishing Hypothesis*.

I read this at once with great admiration and delight, and wrote to Crick right away:

> I think you bring together an incredible range of observations from different disciplines into a single, brilliant clear focus.... I am particularly and personally grateful that you make such a full and generous reference to the Colorblind Painter whom Bob Wasserman and I studied. I still cherish that marvelous letter you sent me about him. When Semir [Zeki] developed his new technique for PET scanning V4 etc in humans, we did our utmost to get Mr. I. to him, but sadly, Mr. I. became acutely ill at this time with bronchogenic carcinoma and brain metastases, and died within a few weeks (we were not able to get a post-mortem). So it never became clear exactly what happened.

I enclosed a copy of my new article, "To See and Not See," saying that here, too, Bob Wasserman and Ralph Siegel had been invaluable research collaborators, and that we especially hoped to get serial PET scans as this patient, Virgil (who was born virtually blind and given vision through eye surgery as an adult), struggled to establish basic visual perceptions in the visual tumult suddenly loosed on him. (Though here, too, the patient, as with Mr. I., became unable, owing to an unrelated illness, to have such scans.) "I know your own central interests lie in vision, and the ways in which this can illuminate the fundamentals of mind and brain," I wrote, "and in my own rambling, clinical way, I find it is my own favorite subject, too."

The following year, in June 1994, I met with Ralph Siegel and Francis Crick for dinner in New York. As with that first dinner in 1986, I cannot remember what we ate, only that the talk ranged in all directions. Ralph talked about his current work with visual perception in monkeys, and his thoughts on the fundamental role of chaos at the neuronal level (we had worked together writing about chaos and self-organization in the phenomena of visual migraines, as well as chaos in parkinsonism). Francis spoke about his expanding work with Koch and their latest theories about the neural correlates of consciousness, and I spoke about my upcoming visit to Pingelap, an island in the South Pacific with a genetically isolated population of people born completely colorblind—I planned to travel there with Bob Wasserman and a Norwegian perceptual psychologist, Knut Nordby, who, like the Pingelapese, had been born without color receptors in his retinas.

In February 1995 I sent Francis my new book, *An Anthropologist on Mars*, which contained an expanded version of "The Case of the Colorblind Painter," much amplified, in part, through my discussions with him on the case. (He had immediately assented to my quoting from some of his letters in the revised version, adding that he liked it even more than the original, "if only because you have conveyed more of Mr. I.'s personality.") I also told him something of my experiences in Pingelap, and how Knut and I tried to imagine what changes might have occurred in his brain in response to his achromatopsia. Would the color-constructing centers in his brain have atrophied, in the absence of any color receptors in his retinas? Would his V4 areas have been reallocated for other visual functions? Or were they, perhaps, still awaiting an input, an input which might be provided by direct electrical or magnetic stimulation? And if this could be done, would he, for the first time in his life, see color? Would he know it was color, or would this visual experience be too novel, too confounding, to categorize? Questions like these, I knew, would fascinate Francis too.

Francis and I continued to correspond on various subjects, and I would always try to see him when I visited La Jolla. From 1997 to 2001, I was preoccupied with my memoir *Uncle Tungsten*, and less intensely with matters of visual consciousness. I continued to see a stream of patients, however, and I often carried on a sort of mental dialogue with Francis whenever puzzling problems came up with regard to visual perception or awareness. What, I would wonder, would Francis think of this—how would he attempt to explain it?

2

Francis's nonstop creativity—the incandescence that struck me when I first met him in 1986, allied to the way in which he always looked forward, saw years or decades of work ahead for himself and others—made one think of him as immortal. Indeed, well into his eighties, he continued to pour out a stream of brilliant and provocative papers, showing none of the fatigue, or fallings-off, or repetitions, of old age. It was in some ways a shock, therefore, early in 2003, to learn that he had run into serious medical problems. Perhaps this was in the back of my mind when I wrote to him in May of 2003—but it was not the main reason why I wanted to make contact with him again.

I had found myself thinking of time the previous month—time and perception, time and consciousness, time and memory, time and music, time and animal movement. I had returned, in particular, to the question of whether the apparently continuous passage of time and movement given to us by our eyes was an illusion—whether in fact our visual experience consisted of a series of "moments" which were then welded together by some higher mechanism in the brain. I found myself referring again to the "cinematographic" sequences of stills described to me by migraine patients, and which I myself had on occasion experienced. When I mentioned to Ralph Siegel that I had started writing on all this, he said, "You have to read Crick and Koch's latest paper—it came out just a couple of weeks ago in *Nature Neuroscience*. They propose in it that visual awareness really consists of a sequence of 'snapshots'—you are all thinking along the same lines."

I had already written a rough manuscript of an essay on time when I heard this, but now I read Crick and Koch's paper, "A Framework for Consciousness," with minute attention.[2] It was this which stimulated me to write to both Francis and Christof (whom I had seen a few weeks earlier at Caltech), enclosing a draft of my article (entitled, at that point, "Perceptual Moments"). I threw in, for good measure, a copy of *Uncle Tungsten*, and some other recent articles dealing with our favorite topic of vision. On June 5, 2003, Francis sent me a long letter, full of intellectual fire and cheerfulness, and with no hint of his illness.

> I have enjoyed reading the account of your early years. I also was helped by an uncle to do some elementary chemistry and

---

2. *Nature Neuroscience*, February 2003.

glass blowing, though I never had your fascination with metals. Like you I was very impressed by the Periodic Table and by ideas about the structures of the atom. In fact, in my last year at Mill Hill [his school] I gave a talk on how the "Bohr atom," plus quantum mechanics, explained the Periodic Table, though I'm not sure how much of all that I really understood.

I was intrigued by Francis's reactions to *Uncle Tungsten*, and wrote back to ask him how much "continuity" he saw between that teenager at Mill Hill who talked about the Bohr atom, the physicist he had become, his later "double helix" self, and his present self. I quoted a letter that Freud had written to Karl Abraham in 1924—Freud was sixty-eight then—in which he had said,

It is making severe demands on the unity of the personality to try and make me identify myself with the author of the paper on the spinal ganglia of the Petromyzon. Nevertheless I must be he....

In Crick's case, the seeming discontinuity was even greater, for Freud was a biologist from the beginning, even though his first interests were in the anatomy of primitive nervous systems. Francis, in contrast, had taken his undergraduate degree in physics, worked on magnetic mines during the war, and went on to do his doctoral work in physical chemistry. Only then, in his thirties—at an age when most researchers are already stuck in what they are doing—did he have a transformation, a "rebirth," as he was later to call it, and turn to biology. In his autobiography, *What Mad Pursuit*, he speaks of the difference between physics and biology:

Natural selection almost always builds on what went before.... It is the resulting complexity that makes biological organisms so hard to unscramble. The basic laws of physics can usually be expressed in simple mathematical form, and they are probably the same throughout the universe. The laws of biology, by contrast, are often only broad generalizations, since they describe rather elaborate (chemical) mechanisms that natural selection has evolved over millions of years.... I myself knew very little biology, except in a rather general way, till I was over thirty... my first degree was in physics. It took me a little time to adjust to the rather different way of thinking necessary in biology. It was almost as if one had to be born again.

By the middle of 2003, Francis's illness was beginning to take its toll, and I began to receive letters from Christof Koch, who by that time was spending several days a week with him. Indeed, they had become so close, it seemed, that many of their thoughts were dialogic, emerging in the interaction between them, and what Christof wrote to me would condense the thoughts of them both. Many of his sentences would start, "Francis and I do have a few more questions about your own experience.... Francis thinks this.... Myself, I am not sure," and so on.

Crick, in response to my "Perceptual Moments" paper (a version of which was later published in these pages as "In the River of Consciousness"[3]), quizzed me minutely on the rate of visual flicker experienced in migraine auras. It is only now, looking through our correspondence, that I realize these were matters which we discussed when we first met, in 1986. But this, apparently, we both forgot—certainly neither of us made any reference to our earlier letters. It is as if no resolution could be reached at that time, and both of us, in our different ways, shelved the matter, "forgot" it, and put it into our unconscious, where it would cook, incubate, for another fifteen years

---

3. *The New York Review*, January 15, 2004.

before reemerging. Francis and I both had a feeling of complementarity, I think, converging on a problem which had defeated us before, and was now at least getting closer to an answer. My feeling of this was so intense in August of 2003 that I felt I had to make a visit, perhaps a final one, to see Francis in La Jolla.

I was in La Jolla for a week, and made frequent visits to the Salk. There was a very sweet, noncompetitive air there (or so it seemed to me, as an outsider, in my brief visit), an atmosphere which had delighted Francis when he first came there in the mid-1970s, and which had deepened, with his continued presence, ever since. And indeed, he was still, despite his age, a central figure there. Ralph pointed out his car to me, its license plate bearing just four letters: ATCG—the four nucleotides of DNA, and I was happy to see his tall figure one day going into the lab—still very erect, though walking slowly, perhaps painfully, with the aid of a cane.

I made an afternoon presentation one day, and just as I started, I saw Francis enter and take a seat quietly at the back. I noticed that his eyes were closed much of the time, and thought he had fallen asleep—but when I finished, he asked a number of questions so piercing that I realized he had not missed a single word. His closed-eye appearances had deceived many visitors, I was told—but they might then find, to their cost, that these closed eyes veiled the sharpest attention, the clearest and deepest mind, they were ever likely to encounter.

On my last day in La Jolla, when Christof was visiting from Pasadena, we were all invited to come up to the Crick house for lunch with Francis and his wife, Odile. "Coming up" was no idle term— Ralph and I, driving, seemed to ascend continually, around one hairpin bend after another, until we reached the Crick house. It was a brilliantly sunny California day, and we all settled down at a table in front of the swimming pool (a pool where the water was violently blue—not, Francis said, because of the way the pool was painted, or the sky above it, but because the local water contained minute particles which—like dust—diffracted the light). Odile brought us various delicacies—salmon and shrimp, asparagus—and some special dishes which Francis, now on chemotherapy, was limited to eating. Though she did not join the conversation, I knew how closely Odile, an artist, followed all of Francis's work, if only from the fact that it was she who had drawn the double helix in the famous 1953 paper, and, fifty years later, a frozen runner, to illustrate the snapshot hypothesis in the 2003 paper that had so excited me.

Sitting next to Francis, I could see that his shaggy eyebrows had turned whiter and bushier than ever, and this deepened his sage-like and venerable appearance. But this was constantly belied by his twinkling eyes and mischievous sense of humor. Ralph was eager to present his latest work—a new form of optical imaging, which could show structures almost down to the cellular level in the living brain. It had never been possible to visualize brain structure and activity on this scale before, and it was on this "meso" scale that Crick and Edelman, whatever their previous disagreements, now located the functional structures of the brain.

Francis was very excited about Ralph's new technique and his pictures, but at the same time, he fired volleys of piercing questions at him, grilling him, interrogating, in a minute but also in a kindly and constructive way.

Francis's closest relationship, besides Odile, was clearly with Christof, his "son in science," and it was immensely moving to see how the two men, forty or more years apart in age, and so different in temperament and background, had come to respect and love one another so deeply. (Christof is romantically, almost flamboyantly, physical, given to dangerous rock climbing and brilliantly colored shirts. Francis seemed almost ascetically cerebral, his thinking so unswayed by emotional biases and considerations that Christof occasionally compared him to Sherlock Holmes.) Francis spoke with great pride, a father's pride, of Christof's then-forthcoming book *The Quest for Consciousness*,[4] and then of "all the work we will do after it is published." He outlined the dozens of investigations, years of work, which lay ahead—work especially stemming from the convergence of molecular biology with systems neuroscience. I wondered what Christof was thinking, Ralph too, for it was all too clear to us (and must have been clear to Francis too) that his health was declining fast, and that he would never himself be able to see more than the beginning of that vast research scheme. Francis, I felt, had no fear of death, but his acceptance of it was tinged perhaps with sadness that he would not be alive to see the wonderful, almost unimaginable, scientific achievements of the twenty-first century. The central problem of consciousness and its neurobiological basis, he was convinced, would be fully understood, "solved," by 2030. "You will see it," he often said to Ralph, "and you may, Oliver, if you live to my age."

A few months later, in December 2003, I wrote to Francis again, enclosing a copy of the final proof of "In the River of Consciousness," emphasizing how much of it I owed to his paper in *Nature Neuroscience*. (I added that I had just been rereading *Life Itself*, and found it even more wonderful on a second reading, especially since I had become deeply interested in the issues it raised. I enclosed a tiny article I had written for *Natural History* on the possibility of life elsewhere in the universe.)

In January 2004 I received the last letter I would get from Francis. He had read "In the River of Consciousness." "It reads very well," he wrote, "though I think a better title would have been 'Is Consciousness a River?' since the main thrust of the piece is that it may well not be." (I agreed with him.)

"Do come and have lunch again," his letter concluded.

—March 24, 2005

4. Reviewed by John R. Searle, *The New York Review*, January 13, 2005.

ABOUT THE AUTHORS AND SUBJECTS

ANNA AKHMATOVA (1889–1966) was the central figure of the St. Petersburg tradition of Russian poetry for more than half a century. *Requiem*, her tragic masterpiece on the Stalinist terror, describes the system that effectively silenced her from 1925 to 1952.

FRANCIS BACON (1909–1992) was an Anglo-Irish painter. In 1962, the Tate Gallery, London, organized a retrospective of his work. Other exhibitions and retrospectives of his work have been held at major museums throughout the world.

DJUNA BARNES (1892–1982) was an American modernist writer and part of the Paris literary scene in the Twenties and Thirties. She is best known for her novel *Nightwood*.

SAUL BELLOW (1915–2005) was brought up in a Jewish household and was fluent in Yiddish. He won the National Book Award three times, for his novels *The Adventures of Augie March*, *Herzog*, *and Mr. Sammler's Planet*; he won the Pulitzer Prize for *Humboldt's Gift*. In 1976, he was awarded the Nobel Prize in Literature.

ISAIAH BERLIN (1909–1997) was a political philosopher and historian of ideas. Born in Riga, he moved in 1917 with his family to Petrograd, where he witnessed the Russian Revolution. In 1921 he emigrated to England. He was educated at Oxford and became a Fellow of All Souls College, where he was later appointed Professor of Social and Political Theory. He served as the first president of Wolfson College, Oxford, and as president of the British Academy.

CAROLINE BLACKWOOD (1931–1996) was an Anglo-Irish writer whose books include the novels *Great Granny Webster* and *Corrigan*; *On the Perimeter*, an account of the women's anti-nuclear protest at Greenham Common; and *The Last of the Duchess*, about the old age of the Duchess of Windsor.

JOSEPH BRODSKY (1940–1996) was born in Leningrad and moved to the United States when he was exiled from Russia in 1972. His poetry collections include *A Part of Speech* and *To Urania*; his essay collections include *Less Than One*, which won the National Book Critics Circle Award, and *Watermark*. In 1987, he was awarded the Nobel Prize in Literature. He served as U.S. Poet Laureate from 1991 to 1992.

BRUCE CHATWIN (1940–1989) is best known for his travel books *In Patagonia* and *The Songlines*. He also wrote several novels; a collection of his essays, *What Am I Doing Here*, was published after his death.

JOHN CHEEVER (1912–1982) was a frequent contributor to *The New Yorker*. His novel *The Wapshot Chronicle* won the National Book Award; *The Stories of John Cheever* won the American Book Award, the National Book Critics Circle Award, and the Pulitzer Prize.

ROBERT CRAFT (1923–) is an American conductor and writer. He met Igor Stravinsky in 1948, and from then until the composer's death in 1971 continued to work alongside him in a variety of roles that ultimately became a full artistic partnership. His book *An Improbable Life* recalls his life before, during, and after this collaboration.

HART CRANE (1899–1932) published two volumes of poetry in his lifetime, *White Buildings* and *The Bridge*.

FRANCIS CRICK (1916–2004) and fellow scientist James Watson were awarded the 1962 Nobel Prize in Medicine for their discovery of the three-dimensional structure of the DNA molecule, which they determined to be a double helix.

PRUDENCE CROWTHER (1948–), editor of *Don't Tread on Me: The Selected Letters of S. J. Perelman*, is a writer and the copy chief of *Business Week*.

EDWARD DAHLBERG (1900–1977) was an American novelist and essayist. His works include *Bottom Dogs, Do These Bones Live, The Flea of Sodom*, and *Because I Was Flesh*.

F. W. DUPEE (1904–1979) was a literary critic and Professor of English at Columbia University. Among his books are a biography of Henry James and the essay collection *"The King of the Cats" and Other Remarks on Writers and Writing*.

ALBERT EINSTEIN (1879–1955) formulated the theory of relativity and contributed to the development of quantum theory, statistical mechanics, and cosmology. He was awarded the Nobel Prize in Physics in 1921.

JASON EPSTEIN (1928–) is the former editorial director of Random House. He founded Anchor Books, co-founded *The New York Review of Books*, and is the author of *Book Business: Publishing Past Present and Future*.

THOMAS FLANAGAN (1923–2002) was a Professor of English Literature at SUNY–Stony Brook and the author of the novels *The Year of the French*, which won the National Book Critics Circle Award, *The Tenants of Time*, and *The End of the Hunt*. A selection of his essays are collected in *There You Are: Writings on Irish and American Literature and History*.

PAUL GOODMAN (1911–1972) was a social scientist, humanist, anarchist, and pacifist. With the publication of his book *Growing Up Absurd*, he became one of the most influential social critics of the 1960s. He wrote on politics, education, language, and literature; he also wrote novels, stories, poems, and plays.

MAURICE GROSSER (1903–1986) was an American painter of landscape and still life and a writer and art critic for *The Nation*. His artwork has been exhibited at the Whitney Museum of American Art, the Art Institute of Chicago, and the Pennsylvania Academy.

ELIZABETH HARDWICK (1916–) is a literary critic and a co-founder of *The New York Review of Books*. Her books include *Sight-Readings*, *American Fictions*, *Bartleby in Manhattan and Other Essays*, *Seduction and Betrayal*, *Herman Melville*, and the novel *Sleepless Nights*.

SEAMUS HEANEY (1939–) was born in Northern Ireland. He is the author of numerous collections of poetry, several volumes of criticism, and *The Cure at Troy*, a version of Sophocles' *Philoctetes*. He is a foreign member of the American Academy of Arts and Letters; in 1995 he was awarded the Nobel Prize in Literature.

ANTHONY HECHT (1923–2004) was a poet and also the author of *Obbligati: Essays in Criticism* and *The Hidden Law: The Poetry of W. H. Auden*. In 1968, he was awarded the Pulitzer Prize for his poetry collection *The Hard Hours*; he also won the Bollingen Prize, the Prix de Rome, and the Eugenio Montale Award. He was poetry consultant to the Library of Congress from 1982 to 1984.

JOSEPHINE HERBST (1892–1969) was best known for her journalism in radical publications such as *New Masses* and *The Nation*. Her novels include the trilogy *Pity Is Not Enough*, *The Executioner Waits*, and *Rope of Gold*.

MICHAEL IGNATIEFF (1947–) is Director of the Carr Center for Human Rights Policy at the Kennedy School of Government at Harvard. His books include *The Russian Album*, a study of his family's history in imperial Russia and later exile in Europe and Canada, and a biography of Isaiah Berlin.

RANDALL JARRELL (1914–1965) was the author of the novel *Pictures from an Institution*, the children's stories *The Bat Poet* and *The Animal Family*, the essay collection *Poetry and the Age*, and the poetry collection *The Woman at the Washington Zoo*, which won the National Book Award. He taught for many years at the University of North Carolina and was poetry consultant to the Library of Congress from 1956 to 1958.

ALFRED KAZIN (1915–1998) was a writer and teacher. Among his books are *On Native Grounds*, a study of American literature from Howells to Faulkner, and the memoirs *A Walker in the City* and *New York Jew*. In 1996, he received the first Lifetime Award in Literary Criticism from the Truman Capote Literary Trust.

KEN KESEY (1935–2001) was the author of the novels *One Flew Over the Cuckoo's Nest* and *Sometimes a Great Notion*. The latter was published in 1964, the same year he drove across the U.S. with the Merry Pranksters.

ENRIQUE KRAUZE (1947–) is the author of *Mexico: Biography of Power*. He is Editor in Chief of the magazine *Letras Libres* and was, for twenty years, Deputy Editor of *Vuelta*, the magazine founded by Octavio Paz.

STANLEY KUNITZ (1905–) was poetry consultant to the Library of Congress from 1974 to 1976 and U.S. Poet Laureate from 2000 to 2001. His *Selected Poems, 1928–1958* won the Pulitzer Prize, and *Passing Through: The Later Poems, New and Selected* won the National Book Award.

BRAD LEITHAUSER (1953–) is Professor of English at Mt. Holyoke. His books include *Darlington's Fall*, a novel in verse; the novels *The Friends of Freeland* and *A Few Corrections*; the poetry collections *The Mail from Anywhere* and *The Odd Last Thing She Did*; and a collection of essays, *Penchants and Places*.

JÉRÔME LINDON (1926–2001) became director of the small publishing house Les Éditions de Minuit in 1948. A lifelong champion of new writing, he published three Nobel Prize winners: Claude Simon, Elie Wiesel, and Samuel Beckett. He also published the literary review *Critique* and several nonfiction books critical of French involvement in Algeria.

ROBERT LOWELL (1917–1977) twice was awarded the Pulitzer Prize for Poetry. *Lord Weary's Castle*, *Life Studies*, and *For the Union Dead* are among his many volumes of verse.

DWIGHT MACDONALD (1906–1982) became editor of *Partisan Review* in 1937 and later founded the journal *Politics*. His books include *Henry Wallace*, *Memoirs of a Revolutionist*, *Against the American Grain*, *Dwight Macdonald on Movies*, *Politics Past*, and *Discriminations*.

MARY MCCARTHY (1912–1989) was the author of the novels *The Group*, *The Groves of Academe*, and *Birds of America*; among her nonfiction books are *Venice Observed*, *The Stones of Florence*, *Vietnam*, and the autobiographies *Memories of a Catholic Girlhood* and *How I Grew*. A comprehensive collection of her literary, cultural, and political writings was published posthumously in *A Bolt from the Blue and Other Essays*.

LARRY MCMURTRY (1936–) is a novelist, essayist, and screenwriter. Among his many novels are *The Last Picture Show*, *Terms of Endearment*, and *Lonesome Dove*, for which he won the Pulitzer Prize. In 2006, he won the Academy Award for best adapted screenplay, with Diana Ossana, for *Brokeback Mountain*, based on the story by Annie Proulx.

AMEDEO MODIGLIANI (1884–1920) was an Italian Expressionist painter and sculptor. His works were exhibited in the Paris Salon d'Automne in 1907 and 1912 and in the Salon des Indépendants in 1908, 1910, and 1911. From 1909 to 1914, he concentrated on sculpture; most of his paintings date from 1915 to 1919.

ROBERT OPPENHEIMER (1904–1967), the American physicist known as "the father of the atomic bomb," served as the scientific director of the Manhattan Project. Later he advised the Atomic Energy Commission and helped found the American school of theoretical physics while at the University of California, Berkeley.

OCTAVIO PAZ (1914–1998) was born in Mexico City to a family of Spanish and native Mexican descent. A poet, essayist, and diplomat, he founded the magazine *Vuelta* in 1976 and edited it until his death. In 1990, he was awarded the Nobel Prize in Literature.

S. J. PERELMAN (1904–1979) was an American humorist and motion-picture writer. He wrote scripts for Marx Brothers films and musical theater, as well as humor pieces which often appeared in *The New Yorker*. His books include *Westward Ha!* and *The Swiss Family Perelman*.

DARRYL PINCKNEY (1953–) is the author of the novel *High Cotton*, which won the Los Angeles Times Book Prize for Fiction; *Out There: Mavericks of Black Literature*, based on the Alain Locke lectures he gave at Harvard; and *Sold and Gone: African American Literature and U.S. Society*. He received the Harold D. Vursell Award for Distinguished Prose from the American Academy of Arts and Letters in 1994.

THEODORE ROETHKE (1908–1963) published his first collection of poems, *Open House*, in 1941. He was awarded the Pulitzer Prize for Poetry in 1954 for *The Waking*.

OLIVER SACKS (1933–) is a physician and writer. His books include *Awakenings*, *The Man Who Mistook His Wife for a Hat*, *An Anthropologist on Mars*, *The Island of the Colorblind*, and *Uncle Tungsten: Memories of a Chemical Boyhood*. He is Clinical Professor of Neurology at the Albert Einstein College of Medicine, Adjunct Professor of Neurology at the NYU School of Medicine, and consultant neurologist to the Little Sisters of the Poor.

DELMORE SCHWARTZ (1913–1966) published his first short story in *Partisan Review* in 1937. The story was included in his first book, *In Dreams Begin Responsibilities*, which appeared the following year. He went on to write numerous stories, poems, and plays, and to edit *Partisan Review* from 1943 to 1955. In 1960, he became the youngest recipient of the Bollingen Prize, awarded for *Summer Knowledge: New and Selected Poems*.

RICHARD SEAVER (1933–) is President and Editor in Chief of Arcade Publishing. He began his publishing career in Paris, where he cofounded the English-language quarterly *Merlin* in the 1950s. He has translated some forty books from the French.

SUSAN SONTAG (1933–2004) was an American essayist, short story writer, novelist, film and theater director, and human rights activist. Her work addressed subjects ranging from camp, pornographic literature, fascist aesthetics, and photography to AIDS and revolution. Her books include *Against Interpretation*, *On Photography*, *Illness as Metaphor*, *Regarding the Pain of Others*, and the novels *The Volcano Lover* and *In America*.

GERTRUDE STEIN (1874–1946) was an early supporter of Cubism and was interested in applying its theories to her writing. Her works include the novel *The Making of Americans*, the poetry collection *Tender Buttons*, *The Autobiography of Alice B. Toklas*, and two opera librettos scored by Virgil Thomson, *Four Saints in Three Acts* and *The Mother of Us All*.

IGOR STRAVINSKY (1882–1971), the Russian-French-American composer of modern classical music, was also a renowned pianist and conductor. His compositions ranged from symphonies to piano miniatures, as well as ballets, including *The Rite of Spring* and *The Firebird*.

ALICE B. TOKLAS (1877–1967) lived in Paris in the first half of the twentieth century with her companion, Gertrude Stein. Their home was a salon for artists and writers including Pablo Picasso, Henri Matisse, Georges Braque, Sherwood Anderson, and Ernest Hemingway.

TATYANA TOLSTAYA (1951–) was born in St. Petersburg. She is the author of the story collections *On the Golden Porch* and *Sleepwalker in a Fog*, the essay collection *Pushkin's Children: Writings on Russia and Russians*, and the novel *The Slynx*.

DEREK WALCOTT (1930–) is a poet, playwright, essayist, and visual artist. Born in Castries, St. Lucia, he won the Nobel Prize in Literature in 1992. His epic poem *Omeros* is a reworking of Homeric story and tradition into a journey around the Caribbean and beyond to the American West and London.

EDMUND WILSON (1895–1972) wrote for *Vanity Fair*, helped edit *The New Republic*, served as chief book critic for *The New Yorker*, and was a frequent contributor to *The New York Review of Books*. He was the author of more than twenty books, including *Axel's Castle*, *To the Finland Station*, *Patriotic Gore*, and a work of fiction, *Memoirs of Hecate County*.